IN-LAWS

IN-LAWS

A Guide to
Extended-Family Therapy

GLORIA CALL HORSLEY, C.N.S., M.F.C.C.

JOHN WILEY & SONS, INC.

New York • Chichester • Brisbane • Toronto • Singapore

Library of Congress Cataloging-in-Publication Data:

Horsley, Gloria Call.
      In-laws : a guide to extended-family therapy / by Gloria Call
   Horsley.
          p.   cm. — (Wiley series in couples and family dynamics and
   treatment)
      Includes index.
      ISBN 0-471-12914-3 (cloth : alk. paper)
      1. Family psychotherapy.   2. Parents-in-law.   I. Title.
   II. Series.
   RC488.5.H634   1996
   616.89'156—dc20   95-15343

This book is dedicated to my husband, Phil, my daughters, Heidi, Rebecca, and Heather, to their husbands—my sons-in-law—and to my grandchildren, Eliza and Scott, who were the inspiration for this book.

Series Preface

Our ability to form strong interpersonal bonds with romantic partners, children, parents, siblings, and other relations is one of the key qualities that defines our humanity. These relationships shape who we are and what we become—they can be a source of great gratification, or tremendous pain. Yet, only in the mid-20th century did behavioral and social scientists really begin focusing on couples and family dynamics, and only in the past several decades have the theory and findings that emerged from those studies been used to develop effective therapeutic interventions for troubled couples and families.

We have made great progress in understanding the structure, function, and interactional patterns of couples and families—and have made tremendous strides in treatment. However, as we stand poised on the beginning of a new millennium, it seems quite clear that both intimate partnerships and family relationships are in a period of tremendous flux. Economic factors are changing work patterns, parenting responsibilities, and relational dynamics. Modern medicine has helped lengthen the life span, giving rise to the need for transgenerational caretaking. Cohabitation, divorce, and remarriage are quite commonplace, and these social changes make it necessary for us to rethink and broaden our definition of what constitutes a family.

Thus, it is no longer enough simply to embrace the concept of the family as a system. In order to understand and effectively treat the evolving family, our theoretical formulations and clinical interventions must be informed by an understanding of ethnicity, culture, religion, gender, sexual preference, family life cycle, socioeconomic status, education, physical and mental health, values, and belief systems.

The purpose of the *Wiley Series in Couples and Family Dynamics and Treatment* is to provide a forum for cutting-edge relational and family theory, practice, and research. Its scope is intended to be broad, diverse, and international, but all books published in this series share a common mission: to reflect on the past, offer state-of-the-art information on the present, and speculate on, as well as attempt to shape, the future of the field.

FLORENCE W. KASLOW
Florida Couples and Family Institute

Preface

In-law relationships present an interesting paradox: Although they have an unlimited potential to cause problems, these relationships, when accorded the attention they deserve, also have the ability to add great joy to peoples' lives. Coping with in-law relationships is an unaddressed problem area for many of the individuals and couples who consult therapists for help with troubled relationships and marriages. Because these problems are so deeply embedded in the very fiber of the family, they are often not recognized.

Many people believe that, if ignored, their in-law problems will magically disappear. This has not been my experience during more than a decade of individual and family counseling. Without proactive steps to strengthen and build good in-law relationships, clients inevitably experience a negative reinforcement, not unlike a child touching a hot stove. The painful burn teaches the child to keep his or her hands away from the heat or to avoid the stove altogether. Similarly, when each contact with their in-laws is fraught with pain and distress, extended family members eventually find themselves less capable of being together, which fosters physical and emotional cutoffs (Bowen, 1978).

It doesn't have to be that way. With time and maturity, the child who was burned by the stove can ideally learn to use it as a resource. Rather than simply "avoiding the heat," clients can share nurturing and mutually fulfilling family relationships with their in-laws.

In the past eight years, my three daughters were married, and I increasingly found myself focusing on my relationships with my new sons-in-law. Concurrently, I began to notice many parallels with my clients and their extended families, which stimulated me to consider the application of my training and theoretical knowledge to in-law relationships. My basic approach to family therapy is influenced by three years of training with Drs. Judith Landau-Stanton and Duncan Stanton at the University of Rochester Medical Center Family Therapy Training Program, which focused on a short-term, problem-centered therapeutic model (Horsley, 1988; Landau-Stanton, Clements, & Stanton, 1993; Landau-Stanton, Horsley, Stanton, & Watson, 1994).

Being an in-law is difficult. Clients sometimes lose the battle before they even know they are in a fight. Long-term, deep-seated family problems are difficult for families to face, and therapy requires a great deal of energy, both from the family and from the therapist. But when treated early, many intrafamily problems can be improved, or avoided altogether. When in-law relationships are kept clear of hostilities and resentments, mutually satisfying interactions are possible with even the most difficult relatives. In this world of diminishing resources, it seems prudent to maximize every resource—especially those of family. Therapists can go a long way in helping clients to value their in-law relationships and to use these relationships as wisely as possible.

This book is primarily directed toward clinicians who work with individuals and their extended families, including newly married couples (children-in-law), their parents (parents-in-law), and siblings (brothers- and sisters-in-law). The book provides these therapists with useful tools for helping clients to start new in-law relationships on firm footing and then to keep them strong. For in-law relationships that are already out of kilter, the book offers practical techniques to get them back into balance. The material in these pages will be equally useful to therapists who must deal with their own in-law issues. Therapists may also find the information beneficial when working with individual clients who are not interested in doing family therapy or family-of-origin work.

GLORIA C. HORSLEY

Acknowledgments

I would like to acknowledge Phil, my husband of 35 years, for his support and encouragement throughout my education and the establishment of my professional career.

I thank our three daughters and their husbands for their encouragement all along the way. I also acknowledge the silent support of our son, Scott, who although no longer with us, continues to be a strong force in our lives.

Deep appreciation is also extended to Beverly McManus, my friend and editor, for her excellent editorial skills and encouragement throughout this endeavor. Thanks also to her daughters, Emily and Mary Ella, for sharing their mother's creative energy with me and this book.

Thanks to Kelly Franklin, my editor at Wiley, for her enthusiastic support of a first-time author.

Thanks to Karen Lau, whose tireless and exacting standards have so added to achieving the goal. Her speed and accuracy, along with unfailing good humor, are much appreciated.

Thanks to Gena Alder for her creative graphic support.

And thanks above all to Florence Kaslow and our fortuitous meeting. Her encouragement from the inception of this idea made this book evolve from a lunch conversation into the finished distillation of the work and lives of many therapists, researchers, and in-laws.

Appreciation is also given to Judith Landau-Stanton, who has been an inspiration to me not only as a professional, but as a mentor whose ideas and friendship have been invaluable.

Thanks go to Dr. Marguerite McCorkle, Director of Research, Mental Research Institute (MRI), Palo Alto, California, for her assistance in designing my in-law research.

Thanks to my supportive friends and colleagues, Mary Insel, Mary Dean, and Cynthia Hart. A special thanks to Trev Blazzard for his expertise in legal and financial issues. And to my grandmother Mamie Peters Call and my sister-in-law Joan Haskins whose love for writing has inspired me.

And last but not least, thanks to my friends, family, and clients, whose in-law stories fill this book.

G.C.H.

Contents

CHAPTER 1

Providing Therapy to In-Laws

PUTTING IN-LAWS INTO PERSPECTIVE

In-law relationships can have a major impact on the success or failure of a marriage. Sometimes, the mere mention of the word *in-law* can strike fear and quaking in the hearts of therapists as well as clients. This book takes an interior look at the relationships that work and those that do not, and explores the secrets of the best in-law relationships.

Being a successful in-law is worth the effort. Whether a parent-in-law, child-in-law, sibling-in-law, or ex-in-law, each person within a family system has the opportunity to add richness or sorrow to the relationship. During my training in a community mental health center and hospital, I was surprised to discover that extended families often were viewed negatively by some of the staff members, and were perceived as an annoyance—almost a toxic agent— rather than a resource. One resident in psychiatry told me he did not work with families; they "presented too many variables." Until then, I had never thought of a person as a variable!

In therapy sessions with troubled individuals or couples, a therapist frequently hears comments like these, regarding in-laws:*

> *The only time we hear from our daughter and son-in-law is when they want money or a free dinner.*—Gladys, 49, painter

> *The holidays are a nightmare. We spend our whole vacation dragging the children from one in-law to another and when it's time to go home we hear, "You didn't spend enough time with us." I'm glad we live 2,000 miles away.*—Hugh, 35, investment adviser

> *Is it any wonder that we got divorced? Whenever we had a disagreement he would run home for family support. It got to the point where they all hated me.*—Catherine, 31, lawyer

---

* To protect the privacy of persons mentioned or quoted, names and identifying characteristics have been changed throughout the book.

My mother-in-law lived with us for one year, and I will tell you, it almost destroyed our family.—Diane, 43, insurance executive

My in-laws were a major problem in our relationship. If it hadn't been for pressure from her family over my being in jail, I know she wouldn't have filed for divorce.—Ryan, 38, dentist

My brother and I had been very close, but after he married Susan, she made it clear that he was "her man," and there was no room for another woman, including a sister.—Meadow, 21, student

Since I separated from my wife, my father-in-law won't even speak to me. It really makes me sad; after all, we will always have the kids in common.—Martin, 35, plumber

The adage is true: When you marry a person, you marry his or her entire family. Families are getting bigger, older, and more complicated. People are living longer and are healthier and more active than they were in the past. With the high divorce and remarriage rate, blended families are increasing the spectrum of in-law relationships. How can parents-in-law and children-in-law see each other as resources and enhancements, rather than as annoyances and nuisances or, in a more negative light, as destructive forces?

Therapists need a range of techniques to help their clients learn how to avoid the pitfalls that await those who are unaware that rewarding in-law relationships require effort. We will explore in-law relationships from the point before one even becomes an in-law (when many factors can make or break a relationship) through the life cycle changes, to the end of the relationship, whether through divorce or death.

We will examine the stages transited as a new in-law is accepted (or not) into a family, and look at the in-law problems that begin with the marriage. What strategies will avoid the "wedding bell blues," and how do expectations change as the relationship grows? Family loyalties, secrets, and myths are realities that can change with the addition of new in-laws. Cultural and ethnic variables come into play as new members from different backgrounds are added to the family. Transformation of the in-law relationship may occur during expected (and unexpected) life-cycle changes, or as an effect of the aging process. We will look at the richly textured family issues of siblings-in-law. What techniques will mend rifts and heal long-standing wounds in the in-law spectrum? We will delve into some special in-law issues that many families encounter, including divorce and its repercussions. Although not typically included in therapeutic literature, financial and legal considerations—including the blending of finances between two previously married families, gifts, guardianship agreements, and wills—are increasingly faced by therapists and are explored here. The final chapter offers an in-law inventory—a look at the qualities of positive in-law relationships and at some useful tools that allow therapists and their clients to detect potential problems before they arise, thereby building strong bonds from the earliest point possible.

BINDING CONTRACTS: THE HISTORICAL PERSPECTIVE OF THE IN-LAW RELATIONSHIP

Until a couple faces divorce, they seldom think of their marriage license as being a binding contract that is subject to the laws of the state or jurisdiction where they were married. Their marriage, made within their state and sanctioned by its laws, also connects them to relationships with their in-laws. A perusal of the history of other civilizations reveals that as a society becomes more sophisticated, legal rulings are made to deal with the complex matters that cannot be solved informally. As a result, we have the idea of social relationships being recognized "in-the-law." Black's Law Dictionary (1990) defines the word *in-law*: "Implied by law; Presumed by law to be so or to exist; A relative by marriage." Indicating the seriousness with which the State has traditionally viewed the marriage contract, Justice Field said in 1888 that "marriage, as creating the most important relation in life, as having more to do with the morals and civilization of a people than any other institution, has always been subject to the control of the legislature" (Krause, 1986).

Acknowledging the in-law connection is important, because people are constantly influenced directly and indirectly by their in-laws. In her crosssectional sociological study of White, native-born Americans, Komarovsky (1962) found that men and women acquired their concepts of marital roles from their parental families. She also found that, of the 46 couples studied, 36% named in-laws as having an effect on their socialization into their marital roles.

In-laws are also important in other ways. They show individuals where their partners have come from and preview where they may be going. Extended families, including in-laws, also serve as important resources for financial, physical, and emotional support.

Recognition of in-law status is a significant factor in numerous relationships in the United States, where 2.4 million people marry each year (Famighetti, 1994). If we consider the fact that a majority of the parents of these newlyweds are still living, this means there are upward of 9.6 million new in-law relationships created every year—and this accounts for only the parents of the children who married. Imagine how large the number grows if we also consider siblings, stepfamilies, and the like. In *The Wife In-law Trap,* Cryster (1990) extended the in-law web to include the ex-husband's second wife (the *wife-in-law*), and reported survey data on how 93 women in 63 cities across the nation deal with their wives-in-law. With divorces and remarriages, the number of potential in-laws soars exponentially.

Many people believe that extended families are at best neutral, and at worst harmful, and that the formation of a nuclear family includes making a physical and emotional break from the in-laws. The degree and extent of in-law problems throughout our society would argue that extended families are a fact of life and must be dealt with.

 In a survey of 7,000 divorced Roman Catholics in St. Louis, Missouri, in-laws were reported to be the greatest single cause of marital breakup during the first year of marriage; in subsequent years, they became less important (Duvall, 1954). This underscores the importance of dealing with these issues at the outset of the relationship. A study of 100 Montana ranch families indicated that fully one-third of the women were having problems with their in-laws (Marotz-Baden & Cowan, 1987). Given the sheer numbers of in-laws and the potential for problems in the relationships, it is essential that we expend some energy exploring and improving the quality of in-law ties.

When I told a colleague at a professional meeting that I was writing a book on in-laws, she commented, "That's interesting, but I'm not in that category yet, as I'm not married." At this, I asked, "You don't have married siblings?" She stated that she had two married brothers, and in a rather chagrined manner, added, "I guess that makes me an in-law, doesn't it?" It is easy to think of in-laws as being only the parents of the partners we marry, rather than looking at the fact that we are the children-in-law to our spouse's parents, and we have in-law relationships with our sisters' and/or brothers' spouses.

The time has come for a paradigm shift regarding extended family relationships. To change attitudes, mental health practitioners might begin by looking at the basic parent–child relationship, including the accompanying myths and stories. The time for transforming the stories and in-law jokes to a more constructive genre is long overdue. It is the premise of this book that people can enrich their family lives by changing the perspectives they hold toward themselves and their in-laws.

WORKING WITH FAMILY NETWORKS

Typical problems related to in-laws include lack of permission to marry; disapproval of child's choice of spouse; competition by parent or sibling with in-law for partner; parents' desire to maintain close relationship with son or daughter and to exclude his or her spouse; arguments around where to spend holidays and vacations; allocation to each family of scarce resources in terms of time, money, and energy; and grandchildren—who does or does not get to baby-sit. These issues (and many more) will be covered throughout this book.

Setting Up an In-Law Therapy Session

When presenting problems include the in-laws, it is my preference to have the extended family join the therapy. Generally, before therapists see in-laws in therapy, they have already seen an individual, a couple, or the nuclear family. During the course of therapy, the in-laws are identified by the therapist or the client as possible resources or as part of the family problem. If in-laws are an important issue, the therapist can let clients know that when they feel comfortable, the in-laws will be invited to join the session. The therapist will already have gathered some data about the in-laws, and perhaps will have formed some initial impressions. It often takes two or three sessions to build up the trust that couples or individuals need in order to enlarge the network to include the in-laws. Once that trust is established, the therapist stresses that having the in-laws in therapy can help to loosen rigid boundaries, and can give the family a better understanding of each member's desires and goals. Framo (1992) states that one session with the entire family of origin, including parents and siblings, can do as much as a whole long-term course of individual therapy. He feels that families should be able to work out their problems face-to-face. Whitaker and Keith (1981) also believe in working with three generations in order to increase the therapeutic power; however, the works of Framo and of Whitaker and Keith focus on blood relatives, rather than in-laws. It is my experience that work with the in-laws present (with the session framed as an in-law session) can be equally as powerful as those with birth parents and siblings.

Who to Include in Therapy

After the client and therapist have decided that an in-law session could be productive, they will want to discuss who should be included in in-law therapy. All interested parties should be invited to the session. Stanton (1981b) calls interested parties the *systems of impact*. It is important to avoid inviting only those the therapist would consider *key players* (Landau-Stanton et al., 1994), because individuals who are not as involved with the problem can often give some important observations that may be more easily heard by those experiencing emotional distress. If the idea of a large network stresses the therapist, it might be remembered that when a situation in therapy is difficult, enlargement of the therapeutic system is encouraged (Sluzki, 1978). At that point, another therapist (or perhaps even a priest or other member of the clergy who has family counseling skills) could be invited to join the session.

It is not always possible for the therapist to include the entire extended in-law network. Some in-laws may not be available or may be unwilling to be involved in the therapeutic process; others may fear that family secrets will be divulged. There may be a history of sexual or physical abuse that would make it unwise to invite the entire family (Framo, 1992). In cases where the in-laws cannot or will not attend, I often use material that appears in this book, including handouts of some of the questions found at the end of each chapter, to serve as a bridge between those who do and those who do not attend the session.

A Grounded Therapeutic Approach

In doing therapy with in-law systems, it is as important for the therapist to have a clear sense of his or her own philosophy of therapy as it is to set realistic goals. In-laws who are invited into therapy sessions often ask, "Why am I here and how can I help?" Therapists can show their respect to those who agree to participate by being able to say, "This is what I do and why I am doing it." In-laws don't want their time wasted and they want to feel safe. When the therapist can explain his or her own philosophy of therapy, it serves as a grounding for both the therapist and the family.

The therapist's philosophy and goals for in-law therapy can serve as a compass or guide. This compass can help therapists to reorient themselves, somewhat like the *you are here* maps in shopping centers. Therapists who have a firm grounding in their own general philosophy will have a better chance of helping the in-laws differentiate and define themselves within their family system.

THERAPEUTIC TECHNIQUES

While doing in-law therapy, I use a variety of therapeutic approaches, depending on the problem and the requirements of the individuals or families involved. However, I have found Bowen's differentiation of self (Bowen, 1976; Kerr & Bowen, 1988) to be a good *container* for a variety of therapeutic techniques. My goal in therapy, no matter which technique or theory I am using, is the gradual differentiation of each individual in-law from the family emotional system (Bowen, 1978). I believe the goal of all therapy is to help individuals to understand who they are within the boundaries of their family. Over the ancient Greek temple at Delphi is the command, *Gnothi Seauton* (Know Thyself). The goal I hope to achieve in in-law therapy is differentiation within the group: each client knows who he or she is within the in-law system. Erickson (1950), in his *stages of man,* termed this *interdependence,* as opposed to dependence or isolation.

To promote self-knowledge and individual differentiation, I use a problem-oriented short-term model (Haley, 1976; Horsley, 1988; Landau-Stanton et al., 1994). I draw on a variety of theories and techniques, including Family Evaluation (Kerr & Bowen, 1988); Network Therapy (Speck & Attneave, 1973);

Narrative Therapy (O'Hanlon, 1994; White, 1989); Family of Origin Therapy (Framo, 1976, 1992); Family Sculpturing (Nerin, 1993; Satir, 1964; Simon, 1972); and Contextual Therapy (Boszormenyi-Nagy & Spark, 1973; Van Heusden & Van Den Eerenbeetmt, 1986). Interventions taken from these and other models will be described more fully in the rest of the chapter and throughout the book.

CONTEXTS OF IN-LAW THERAPY

When setting up in-law therapy, I have found two to four sessions, each two hours in length, to be the most workable format. It is unrealistic to expect that in-laws can make themselves available for more than two to four sessions. I generally conduct in-law therapy in one of the following contexts:

1. **Dedicated in-law therapy:** All of the in-laws are seen together for one to three sessions.
2. **Partial in-law therapy:** Parts of the in-law system are seen at each of two to four in-law sessions. Partial therapy usually occurs because some in-laws cannot make it to all sessions, or because it is not appropriate or desirable for both sets of in-laws to be seen concurrently. Unavailable in-laws may be included with conference calls, or sessions can be videotaped and viewed later.
3. **Ongoing therapy with in-law interventions:** During the course of individual, couples, or family therapy, an in-law problem may be identified, and in-laws are then asked to attend one or two sessions or to complete a homework assignment to deal with in-law problems.
4. **Network therapy:** The entire support community, including the in-laws, is present, usually for two or three sessions.

The following four cases illustrate how I use theory and each of the four in-law context therapeutic techniques. Each case demonstrates some (but not all) of the techniques and models mentioned previously.

Dedicated In-Law Therapy: The March Family

Margaret, a 26-year-old filmmaker, called me and complained that her mother-in-law was making too many demands on her husband's time. Margaret had recently married Lynn, a 27-year-old sales representative. Lynn's father had died of a heart attack one year previously, and because Lynn was an only child, his mother was highly dependent on him and asked him to drive her everywhere. Margaret, the oldest of three daughters, resented the demands made on Lynn.

Prior to the marriage, Margaret had enjoyed her future mother-in-law and had spent a good deal of time just hanging out with her, because her future husband lived at home. After the marriage, the couple bought a small home 30 miles away from Lynn's mother. When the couple returned from their honeymoon, they waited several days to contact the mother-in-law. Within the week, the mother-in-law telephoned her son at his office, demanding to know why he had not contacted her and wanting to know when they were coming to visit. The couple went over to the mother-in-law's house the next evening and, as Margaret put it, "All hell broke loose." The mother-in-law let it be known that she had expected Lynn to take a vacation day from work and take her to the doctor. As a dutiful son of a widowed mother, Lynn told his mother that he would. When the couple left the mother-in-law's house, Margaret blew up and told Lynn that she had married him and not his mother. She further stated that Lynn's mother needed to realize that Lynn was someone else's husband now— and not his mother's boy. Lynn became defensive and said that Margaret had to consider that his mother was dealing with his father's death. Margaret said that since it had been one year since his death, her mother-in-law had to realize that life goes on. When Margaret telephoned me, the couple had not spoken for three days. I suggested that we have a joint session with Lynn's mother.

Taking an in-law problem-oriented approach (Haley, 1976), I identified the problem as lack of differentiation of self between Lynn and his mother, exacerbated by two factors: Lynn and Margaret's recent marriage, and the death of Lynn's father one year previously. The lack of differentiation caused Lynn and Margaret to be pulled into an emotional triangle with the mother-in-law. To deal with this differentiation problem, I planned six hours of therapy over three weeks, with one two-hour session per week. The following is an outline of the therapy content and a brief description of the therapy process. Recognizing that this is a distillation of some very rich and complex theories and techniques, it is my hope that the reader will gain from it a flavor for my work and will explore more deeply those therapeutic techniques that seem most appropriate for the client situation.

Using the theories of Framo (1976, 1992) regarding the importance of the family of origin and their views, I invited the extended family into the session. During the first session, I constructed on a large easel a genogram— a diagram of the family tree (McGoldrick & Gerson, 1985). The process of constructing the genogram helped us to look at the history and dynamics of in-laws in the family. Among other issues, we discussed permission to marry, how the death of Lynn's father left a void in the family, what it meant to the family to experience such a loss, and how it was for Margaret to live with the loss, having never known her father-in-law. We also discussed how the new marriage, with the introduction of a daughter-in-law, could represent for Lynn's mother an addition of a new family member, as well as the lost role of her only child. Mrs. March said that she had given the couple permission to marry, but that she wasn't sure that she had really given Lynn permission to leave home. She thought of the marriage as gaining a daughter, not losing a son.

While constructing genograms, I also consider the work of White and Epston (1989), in which they see therapy as a process of reauthoring the lives of people who present problems (Tomm, 1989). I am very interested in White and Epston's ideas of externalizing problems. Throughout construction of the genogram, I encouraged the March family to tell their in-law stories and jokes, to process them, and to find meaning in them. Because the March family is a high-functioning family, we discussed the idea of reauthoring and explored how in-law stories, which often have a negative bent, can be rewritten to be empowering and uplifting, and can promote in-law competence and wellness. We also discussed how, in the reauthoring, the focus is on the problem and not on the persons depicted in the stories.

Mrs. March told a story of how her mother-in-law had always been seen as having fragile health and a poor nervous system. She was so nervous that she could not drive, and was totally dependent on her husband, son, or friends to take her anywhere that was beyond walking distance. The story went that her husband took her out to teach her to drive and she almost ran into a car. From that day on, she never got behind the wheel. Mrs. March said that the incident had affected the entire family, and that her sister-in-law was also too nervous to drive.

We discussed the problem posed by this in-law story. We decided the story had a negative bent that made the women in the family look fragile and dependent. We then looked for a unique outcome. When *wasn't* Mrs. March's mother-in-law dependent and fragile? Mrs. March said that her mother-in-law was in fact a very independent woman in other areas of her life and, considering that she couldn't drive, was highly active in the community. She said that now that she thought about it, in a way not driving had been a plus: her father-in-law ran most of the bothersome errands such as grocery shopping or picking up the laundry.

It was interesting that Mrs. March picked a driving story. It represented the idea of being dependent on others to drive, which was Margaret's original complaint about her mother-in-law. We went on to discuss how Mrs. March's husband used to annoy her because he thought she should wait for him to take her places. Mrs. March said that she valued her independence and wanted her story to be that of an independent in-law. Lynn said that he and Margaret would help her to build on that story.

According to Beck (1976), if clients are to attach meaning to their experiences, they must make a connection between meaningful events and their thoughts and feelings. To help individuals to frame their experiences and events in an in-law context, I often use an educational component that helps clients in in-law therapy make this cognitive connection.

With Margaret's mother-in-law, I did some grief and loss education around the fact that grieving for a spouse is a four-year process and that the marriage of a child can also be a loss. Mrs. March was able to make the connection that her strong desire to have her son and daughter-in-law constantly involved in her life was related to the loss of her husband and that wanting to replace the lost object is a normal part of the grieving process (Worden, 1982). We also discussed the fact that the grieving process would be stressful during anniversary dates, holidays, and family gatherings such as reunions and birthday celebrations.

At the session held one week later, I used several structural and strategic techniques (Aponte & VanDeusen, 1981; Stanton, 1981a, 1981b), including moving participants from one chair to another during the therapy session and giving homework assignments. Structural and strategic approaches solve problems in the context of the therapeutic environment when the therapist identifies the problem and tailors an intervention specifically for the problem. An example of a structural approach regarding enmeshment or lack of differentiation of mother-in-law with her son was reflected by the fact that Mrs. March took the chair next to her son during therapy. Using a structural intervention during the therapy session, I asked Mrs. March to move her chair to sit next to me, facing the couple, rather than sit next to them. Mrs. March and I then discussed how she met her husband and what she felt were the keys to a happy marriage, as well as what advice she as a mother-in-law might want to give the couple. This intervention changed the physical dynamic in the room to reflect the needed change in the relationship, and it empowered Mrs. March as a mother-in-law and encouraged her to take on a new role as trusted adviser to the couple.

At the end of the session, I gave the family a homework assignment aimed at increasing differentiation between mother and son. The assignment was in response to the fact that Mrs. March had previously stated that she didn't miss some things about her son, like his messy habits, but that she was pleased that this behavior had been outgrown. At that point, Margaret said that she wished that were the case, because she was constantly picking up after him. Because Mrs. March missed her son and wanted him to spend more time in her home, she acted as though she did not believe her daughter-in-law. I suggested the Paradoxical Strategic intervention of prescribing the symptom (Rohrbaugh, Tennen, Press, & White, 1981); the therapist prescribes an action that is in apparent opposition to the goal. The goal here was to help individual family members to differentiate—to "detriangle" Mrs. March, her son, and her daughter-in-law. The desired behavioral outcome was decreased demands for contact with her daughter-in-law and son and especially with her son.

As the homework assignment, Lynn was to continue to spend as much time as possible with Mrs. March, but because he couldn't be with her all of the time (Mrs. March worked), Lynn was to leave signs of his presence around the house. Lynn, Margaret, and I discussed the details in private. Mrs. March was assigned to report back the following week about how she knew Lynn had been there. Prior to the next session, I instructed Margaret to pick up Lynn's dirty clothes and shoes and put them in a bag for Lynn to take to his mother's house, where he would leave them strewn around his old room. He would then raid the icebox and leave his dirty dishes in the sink.

At the last session, I checked up on the homework assignment. Mrs. March was somewhat amused but was also a bit angry about the extra work caused by Lynn's dishes in the sink (especially the burned eggs in the pan) and the dirty clothing. She had to admit to her daughter-in-law that she guessed that Lynn was not perfect after all and that, just maybe, there were some good points about having a child married and out of the house. She conceded that she would appreciate it if he didn't revert back to his teenage years.

After discussing the homework assignment, I suggested that we do what is termed a family in-law sculpture. The sculpture (or reconstruction) is based on the work of Satir (1988) and Nerin (1993). I asked each family member to stand, and I assigned one family member (Lynn) to be the "director" or artist, while I stood in for that person. Lynn, as director, then positioned the others as he saw them at the present time in their in-law relationship. The participants then commented about how they felt in that positioning. A second sculpture was done: the director placed the in-law family members the way the director *would like* things to look. After each sculpture, I asked participants to comment only on their feelings; asking questions of the director or challenging the director's judgment was not allowed. This lighthearted and creative activity is often a favorite of families. As a therapist, I find it diagnostic as well as therapeutic.

Lynn's first in-law sculpture was highly revealing. In showing how the situation was at the present, he placed me as his surrogate in the center and had Mrs. March and Margaret standing on each side, with each holding onto one of my hands. It was a sculpture of motion: at times Margaret would pull on me, and at other times Mrs. March would pull. Each of the participants was asked about the sculpture. Mrs. March said that she felt distanced from her daughter-in-law and off balance with the pushing and pulling. Margaret said that she resented the unexpectedness and unpredictability of her husband's pulling away. She didn't know whether her mother-in-law or her husband was causing the pull. As a surrogate for Lynn, I felt highly off balance and annoyed; I had no control over which direction I could go, and I felt torn between and by the two women in my life.

In the second sculpture, Lynn showed how he would like things to be. He placed Margaret and me in the center of the room, alongside each other and holding hands. Tears began to fill his eyes when he said what he really wanted was for his mother and father to be standing holding hands in front of us. At that point, everyone choked up. I suggested that his father would always be with them in memory and spirit, and I asked Lynn to move a stepladder behind his mother and to put a wooden bust on it to represent his father. This being done, Lynn had Margaret and me take hold of the mother-in-law's hands, making a circle of love and support. Everyone expressed comfort and support from this sculpture. After the sculpture session was completed, it seemed appropriate to wrap up the therapy with a psychoeducational model.

We discussed the predictable stages of in-law relationships (these concepts are detailed in Chapter 2). Tasks related to the in-law life cycle include empowering in-laws, building on strengths, and dealing with the empty nest and the death of an in-law (Chapter 5). To give this family some strategic tools for future reference, we looked at some ways to mend broken or bruised in-law relationships, taking into consideration personality variables in in-law relationships (these are covered in Chapter 7).

After completing the three two-hour in-law dedicated sessions, Margaret, Lynn, and Mrs. March said that they now saw in-law relationships as distinct, unique, and an important part of the family system; they were not to be ignored or swept under the rug. Mrs. March thanked her daughter-in-law for arranging the in-law therapy, and said that she could see how misunderstandings had been created by the loss of Mr. March as well as the marriage of a son and the introduction of a new daughter-in-law. Margaret in turn thanked her mother-in-law for being willing to attend therapy. They all vowed to support one another and to keep their in-law communications open.

Partial In-Law Therapy

The next case demonstrates a therapeutic situation where various parts of the family come into different sessions to deal with the problem. The first session was with the couple, Todd and Candy. The second session included Lex, Candy's brother. The last two sessions included all of the above as well as the parents-in-law. I did not attend the last two sessions, which were coordinated by an expert in alcoholic interventions. The identified problem was the father-in-law's need for financial support because of his alcoholism. Although in most families the parents-in-law have the economic clout, this is not so in all cases. The Berry family is an example.

Todd Berry made an appointment for himself and his wife, Candy, to discuss his anger at being asked to pitch in to support his alcoholic father-in-law and his mother-in-law. What really frosted Todd was that he hadn't been given a choice; Lex, Candy's older brother, demanded that they provide financial support. Todd said that his brother-in-law just didn't get it and that giving the father-in-law financial support was making him dependent and enabling him to continue drinking. Candy felt caught in the middle between her loyalty to her brother and parents, and her loyalty to Todd. Both Todd and Candy saw Lex as overbearing, always running around telling everyone in the family what to do. Todd saw his parents-in-law as being made into infants by their dependency on Lex.

In-law loyalties and hierarchies (Boszormenyi-Nagy & Spark, 1973; Van Heusden & Van Den Eerenbeetmt, 1986) played an important part in formulation of this case. Lex's loyalty to his parents kept them firmly bound in family emotional systems. The age hierarchies had been switched: Lex had become the economic supporter of his parents and expected his sister and brother-in-law to share the obligation. Todd, as an in-law, brought a fresh point of view. He recognized that his father-in-law was an alcoholic and needed to be confronted—an illustration of how in-laws can bring in new information and what Bateson (1980) termed *the news of difference*. This case also demonstrates the power of economics among in-laws, with the in-laws who give the economic support having a disproportionate amount of influence.

I suggested to the couple that at the next session we have Lex and the parents-in-law join us to see whether we could begin to free up the family emotional system. Lex said that he would come in but he did not think it was appropriate to involve his parents.

During the session, Candy told Lex of her conflict of loyalty between her birth family and Todd, and said that she didn't want her marriage to end in divorce, as did Lex's marriage. Candy further stated that she appreciated the sacrifices Lex made for her parents but she felt the price he had paid for his loyalty was too high. Todd then talked about his concern and love for the father-in-law, but warned that if the family didn't stop denying the alcoholism, the father-in-law would die.

Although at first defensive, after a discussion of the signs of alcoholism, Lex had to admit that his father was an alcoholic. He further admitted that he was tired of trying to hold things together in the family. They all agreed that the father-in-law should stop drinking and get a steady job. I suggested that they contact an alcohol counselor and do an alcohol intervention. I stayed in contact with the family. The first intervention was not successful because the father-in-law refused treatment. The family then upped the ante: Lex told his father that if he did not go in for treatment, he would encourage his mother to leave him and would financially support her but would cut off support of the father. When I last spoke to Todd, his father-in-law was in a 30-day residential treatment program. Sometimes it takes the perspective of an outsider—in this case, an in-law—to point out the changes that need to be made in the family.

Ongoing Therapy with In-Law Interventions

In the next case, a mother-in-law problem was embedded into a couple's crisis and was dealt with without the actual presence of the in-law.

I had seen Nell, a clothing designer and mother of three-year-old Jessica, for one year in individual therapy before she told me that she wanted to leave her husband Kenneth for another man. Her initial presenting problem had been depression and frustration related to her move to the Bay Area. She had lost family support and was frustrated with Kenneth's lack of availability during a demanding medical residency. Nell had not yet disclosed her feelings to her husband.

I suggested to Nell that before things went any further, Kenneth should join us to talk about the problem. Nell agreed, as long as she could disclose her plan to Kenneth in the office. The couple came to therapy several days later, and, at the session, Nell told Kenneth that she was in love with her old high school boyfriend Lorin. Kenneth began to cry and said that he had suspected something, because Lorin had kept in touch with Nell since their marriage and in the last month had called her weekly from his home in Colorado. Nell said that Lorin had recently broken up with his long-time companion, and had begged Nell to leave Kenneth, saying it was "now or never." Kenneth, who loved Nell deeply, had been aware of Nell's intimate friendship with Lorin, but they had agreed that their marriage would end it. Kenneth begged her not to leave him and Jessica. Nell said she was torn because she loved them all and feared losing custody of Jessica.

In the next session, I learned that when he got home from the first session, Kenneth had called Nell's mother for emotional support. Kenneth said that at first she was great. She said he was a wonderful man and confessed that she had always been uncomfortable with the relationship between Nell and Lorin. After completing her conversation with Kenneth, the mother-in-law called Nell and read her the riot act. Nell hung up on her mother and refused to answer any subsequent calls or letters.

When Nell would not respond, her mother began making frequent calls to the hospital where Kenneth was doing his residency. The calls were long distance from New Mexico, so the hospital staff was always anxious to track him down. His mother-in-law demanded to know why Nell wouldn't answer her calls. Kenneth discovered during one very emotional call that his mother-in-law had even threatened to go to court to try to win custody of Jessica. She wanted to know how much free time he had to spend with her grandchild because it sounded like he was at the hospital the majority of the time, leaving her granddaughter with an unfit parent. Kenneth said that he tried to stay calm because he was in the medical residents' lounge and didn't want to make a scene. He just said, "Jessica is fine, and Nell is a good mother. I really can't talk now."

At this point in the therapy session, I discussed with Kenneth and Nell how they had drawn the mother-in-law into an emotional triangle. I told them that it might be helpful for me to teach them the rudiments of transactional analysis (see Chapter 8), and I showed them how knowledge of the ego states can be used to detriangle (differentiate) the emotional system.

During a therapy session for the couple, I drew a triangle (Figure 1.1) on a large pad and discussed with Nell and Kenneth the idea of emotional

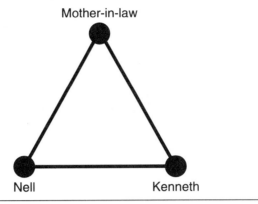

Figure 1.1   Nell's Triangle

triangles and how, when the stress between Nell and her mother was too great, Nell's mother triangled in Kenneth by telephoning him at the hospital. However, I also pointed out to Kenneth that he was responsible for the original triangle when he contacted his mother-in-law to intercede in the stress between himself and Nell.

Kenneth then asked what steps could be taken to get out of this triangle. I suggested that he might respond in a different manner when talking to his mother-in-law. Using the theories of transactional analysis (Barnes, 1977; Berne, 1961), Kenneth could identify, analyze, and change problematic mother-in-law communications. We then discussed the three ego states (Parent, Adult, Child) and I drew these on the pad (Figure 1.2). Kenneth felt that his mother-in-law was speaking to him as a Punishing Parent when she accused him and Nell of not being responsible parents. The mother-in-law's

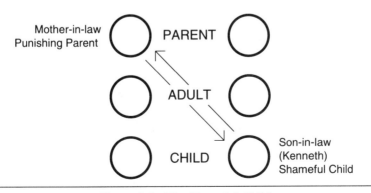

Figure 1.2   The Shameful Child

speaking to him as a Parent made Kenneth feel like a Shameful Child, unable to take care of himself or his family.

Nell said that she had the same feeling when her mother told her that she was an embarrassment to the whole family. Both Kenneth and Nell wanted to respond to Nell's mother in an Adult manner, although they recognized that they could easily put themselves into the Punishing Parent role by framing Nell's mother's reaction as unresponsive and infantile. However, they recognized that, in the long run, the short-term satisfaction would not be worth sacrificing future family relationships.

Kenneth and Nell decided that they would respond in an Adult manner but would keep the mother-in-law in a Caring Grandparent role, thus recognizing her concern for her granddaughter. The couple made an Adult decision to take the Responsible Child stance, putting the mother-in-law in the role of a Caring Grandparent rather than a Punishing Parent. They felt that emphasizing the value of the role of Caring Grandparent would help her decrease her involvement with the couple's problems. This would acknowledge a relationship that was of vital concern to all of the parties involved (Figure 1.3).

Because Kenneth was the member least caught up in the family emotional system, he agreed to make the first attempt at changing the family dynamics. The couple's plan was to have Kenneth telephone his mother-in-law that evening while Nell was at book club. To stay in the Responsible Child role, he would try to exchange information with his mother-in-law and not keep her guessing. He told his mother-in-law that he just wanted to call her because Nell and he knew that she was a very Caring Grandparent. He told her about Jessica's day care and put Jessica on the line to say hello. He said that Nell was fine and that they were going to counseling and were hopeful that things would work out. His mother-in-law was very responsive to the new triangle of grandmother, grandchild, and parents (Figure 1.4).

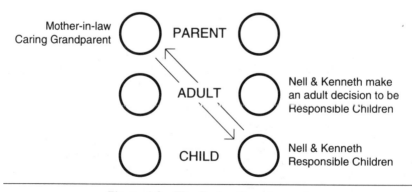

Figure 1.3   The Caring Grandparent

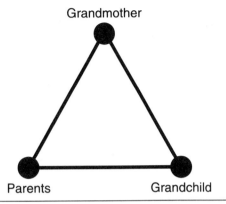

Figure 1.4   A Healthy Triangle

Kenneth ended the conversation by saying that either he or Nell would call her the following Sunday and that it was better if he called her, as it was difficult to talk at the hospital. Kenneth also told his mother-in-law he would send her some of Jessica's artwork.

At the next session, I asked Kenneth how it had gone. He said that his mother-in-law was at first suspicious and a bit guarded, but after speaking with Jessica she had melted like butter. She said she could understand about calling Kenneth at work and that she would look forward to hearing from them the following Sunday. I continued to counsel with the couple for several months. Nell decided that leaving her family for Lorin was too high a price to pay, and shortly thereafter, Kenneth finished his residency and the family moved to New Mexico. One year later I received a Christmas card with a picture of the smiling faces of Kenneth, Nell, Jessica, and their new baby boy, Christopher.

Network Therapy

To deal with differentiation problems where individuals are so poorly differentiated that they are not only in the family in-law soup but in the community stew, I suggest network therapy. In network therapy, as described by Speck and Attneave (1973), the individual's or couple's community is asked to come in to support the family. I use this approach in very complex cases, where there is abuse, alcoholism, or a possibility of suicide. In the following case, the couple was at risk of having their children removed from their home by the child protective agency.

I was called by a Baptist minister who requested that I see Jean and Louis Babcock, a slightly retarded couple who had gone to him as a result of a child protective referral. The child protective counselor was ready to put the couple's two children (Alexis, 2, and Biff, 4) into foster care. Because this was a crisis situation, I suggested we have a large session, with all interested and involved parties present, and the couple agreed to three network sessions. Included in the sessions were the couple, their two children, their pediatrician, the minister, the president of the church's women's auxiliary, two child protective agency workers, and the paternal in-laws. The father-in-law attended only the first session. The maternal in-laws did not live in the area.

The couple had been reported by a neighbor, who said that the children were walking outside their apartment in the snow without shoes. Jean, who presented as being depressed and discouraged, said that she didn't have enough energy to put shoes on the children. On the morning they were reported, Louis had slapped her. She said Louis was also often verbally threatening. Louis justified his actions by saying that yelling or slapping was the only way to get her moving. The network offered suggestions as to how the family could better function. Louis was referred to a 30-day group program for Men Overcoming Violence, to help him learn techniques for dealing with his anger.

Louis agreed to stop the emotional and physical abuse while in therapy, but said that stopping it on a permanent basis would be a more difficult matter. Neither Louis's father nor his mother was willing to stand up to Louis and tell him to stop the abuse, even though they helped the family financially and had a great deal of sway with Louis. During the third and last session, the reason for a lack of a clear message from his parents, that abuse would not be tolerated, became clear: the mother-in-law had herself been abused by her husband when her children were young, and to stand up for Jean would be to confront her husband and her own marriage. At this point, it became clear that I needed to find a strategy to have the mother-in-law empower herself, give up the loyalty to her husband, and come to her daughter-in-law's defense.

One of the mother-in-law's most valued assets was her orderly and lovely home, which she would not allow the grandchildren to visit without supervision. The mother-in-law expressed great concern for Jean and the children and said that she would do anything to help them. I suggested to the network that they might all help when there was a problem. If Louis became hostile, Jean could call the minister and he could contact the women's organization president who would then drive Jean and the children to the mother-in-law's house where they would be safe. The mother-in-law said that would be fine; however, she worked and she was unwilling to let anyone have a key.

I then suggested that since I knew that, as a good mother-in-law, she wouldn't want anything to happen to her daughter-in-law or the grandchildren, Jean and the children could go to the house when things got bad and sit on the porch, wrapped in blankets, until the mother-in-law got home. She said absolutely not: it would embarrass her if the neighbors should see them. I then suggested that Jean could break a small window and get into the house. At that point, the ante had been upped enough and the mother-in-law turned to Louis and said in a very firm voice, "I want you to stop slapping your wife and threatening her." We now had a beginning for a change in a cycle of family abuse, with a mother-in-law standing up for a daughter-in-law, although her reaction was linked to concern for herself and her orderly home.

When I last heard from the minister, the couple was still together with the children. Jean had called the minister on several occasions; each time, Louis had backed down and left the house until he cooled down. The couple had been frightened by the child protective agency report and were attending parenting classes recommended by the pediatrician. The minister said that he was in contact with the in-laws on a monthly basis.

By expanding the network to include church and community, the mother-in-law was drawn into therapy, a situation she had previously been reluctant to be engaged in. This expanded network gave the mother-in-law the support she needed to confront her own abuse, and the social stigma of the community's awareness of what was taking place between Louis and Jean spurred her to action. Although she had previously been able to ignore the family secret of abuse, the mother-in-law now was forced to feel the repercussions of her son's unwillingness to control his temper. Imagining her grandchildren wreaking havoc in her unprotected house forced her hand, and she was able to draw on her own experience to give her daughter-in-law the protection she herself had never received.

ISSUING AN INVITATION TO THE IN-LAWS

Staying problem-oriented, rather than person-oriented, is important when inviting in-law family members to attend therapy (Landau-Stanton et al., 1994). Using Whitaker and Keith's (1981) idea of the therapist asking for the family members' help in dealing with the family's problems can be very effective in getting in-laws to attend therapy. Whitaker (1976) suggested that the therapist enlist the participation of extended family members by framing the sessions as an opportunity to help the client or clients. This approach is equally useful in gaining the support of in-laws. And, indeed, the in-laws' input and perspective on problems can be a most valuable resource. If in-laws cannot physically attend a session, the therapist may wish to consider including them with telephone conference calls during the sessions (Stanton & Todd, 1982).

Family therapy that includes the in-laws can be fun as well as rewarding. However, it can also be difficult, especially for a therapist not trained to think in terms of systems and networks. In any type of therapy, it is desirable for the therapist to have a practice grounded in theory, and this becomes essential when working with large family systems and when dealing with the number and variety of techniques presented in this book. When the therapist combines multiple techniques and a number of people, including the nuclear family and the extended family, the options and agendas at play are increased exponentially. Without a broad perspective, the therapist can easily get lost in dealing with the content of the therapeutic model, rather than addressing the family process. The techniques mentioned above, and additional in-law interventions, are discussed in more detail throughout this book. Although the therapist may use a variety of interventions and techniques, it is important to maintain an overall philosophy of therapy.

CHECKLIST

Therapeutic Options to Consider in In-Law Therapy

The therapist may wish to consider one or more of the following techniques:

1. Stay oriented to the in-law problem.
2. Help clients work on differentiation of self within the family of origin as well as within the in-law emotional system.
3. Construct an in-law genogram to help clients understand family patterns of behavior.
4. Give homework assignments that have a strategic focus and are tailored specifically for the identified in-law problems.
5. Ask clients to take different seats in the room to reflect desired changes in in-law dynamics.
6. Help clients, through in-law education and information, to use their cognitive ability to make a connection between thoughts and feelings.
7. Use the three ego states—Parent, Adult, and Child—to help clients analyze their in-law communication patterns.
8. Encourage clients to identify when in-laws have been recruited into unproductive emotional triangles. Encourage productive triangles.
9. Conduct a family sculpture showing how the family currently relates to the in-laws and then a second sculpture showing how they would like the relationship to be.
10. Identify and discuss family in-law loyalties and gender hierarchies.
11. If the in-law problems are very serious, consider (with the family's consent) inviting the larger community.

CHAPTER 2

Becoming an In-Law

By the time people are old enough to marry, they have developed patterns of communication and acceptance within their childhood families. In contrast, in-laws usually come together without benefit of much previous interpersonal acquaintance, and they share few of the time-established modes of accommodation. Yet, upon marriage, all are thrown into close contact with the other side of the family and have only their previous experiences and sets to use as guideposts.

INTEGRATING A NEW MEMBER INTO THE KINSHIP

How do family members organize themselves around accepting a new member into the family? How does the new member organize himself or herself into the family? Unfortunately, many couples do not recognize the dramatic changes that occur with the marriage and how the change in status creates corresponding requirements for changed behavior. As a couple moves through the cycles of their relationship, there are predictable—as well as unpredictable—stages that must be worked through if the relationship is to thrive. These stages are covered later in this chapter.

The progression through the stages may bring some surprises for future parents-in-law and children-in-law, who often say, "We got along so well before the wedding and then there was a big change." They may be reflecting Satir's (1964) idea of pseudo-self, the pleasant, amicable person we can be toward those with whom we are acquainted and whom we do not see on a regular basis. The *face* people present to those they infrequently meet can become fatiguing when it must be assumed over the long haul. Indeed, it is not reasonable to expect people to be on their company-best behavior at all times, and as in-laws get to know each other better, care must be taken that all parties feel relaxed enough to show their true selves, which can include the disagreeable along with the charming. Only with true acceptance of the other can this relaxation occur, and paradoxically, it is only when people can relax with each other (thus being free to show their unattractive attributes) that true friendship—or kinship—can develop.

Duvall (1954) postulates that when people marry, they change their sense of who they are and to whom they belong. No longer their parents' little girl or boy, they are now the husband's wife (or wife's husband). Where once the loyalties were to father and mother and to their family of origin's way of life, now the loyalties must shift, to center in those held in common with the spouse. Beck (1988) finds that a heavy investment of one partner with the family of origin can cause emotional strain for the couple. A shifting of loyalties is necessarily a difficult assignment in even the best of situations. "Sometimes it is almost shattering" (Duvall, 1954, p. 294). (These shattering shifts in loyalty are covered in Chapter 4.)

"WE DON'T ASK FOR MUCH . . .": EXPECTATIONS OF THE RELATIONSHIP

Therapists who work with extended families know that all families have different expectations of how the in-law relationship will work. For some, there are expectations that the newly married couple will come over every Sunday for dinner. For others, there is the expectation that the unmarried sisters- or brothers-in-law will baby-sit. There may also be expectations that family members will continually be available by telephone, or will call on a daily or weekly basis, or will be on hand during times of crisis.

> When Bill's father lost his eyesight, my mother-in-law expected Bill to drive him to appointments every week. She said, "In our family, we take care of our own."—Marilyn, 43, school teacher

Therapists can help the family to develop creative solutions, like this one:

> Early on, they treated me like an honored guest, but later, I found out what it was like to be a member of the family, smothered with love. Belinda and I have an agreement: I stay with the in-laws for only two hours, and then leave to pursue my own interests. We live five miles away, and as far as I'm concerned, it's too darn close.—Edward, 30, computer programmer

The parents-in-law, though initially not particularly happy about this arrangement, have accepted the limits imposed by their son-in-law.

Geographic proximity may or may not pose difficult challenges. One would think that the closer in-laws live to each other, the more day-to-day pressure may occur; however, if they live far away, holidays and vacations can become monumental problems (more on this topic in Chapter 4). In their research at the Mental Research Institute in Palo Alto, California, Falcon and Graham (1993) found that problems between in-laws were not related to geographical distance; living close to one's in-laws doesn't necessarily mean one will have problems. This is echoed by Marotz-Baden and Cowan (1987), who found in a study of 100 mothers-in-law from two-generation farm and ranch families in Montana, that neither physical proximity nor length of marriage increased stress levels for either group of women. It may be that people living in closer proximity work out their problems, while those who visit infrequently just grin and bear them.

THE NEED FOR FLEXIBILITY

When does one become an in-law? A couple who is living together prior to marriage can encounter situations that raise many questions of social and legal importance. How do parents introduce their young adult child's live-in partner? How does an adolescent conceptualize a parent's cohabitating partner and, perhaps, the partner's own children? Cohabitation issues are very delicate and very complex.

For example, Mary and Fred came into therapy to discuss Mary's problems with Lucy, the fiancée of their 21-year-old son, Mick. Several months prior to our session, Mary and Fred had a major, relationship-threatening disagreement about whether to let Mick sleep with Lucy, at that time his live-in girlfriend, during visits to the family home. Mary felt that it would be wrong to let them share the same bed, because of the example it would set for their 16-year-old daughter, who was still living at home. Fred felt that Mary was old-fashioned: the couple was living together anyway, so what would be the difference? Mary held her ground and told Mick that he was welcome to bring Lucy home but that they would have separate bedrooms. Mick became angry and felt he was being treated like a child. Lucy, on the other hand, took the entire scenario as a judgment on herself—that she did not live up to her future mother-in-law's moral standards. The lines were drawn and the seeds of in-law hostility were sown, even before the marriage began. Without being brought into the discussion, Lucy and her future mother-in-law were pitted against each other.

In the therapy session, Mary revealed that she was devastated because Lucy was not speaking to her. I pointed out that it was important for the original confrontation regarding Mary's disapproval to be dealt with and openly discussed if the future in-laws wanted to live in harmony. I encouraged them to invite Mick and Lucy to attend the next session. My goal for the session was alignment of age hierarchies.

During the session, I supported Mick in taking the lead to resolve the issue with his parents, and encouraged Lucy to take a low profile. As a new member of the family, Lucy was, I felt, a high-risk target, and thus not able to state her case without fear of rejection. Because she seemingly didn't have an advocate within Mick's clan, the relatives had little fear of rebuke when they focused their animosity on Lucy. During the session, the family discussed the idea that although cohabiting relationships may not be a problem for some couples and their families, they may become an issue if all parties are not in agreement. At the end of the session, Lucy and Mick decided to consider their parents' (and future in-laws') values and opinions and chose to be discreet about their sexual relationship. Mary and Fred concurred that they were old-fashioned, and promised to try to be more flexible.

Lucy and Mick's story highlights the fact that decisions made early in a relationship and prior to marriage can impact how in-laws react to one another during later years, when previous hurts or slights are not only remembered, but take on the ominous glow of grudges that are all too often held tight to the heart. As this case demonstrates, the answer to the query, "When does one become an in-law?" is not clear-cut. It is important to encourage clients to address issues as they arise, early in the relationship—even if no formal announcements of wedding plans have been made.

In premarital counseling, I suggest to couples that they should view their commitment to the in-law relationship as *in for the long haul.* Although temporary arrangements can be addressed and limits can be set, the couple might wish to bear in mind that these rapidly become expectations of how the relationship will work throughout its course. It is important to discuss the expectations of the relationship early on and, if possible, to start with a clean slate as far as moral judgments are concerned. The living arrangements of the parents' generation may have clearly included sex only within the confines of marriage; however, given the less formal cohabiting situations of many children, it would seem wiser for clients to err on the side of friendliness and to presume a future in-law status, than to assume that a relationship is only transient. Such assumptions often mean the child's partner is not accorded the respect due a serious commitment.

The best in-law relationships at this point employ a lot of flexibility—and love—to determine how much closeness and distancing can and will be tolerated. Therapists might take into account the religious, ethnic, and socio-cultural factors that influence their clients' attitudes and behaviors, and not stand in judgment of the clients' belief system or overly identify with the younger (or older) couple's values.

Mutual respect and understanding play important roles here, as does the willingness of all the parties concerned to forge a healthy relationship from the beginning. Still, if parents do not approve of some of the activities of their unmarried children, many therapists encourage the parents to set some limits, including saying, "Not in my house." For example, Suzanne, age 40, who had only recently become Richard's second wife, called to make an appointment to come into therapy with her husband. During the session, she stated that she was appalled when Richard allowed his 19-year-old daughter, Sarah, to invite her boyfriend and friends over for cocktails during a summer college break. Suzanne felt this was highly inappropriate. Richard said, "Hell, we drank when we were that age." Suzanne and Richard both held their ground and agreed to disagree, and Suzanne continued to harass Sarah and her boyfriend about the partying. A year later, Sarah and her boyfriend began living together, and they were married the following year. At last report, Suzanne and her stepdaughter and son-in-law continue to have a strained relationship.

The situation becomes increasingly difficult when, as with Suzanne and Richard, the parents are in complete disagreement, whether with regard to alcohol use, sleeping arrangements of their unmarried children, or other issues about which they feel strongly. Therapists can counsel clients to give themselves enough time to have a complete discussion on the topic, and then to avoid a knee-jerk response, even if the partner's viewpoint is already resolute. Parents are cautioned that quick responses to initial requests often return to haunt them. Finally, if the couple cannot reach resolution between themselves, it is important that they fight it out in private, and then present the children and in-laws with an agreement to disagree or with a united front.

Should one or the other parent decide that he or she absolutely cannot agree with a request from their unmarried children, it is important that responsibility be held by the parent. Parents can express their feelings with comments like: "I appreciate your request and the fact that you would consider my feelings enough to ask, but frankly I would not be comfortable having you sleeping together in my house. Call me a prude, but that is the way I feel." In this way, the parent will be owning the problem, rather than dumping it on a future in-law.

BUILDING THE NEW RELATIONSHIP: NEGOTIATING SOME PREDICTABLE STAGES

When working with extended families, I find it useful to employ the small-group model proposed by Tuckman (1965; Tuckman & Jensen, 1977) in order to help clients understand the process of integrating a new in-law into the family. Tuckman identified six stages that a small group typically transits before its members reach cohesion and can work well together: (a) forming, (b) storming, (c) norming, (d) performing, (e) conforming, and (f) adjourning. I have adapted his small-group approach to in-law therapy by merging the performing and conforming stages and by dropping the adjourning stage to reflect the fact that families rarely adjourn, but, instead, continue to work through these stages as new life changes present themselves.

When I work with family groups and individuals who are embroiled in seemingly unresolvable issues, it is helpful to acquaint the clients with these predictable stages. I explain the typical events that occur in each stage and illustrate these, when possible, with examples from my clients' own relationships.

These stages represent constellations of typical activities that occur at predictable points in a relationship. It is important to note that, with extended families, it is not the relationship that moves through the stages. Instead, each stage can be viewed as the cluster of issues that make up the relationship and must be dealt with in the day-to-day course of living. Below, the narratives of clients supply examples of each of the stages. The issues that are often encountered in each stage are then explored.

Forming: Getting Acquainted

We got along so well with our son-in-law before he married our daughter, and then there was a big change. I can see what they mean when they say, "Familiarity breeds contempt."—Hart, 52, marketing director

The first stage is the getting-acquainted or forming stage. This is the dating period, with introductions to parents and invitations to formal and informal family events. At this point (usually prior to marriage), each person puts his or her best foot forward. Only later to we hear such statements as this:

I loved having my boyfriend's sister stay with us at our apartment in Boston, but after we married she became a real pain. I now know what they mean when they say that "Relatives, like fish, stink after three days."—Diane, 43, insurance executive

One of the principal ways to deal with an in-law relationship in the forming stage is to recognize and honor differences. Various theories have been developed to analyze the myriad personality differences that abound in the human family. For example, Myers and Myers (1980) identified 16 personality types, and the Enneagram presents a system of 9 personality types (Baron & Wagele, 1994; Palmer, 1995). With the plethora of personalities with which they might interact, is it any wonder people can't figure out their in-laws? But this figuring out can help clients to recognize the differences in worldview and approach of each personality type, especially if differing opinions are present in in-law conflicts. If no accord can be reached, a recognition of these in-law differences allows the individuals to gracefully agree to disagree. In sessions, I help clients identify how their outlook in life is fundamentally different from their family members' or in-laws' perspectives.

When I met Henry's parents, I wasn't sure about them. I didn't agree with them on religion, politics, or even how to cook a pot roast. I really wasn't even sure if I liked them. But then I had to remember they had raised Henry, and I loved him, so there must be something good about them. At that point, I began to enjoy their differences, and to love them, too.—Rita, 50, doctor

I can tell you I was really shocked when my son-in-law informed me that he was a Socialist. My father would have turned over in his grave; he didn't even like Roosevelt.—Crede, 57, banker

As the in-law relationship proceeds through this initial forming phase, it is useful for the therapist to discuss with the client the concept of scarce resources. Although we often don't think about it, we all have a need and a desire to preserve what we may consider limited resources. This is of course more true for some individuals than it is for others—people who spend a lot of silent time thinking or planning, or those who have perfectionist tendencies, can be very tight with their resources. Primary among the more scarce family resources would be tangibles such as money, represented by requests for the family car (along with the gas tank that always seems to come back empty), loans of cash, invitations to dine out, trips, and family outings. Intangible resources such as time, energy, and privacy must also be considered.

Integrating a new member into the family requires a good deal of all these resources, but especially time and energy. The therapist can encourage individuals to take the time to identify their problem areas and to get to know each other in the process, but they must be willing to expend the energy and time needed to work out solutions if the family is to develop a level of comfort. If there are unresolved problems, working them out is an energy-intensive (and time-consuming) process. One of the primary reasons that most in-law relationships remain unresolved is because someone gets discouraged and feels that "working it out" is just not worth the investment of effort. This happened with one of my female clients, who said:

It's hard coming into the family as the second daughter-in-law. When I married my husband, my sister-in-law was treated as the daughter my in-laws never had. I felt like an outsider. I tried everything—fixing meals, cleaning up, giving gifts, writing cards, spending holidays with them. Nothing worked. I finally gave up. I just ran out of gas. After a couple of years, my sister-in-law divorced her husband and left the family. They treat me better now, so I guess it all worked out in the end.—Gladys, 49, painter

Had this client consulted me at the point when she "ran out of gas," I might have encouraged her to try to understand the different outlook held by her in-laws, and to discuss the issues directly. If this approach did not work, I would have recommended that her husband (who, as the biological child, had more power) step in and discuss the treatment of his wife directly with his parents.

Storming: Shaking Out the Rules of the House

Following the getting-to-know-you forming stage comes the shaking out, or storming, stage, when the initial expectations of the in-law relationship change. This often takes place after the first year of the relationship. By this time, the "honeymoon" is definitely over and all the little idiosyncrasies and annoyances have been discovered. Many people at this point are fatigued with having to behave at their *company best* and decide to just be themselves and let it all hang out, warts and all. The mother-in-law and father-in-law (who were so wonderful during the first year) have been found to be imperfect and may have even shown some annoyance. By this time there have been comparisons by the couple of each other's in-laws and some of the negative traits discovered have been magnified. The parents-in-law also have seen the downside of the new bride or groom.

At this stage, the family works on setting new family rules and guidelines, and the degree to which many expectations are clarified and agreed on will have a lasting impact on the developing relationship. It is important to note that some families never make it through the storming stage, and never develop a sense of normality regarding what is or is not acceptable for the family. If the family does not have many family rules that are clear, or has many unwritten family rules, it may be difficult for the in-law to know how he or she can fit into the family and then be able to make the adjustments necessary to become comfortable.

Early in a marriage, in many families, the majority of time spent with the newlyweds is in the home of the parents, thus creating numerous uncomfortable in-law situations. The traditional lines of social decorum become muddied in the newly formed relationship. The new member of the family may wonder: What do I do when I need a drink of water? Can I rummage through the refrigerator? Can I open a can of tuna and make a sandwich? Can I help myself to the beer? Do I put the dishes in the dishwasher? Should I expect the in-laws to treat me like a houseguest or like a member of the family? Does the entire family drink out of the glass that's on the sink? Where are the glasses kept in the cupboard? What's the family's eating schedule? How much do they eat? Am I expected to eat everything on my plate? Should I volunteer to do the cooking and food shopping?

For the parents-in-law, there are also questions to be answered regarding expectations of the new in-laws. Can I ask them to take out the garbage? What should I say when they put their feet on the coffee table? Do I mention the long-distance charges they keep running up on my phone bill? Should I invite their parents to the big family barbecue? What if they or their family smokes—should I say something in advance?

Although it's great to have them come, I always have so much extra work to do while they're here and I hope that they don't come again too soon.—Barbara, 58, retired nurse

Some families completely skip the forming stage and go directly to storming. For example, for fearful individuals, every change has the potential to become a major issue, and these in-laws are unable to negotiate the forming stage. More angry in-laws may try to avoid conflict so as not to show their innate hostility. Some in-laws may not be pleased with the prospect of a serious relationship, or for various reasons may not approve of the person chosen. In these cases, the significant other has often had only minimal contact with the extended family and dating was done on the sly. When the couple decides to live together or when marriage plans are announced, the family moves directly into the storming phase.

In the storming phase, everyone—from Mom and Dad to Aunt Martha—seems to have a say. Roles begin to be redefined. Parents-in-law often make statements like, "Treat this like your own home," and then make cracks that the new child-in-law never puts the glasses in the dishwasher.

Some potential parents-in-law may not be ready to have their son or daughter take on the role of husband or wife, thereby giving up their primary role of child. In talking about the new couple, McGoldrick (1980) states that the new family members (in-laws) are often used as scapegoats to relieve family tension. Indeed, it is less risky to hate one's in-laws than to confront one's own blood relatives. For example, if the son or daughter stands up for his or her spouse, the family may see the spouse as an interloper, and therefore a low-risk target, as in Lucy and Mick's case, related earlier in this chapter. The spouse may then become the repository of anger, frustration, and resentment. It is especially important for parents and siblings to remember that they may lose contact with their child or sibling if they slight their new in-law.

My mother-in-law delegated me to be the keeper of the pocketbooks and purses at my brother-in-law's wedding rehearsal. She told me to sit on the back row of the church. After three years of marriage, my husband finally took a stand, and told his mother that if she didn't treat me like a member of the family, she wouldn't see him again. Her behavior changed 180 degrees. She now treats me like a special guest.—Emma, 31, social worker

In *The Family Life Cycle,* McCullough (1980) states, in a chapter entitled "Launching Children and Moving On," that if children have established their personality and beliefs separate from their birth family, they have difficulty incorporating their spouses into the family. Indeed, the child may choose a mate who will help them fend off the family and may become a wedge between the mate and the family. McCullough also states that difficulties with in-laws are often reflections of problems the family had prior to the marriage. Not accepting in-laws into the family may be a way for the parents to try to continue to hold on to the child. As seen in the following vignette, holding on too hard may risk the entire relationship. The idea is to hold, but with an open hand that can also let go.

My mother-in-law and I fought from day one. She wanted to protect her turf and run her daughter's life and so did I. My wife ended up dumping both of us.—Richard, 46, Army officer

In this relationship the wife felt trapped and overly controlled, and the husband and mother-in-law did not know how to let go. After a year's separation and extensive work on family-of-origin issues, Richard felt ready to ask for a reconciliation, and his wife agreed to attend. She discussed her need for independence, but admitted that, in light of her continuing love for her husband, she really did not want the divorce. The husband agreed to work on some issues with his mother-in-law to avoid the conflicts, and the mother-in-law was included in some subsequent sessions. She conceded that she preferred the stability of her daughter's marriage to constant bickering with the son-in-law, and the marriage appears to be back on track.

The key for successfully navigating the forming and storming stages is negotiation. Here, the therapist can help families identify the most important issues, and then, working from the most absurd resolution to the most agreeable one, help the families reach consensus. Negotiation requires a commitment of time and energy. Prior to it, all the parties should agree to stay the course until resolution is reached, even if only one issue is addressed during each session. The family should prioritize the issues in advance, so that the most important ones will be dealt with first. Theoretically, this approach should help the family move more quickly to resolution of easier, subsequent issues. On the other hand if there are severe communication problems a low priority issue may be picked and solved in order to build family confidence in the process.

Another factor that may be dealt with during this stage is the involvement of the spouses' in-laws with each other. Therapists sometimes hear the complaint, "I didn't pick them so why am I expected to love them?" This is often taken even further when the family is expected to tolerate or even love the parents or siblings of the new in-law. An example came up during a couple's therapy session. Jason, a computer programmer, and his wife Sue, a part-time accountant, made it clear that they had in-law problems. During our first session, I suggested that we have a session with their parents. Sue and Jason agreed, but only with the proviso that we have each spouse's in-laws in separate sessions. We learned that Sue's father didn't feel that Jason's parents had really become a part of their family, as he'd hoped they would. He said that Jason's parents had accepted invitations to his home for dinner several times but had never reciprocated the invitations, which made him feel hurt and slighted. Jason defended his parents, stating that the expectation was unrealistic, as his parents "never entertained." During the course of therapy, Sue's father was able to express his feelings and came to realize that his expectations put a great deal of pressure on the young couple.

Unless both sets of parents of a new couple have an established relationship prior to the marriage, the idea of joining two extended families generally requires too much logistical energy. A friend comments, "People moving is the hardest work in the world."

In some cases, one of the children-in-law or parents-in-law wants both sets of parents to bond in a close relationship. For example, when Jane and David married, Jane felt that her parents and David's parents would naturally be great friends, because she and David had so much in common. Jane put on large dinners and invited both sets of in-laws, and she put pressure on her parents to socialize with David's parents on their own. During the course of therapy, Jane came to realize that her strong need for affiliation was not shared by either set of the in-laws, and that she was putting more energy into the bonding of the families than any of the parents-in-law. To everyone's relief, after several years of trying, Jane gave up on family togetherness and began working on her own relationships with individual family members.

Norming: Setting Boundaries and Aligning Age Hierarchies

I really felt like I was part of the family when my wife's folks moved and I was asked to drive their truck for two days. I told them I could only take one day off from work, and they seemed to accept that. Setting my boundaries let me help them without feeling used. —Whit, 28, sales rep

After the family has successfully negotiated the storming phase (or has run out of energy), they then begin to move into the norming phase, where boundaries are set, rules are redefined, and members develop an understanding of where each fits within the in-law system. By the second or third year of the marriage, the couple will have begun to move into developing a state of normalcy within the family. Because the individuals by this point feel comfortable showing their true faces, the in-laws can also be used as a dumping ground for the couple to safely vent their anger and frustration in their efforts toward trying to adapt to each other. At that point, the in-laws, both parents and children, have come to realize what it means to be an in-law and will try to deal with some of the expectations.

Many of the actions and sentiments expressed while limits are being developed in the storming stage can leave bruises. To attain a state of normalcy, the family members may have to go through a ritual of forgiving toward the parents-in-law and the children-in-law after the storming stage has been completed. Then the family can move forward in the norming stage and develop a cordial, warm, and loving relationship. If the family has ambiguous family rules and poorly defined boundaries, the new in-law will find it difficult to know how he or she can fit into the family or make the adjustments necessary to become comfortable.

Defining expectations and rules is an important step during the norming phase, and boundaries may need to be set by the in-law who brings in new skills, or as in the following case, by that in-law's spouse.

> *After a year, I finally had to tell my parents to stop asking Jeff to help them. Mom and Dad just assumed that he would spend his vacation helping Dad fix up the cabin. As the new son-in-law, Jeff felt obligated to help Dad. The funny thing was that they didn't have a clue that Jeff didn't love the work.*—Kitty, 27, secretary

Anyone stepping into a new family quickly discovers that things are not always as they seem. A client may think that the father and mother in the family are jointly making the major decisions, but after looking at the family, may find that one or the other seems to be the policymaker most of the time. It benefits the new in-law to understand the family's age hierarchies, to recognize who has the role of being most in charge of the family, and to be aware of who will be actually making which decisions.

Once the client has discovered the chain of command, he or she may be wise to learn to work with, rather than against, the flow. I recommend that clients learn to respect the existing structure; through understanding the relationship with the new spouse in connection with the structure. Any changes must be made in the context of the structure. For example, if the oldest sister usually plans all the family events and the new brother-in-law wants to put together a day at the horse races, he might consider using his sister-in-law as the sounding board, getting her consensus, and even letting her work out all the details. In this way, they can get to know each other, and learn to work within the existing family system.

Once these roles are clarified and accepted, family members can develop mutual respect for one another. In-laws at this point feel comfortable collaborating on the decision-making process.

> *The first year we were married, my in-laws would ask us to baby-sit when they went out of town. Sure, I'm a teacher, and I love to be with kids, but three young teenagers—give me a break! I finally had to say no. I must say, I was surprised when they said they could understand. I felt so good about it, I told them I would sit once a year if they would give me advance notice.*—Leland, 30, schoolteacher

One of the signs that the in-law relationship has reached the norming stage is when a process has been developed for distributing information and resources, as seen in the above case. Working cooperatively, a team spirit is built, and strong roots for a new kinship are formed. At this point, realigned loyalties and mutual respect allow in-laws the freedom to really be themselves. Rather than causing conflict, differences are negotiated.

Conforming: Reaching Cohesion in the Family Unit

After we had been married for three years, we went to Arkansas to visit my family for Thanksgiving. I was pleased to see that my parents felt comfortable asking Russell to help with the chores, and he felt comfortable just kicking back after they were finished.—Gena, 31, teacher

Conforming occurs for families that have successfully completed the forming, storming, and norming stages, and it is where maximum cohesion is reached. Rules and bonds, both implicit and explicit, have been established and accepted. Minimal social and emotional expectations have been met, and, ideally, the group has laid the foundations to enable them to negotiate future problems, conflicts, or misunderstandings. Once they have reached this stage, the children-in-law and parents-in-law have learned more about give-and-take, and have reached some degree of agreement in their mutual expectations. Although families that have essentially achieved a conforming relationship with the in-laws during the early period of their relationship will have a solid foundation for dealing with future problems, any family is subject to many outside forces and is an open system, and life-cycle changes such as birth, divorce, retirement, and death may shake the system. (This area is explored in Chapter 5.) Awareness of the impact of such changes and an understanding and expectation that flexibility is needed will help clients transit through the ups and downs of extended family life.

NEGOTIATING THE STAGES THROUGHOUT THE RELATIONSHIP: AN ONGOING CYCLE

The constellations of feelings and activities in any given stage do not happen in a linear fashion. Instead, they occur concurrently between different parties in the relationship. For example, the mother of the new husband may be negotiating the storming stage with the new daughter-in-law; her son, who already is very comfortable with his wife's parents, may have reached the norming stage with them; at the same time, his sister, who was best friends with his new bride, is in the conforming stage with her new sister-in-law.

In-laws may thus be storming in one area and conforming in others. The question presents itself: Can the individuals in the family be flexible enough to move through the stages, or will they become stuck in a certain stage? Because patterns of family life change so rapidly from one generation to another today, just growing up in a family may not be enough preparation for what it takes to found one's own family. Helping clients to recognize these expected stages of family growth can be enormously helpful in the establishment of new family units.

Families should also be aware that they will continue to encounter the issues of each of these stages at many points throughout the relationship, when life-cycle changes bring new circumstances to the family. According to Duvall (1954), "Learning to love and accept one's in-laws takes time—it is a process that goes on through living together through real life experiences."

CHECKLIST

What Stage Is the In-Law Relationship Transiting?

Just as medical patients find it beneficial to have their illnesses given a definite diagnosis, many individuals and families in therapy find it helpful to identify the stages they are encountering in the in-law relationship. The questions listed below will help families to determine how their members are processing the issues, and to identify areas where there is danger of getting stuck in any given stage.

Forming

1. Has there been an effort to introduce the new or potential in-law to other family members, or to include him or her in family events?
2. Is the real self or the pseudo-self presented by and to family members?
3. Are the family members aware of differences, and if so, how are they dealing with them? Can family members make allowances for differences? Have they reached the point of honoring the differences?
4. Are new issues discussed among family members?
5. Are individuals willing and able to suspend judgment on issues and individuals? Is there enough individual and family energy available to invest in change?

Storming

1. Are families and individuals putting in the energy needed for change to take place?
2. Have family members discussed their expectations of the new relationship?
3. Is there a desire to work on areas of difference and sameness? Are family members being open and honest regarding the issues?

4. Have family or house rules been identified?

5. Have permission issues around marriage been discussed and worked out (i.e., has permission to marry been given)?

Norming

1. Have family rules and boundaries been processed?

2. Has forgiveness taken place for breaches that occurred in the storming stage?

3. Have individuals and family differences been acknowledged and respected?

4. Are the family roles defined and aligned?

5. Do newcomers to the family understand where the power lies? Can a balance of power be reached?

6. Can family members agree to disagree and live with ambiguity and differences? Is it recognized that all issues will not be resolved?

7. Are global issues, such as staying a part of the in-law's lives, recognized as being more important than one person's being right on any given micro issue?

Conforming

1. Is the family moving with cohesion in the same direction?

2. Has the family made accommodations for new issues and individuals coming into the system?

3. Is there love at home? Can people achieve their goals in a nurturing environment?

4. Does the family structure promote the well-being of individual family members?

5. Has equilibrium been reached—do family members express a tolerable level of comfort with the state of the family?

CHAPTER 3

Developing Relationships: The Marriage and Beyond

PERMISSION TO MARRY: AN ANACHRONISM OR AN INDISPENSABLE ELEMENT FROM THE PAST?

During therapy sessions, I frequently open the discussion by asking couples in crisis if they received their parents' permission to marry. They often reply, "Isn't it a bit old-fashioned to think that a couple needs to get permission from their parents to marry?" The custom may seem out of date, but I believe that marriages should start out with as much going for them as possible, and permission to marry is one aspect that is often overlooked. In fact, I have discovered that a common thread running through many troubled marriages is that the parents had not given permission—either explicit or implicit—to make a potential in-law a member of their family. I hear statements like, "We told them they were too young," "I told them they weren't ready," "We never wanted them to get married," or, "I warned her not to."

Dr. Duncan Stanton of the University of Rochester Medical Center Family Training Program postulates that 80% of the couples in failed marriages had not received permission to succeed in the marriage. According to Dr. Stanton (1981b), this lack of permission originates with the parents. Asking the bride's parents for their daughter's hand in marriage may seem like an outdated gesture; however, if Dr. Stanton's postulation is correct, there is a high correlation between marital difficulty and lack of permission to marry. According to Duvall's (1954) study, there was general agreement that a young man or woman faces more hazards in a marriage of which one or more parents disapprove than are present in a union having the blessing of both sets of parents. Opposition of parents to the marriage is closely related to the breaking up of many engagements. Duvall found a strong correlation between age of the couple and degree of parental interference, and as one might guess, the younger the couple, the more active—both in support and opposition—were the parents. On the basis of the research findings of Duvall, it could be suggested that the initial approval of the parents in courtship is a factor favorable to good in-law relationships in marriage and that initial opposition may precede and be predictive of in-law troubles in marriage.

Receiving explicit as well as implicit permission to marry from both sets of parents may help a young couple to work out difficulties with future in-laws prior to marriage. If the future in-laws refuse to give their blessing to the marriage, at least the couple knows where they stand and differences can then be brought out into the open.

Prior to the 20th century, in America it was expected that parents would assume real responsibility for their children's mate selection and courtship behavior, and for the marriage itself. This is obviously no longer the case; fathers do not ask a potential suitor, "What are your intentions, young man?" followed with "And what are your prospects to support my daughter?" Although they do not play as prominent a role, parents do continue to have a subtle influence in sorting out eligible possibilities (Duvall, 1954).

In their book on family loyalties, Boszormenyi-Nagy and Spark (1973) state that when a couple marries they have to merge their old family commitments with the new. The couple must shift their loyalties from their birth families to one another and deal with the guilt of leaving their parents (this issue is dealt with in Chapter 4). Through the ages, parents in many cultures have arranged their children's marriages, and this is believed to have helped children deal with the guilt of leaving their parents. Although arranged marriages are not the norm in Western culture, parents still impact choice of spouse through positive activities such as parties, weekend outings, and vacations, in order to control their children's circle of activities and influence their choice of friends. To deter what they think may be a poor marriage, parents may also use persuasion, appeals for loyalty, and threats. Marriages are no longer formally arranged by American parents but future in-laws still have an influence on marital choice.

We have moved into what Lash (1977) called an inner-directed self-reliant society where marriages have evolved from parent-controlled to participant-run. However, even though the young couple is making the decision to marry, their contacts with their in-laws will be an integral part of their lives. In a study of elderly people, Shanas et al. (1968) found that 70% of people over 65 in America, England, Denmark, Israel, Poland, and Yugoslavia live within 10 minutes of a son or daughter.

Therapists might suggest that parents think seriously *before* withholding support to a couple who are contemplating marriage. Constructive inquiry or comments may be better received than objections. Over the course of five years, the Minnesota Family and Marriage Group gave marriage compatibility tests to 2,500 young couples, and found that all but a few couples got married regardless of the results of the compatibility testing. The Group then followed the couples over time and found that 80% of the couples who scored in the incompatible range later divorced. The research indicated that most couples will marry despite all objections and that the objections often strengthen their resolve to marry.

Clay and Deborah are an example of a couple who have had negative experience with marital counseling and who did not have parental support to marry. The couple came to me after experiencing a stormy marriage for five years. Although they loved one another, they were considering divorce. Clay said that the impending break up wasn't a surprise; prior to their marriage, all of their friends and future in-laws had told them they were not suited for one another. Rather than discouraging them from marrying each other, these dismal prognostications only encouraged the couple. Clay told me that his mother-in-law went so far as to make appointments for psychological testing, at which time the therapist said that the tests showed them to be highly incompatible. Now, five years and three small children later, they came to me discouraged and resigned to the fact that their parents and friends had been correct—their marriage indeed seemed doomed.

After several individual sessions in which we discussed their differing styles, we had a session with Deborah's parents. During the course of therapy, the psychological testing was mentioned and Deborah's mother laughed with embarrassment and told us, "We all took those tests." She then said that Clay was a "wonderful son-in-law and husband" and that as parents-in-law they would do everything in their power to help the couple work out their relationship. Thus, after five years and lots of conflict, Deborah's mother finally gave marital permission. The point here is not that testing can predict divorce, but that couples marry for reasons other than compatibility. If parents-in-law want to support their children in marriage, they need to realize that their decisions and acceptance have an important impact on the success (or failure) of the marriage. I recently spoke to Clay and Deborah. They continue to work on their marriage, and Clay has pursued individual counseling to work on family-of-origin issues.

Taking a few minutes to discuss with the future parents-in-law the desire to marry their daughter or son can make a big difference in how the relationship gets started. Some parents-in-law, however, will not agree to give permission to the marriage. For example, Roxanne was a single mother with one adult son, Kevin. She was annoyed that Kevin had eloped with Regina, whom she didn't meet until after the honeymoon. Roxanne could never forgive Regina for stealing Kevin from her, and after more than 12 years, continued to harbor a lot of anger and bitterness. Because the couple was living on the other coast, I suggested that Roxanne do some gestalt therapy (Perls, Fefferline, & Goodman, 1972), acting out what she *would* say if Kevin and Regina were present. She soon realized that Regina hadn't stolen Kevin from her; Kevin had left of his own accord many years earlier. Once she got beyond the bitterness, she was able to welcome Regina into the family and reestablish a healthy relationship with Kevin.

Sometimes, resolving an early lack of acceptance takes an enormous amount of energy. Henry came to a session complaining that whenever he had a conflict with his children, they would call his mother-in-law (the children's grandmother) to settle the dispute. He was dismayed that his wife Ann refused to become involved. I suggested that we have an intergenerational family session and that Ann's parents attend the meeting. During the session, her parents revealed that they had never been asked for their daughter's hand in the marriage and that they had never approved of Henry as a son-in-law. After dealing with Henry's resulting anger, and after the parents admitted that they did not want Ann and Henry to divorce, I asked them what Henry would have to do in order to gain their approval to be married to their daughter. Taking the situation to the extreme, I suggested that the couple might want to date and that Henry then could ask Ann's parents for permission to marry her. The in-laws felt that the dating would not be necessary but they conceded that they would like to have him ask for permission to marry their daughter. In a gesture of goodwill toward her parents, Ann and Henry agreed to give her wedding ring to her father for safekeeping until her parents felt that they could give her permission to be married. The parents were pleased and amused when Henry knelt before them and asked for Ann's hand in marriage. They agreed, and this began a joining and forgiveness process for this family.

Many therapists may notice a marked tendency for one spouse to marry a person who has the opposite characteristics. For example, a very artistic and impulsive individual may choose a mate who is compulsive and controlled. During the courtship, the couple is drawn together by their admiration of the qualities they find lacking in their own personalities. However, after the honeymoon is over and the realities of the relationship have had a chance to gel, they spend a great deal of time and energy trying to change those very qualities they once admired in the person they married. If one assumes that the person learned his or her behaviors in the birth family, the parents from whom they were learned may compound the energy of their child. This situation would be especially difficult for a relaxed and easygoing spouse who has unwittingly married into a "Type A" family.

FACTORS AFFECTING IN-LAWS' APPROVAL OR DISAPPROVAL OF CHOICE OF SPOUSE

Nobody is ever good enough for your child.—Doris, 56, housewife

Most parents want to share the benefit of their experience with their children to help them make a better life and have better marriages than they themselves did. Trying to help their children avoid the wrong marriage may be some parents' method of reliving their fondest fantasies of how their own lives should have been. But other parents may relive their disappointments and anger, through becoming too involved in their children's relationships. Landis and Landis (1973) asked 1,062 married people, 155 unhappily married people seeking help through marriage counseling, and 164 divorced people whether both parents had approved of their marriage. Of the married group, 88% stated that both their parents approved. The unhappily married group in counseling and the divorced group reported only a 58% approval rate from both parents.

Many factors may affect the in-laws' approval or disapproval of the choice of spouse, and these primarily are based on early expectations for marital relationships. In my clinical experience, major issues affecting choice of spouse (and approval of the new family member by parents-in-law) are related to age, education, and socioeconomic status, as well as religious, racial, and cultural–ethnic variables. Because of the enormous effect of cultural and ethnicity factors in in-law relationships, this area is covered in depth in Chapter 10. The other factors are briefly discussed here.

Age

Many parents feel that their children are not old enough to get married. This reaction sometimes seems to be related to the age of the parents when they were married, and usually arises when the children are on the younger end of the age spectrum. I often hear comments like, "I was too young when I got married; I should have listened to my parents," or "Had I known what I know today, I would not have gotten married so early."

> In the '60s, while a student at a Southern University, I met 30-year-old Prescott at a civil rights march. I was young, impressionable, and excited to be the girlfriend of a civil rights leader. Those were exciting times and Prescott was full of energy and strength. I just couldn't understand why my dad was so upset. He wrote me a letter stating that he knew that my good training and common sense would win out and that I would break up with Prescott. He further stated that Prescott was too old for me, and that I had school to complete before I got married. Two months later we were married. My parents did not attend the wedding, as Prescott had insisted that it be an interracial event. I will always regret the fact that we did not have more consideration for my parents. Looking back, I know that I was too young and did not have the experience to stand up to Prescott.—Charity, 45, mental health worker

Age gave Charity the perspective she lacked as a college student. Sometimes, age factors work in the opposite direction. Omar, a 73-year-old retired doctor, was contemplating marriage (his first) to a 69-year-old widow. His bride-to-be's children were concerned about the advanced years of both, and feared they would have to take on added responsibilities. Only after Omar pointed out his financial security did the future children-in-law give their blessings to the marriage.

Education

Education may also become an issue in the family. The potential parents-in-law may decide that the children should complete their college education before they marry, and may even make this a requirement before the marriage can take place. When their children decide to marry before earning their degrees, the marriage may be an annoyance to both sets of parents. Some fathers in therapy have demanded to know what the potential spouse is going to do to support their child, particularly if this particular child is a daughter.

> *We sacrificed so that our daughter could earn a college degree and make something of herself. So when she married Ronald, a drum-player with a high-school diploma, we were understandably alarmed. I have to admit that her mother and I were quite satisfied when they split up after three years of marriage. He is still going from gig to gig and can't even support himself, let alone a family.*—Nathan, 61, high-tech executive

Family values differ regarding education. High-achieving parents may wonder what the in-law is going to do to gain more education; blue-collar parents often feel threatened by a college-educated child-in-law. Family members may feel inferior or fear they will be judged critically by the new addition to the family. Siblings-in-law may judge themselves against the new family member's job or degree. Blue-collar parents may also feel that the more educated in-law will take their child away from them.

> *I didn't think it would bother me that my husband has a law degree and I just have an associate degree. But when we go to business functions, I'm in way over my head and I know his friends are wondering what he sees in me. Not to mention his sisters, who all hold master's degrees (guess who never wants to play Trivial Pursuit® at their parties!). I always heard that the wife rises to the social level of her husband, but I don't think it's true.*—Patrice, 37, veterinary aid

> *I'll never forget when I was being fitted for my wedding dress, the seamstress asked me what we were planning to do after the wedding. I was excited about the prospects of our future, and told her that Barney had been accepted to graduate school at an Ivy League college and that we were moving to the East Coast. At that point, my mother said (in a rude voice), "Sometimes I think that's the only reason she is getting married." I felt really hurt, but somehow knew that the comment said more about my mother than it did about me.*—Emma, 31, social worker

Socioeconomic Factors

Although socioeconomic factors can be related to the education issue, the harsh reality of the myth that America is a classless society is all too often felt by in-laws who don't quite measure up to the newcomer's social standing. A child often will bring into the family a potential in-law who is of a higher or lower socioeconomic status. If lower, the child may expect his or her family to help the incoming person to become more educated and more upwardly mobile. The parents-in-law might view such a spouse as a *project:* the child has brought home a spouse for the family to reparent. If the socioeconomic disparity is too great, common ground is rarely found between the families, and, unfortunately, the marriages often end in divorce.

> *Knowing our son-in-law, it seemed like we would fit in with his family, but after going to his parents' home for dinner, I don't know how it will ever work. Their house is enormous, they have servants, and the place just reeks of old money. I don't know how we can ever even attempt to reciprocate socially.*—Gus, 62, security guard

> *Before we were married, I had the feeling that she was ashamed of me. She'd never invited me to her parents' home, but when she finally did, I figured out why she had hesitated. They were a bunch of slobs. It turns out she wasn't ashamed of me, but was embarrassed by her family's poverty. I figured she was a rose amongst the thorns and married her anyway, but now, seven years later, I realize that she's a slob just like the rest of her family. No matter what I do, I can't seem to teach her any class.*—Hugh, 35, investment adviser

Religion

Major issues of marital compatibility are often related to differences in religious values. In the heat of romance, many couples might disregard the fact that much of the family heritage is based on religious celebrations and rituals, especially when offspring enter the picture, and issues such as christening, catechism, communion, and confirmation must be addressed. Clients may deny that they are religious and may say their religion has meant nothing to them for many years. They may even feel surprised at the importance they have suddenly given to their potential in-law's religious beliefs. But when it comes to their children's marriages, many parents suddenly find that they would like them to marry a Catholic, a Jew, a Muslim, a Mormon, or someone from their own religious background. Although some may deem such a preference bigoted, there are valid reasons for desiring religious compatibility.

> *We tried to raise our children without any formal religious training because we wanted them to decide for themselves when they were old enough to understand all the ramifications of religion. Imagine our surprise and dismay when our oldest son fell in love with a very strict Mormon. She insisted on being married*

in their temple, which my husband and I couldn't attend. It turns out that none of my other children will ever marry, and I am still bitter that I was forced to stand outside the doors for their wedding.—Laura, 58, X-ray technician

I always made light of my parents' counsel that "like should marry like." Although our family was always religious, I didn't realize how important my faith was until our first child was born. I was heartsick that my husband, who is agnostic, was unwilling to have our daughter christened in my church. He said, "What does it matter, it's all a bunch of hooey anyway." Now, I'm teaching all my children the importance of marrying someone with the same belief structure they hold. Do you think it will make a difference in their marriage choices? I hope so.—Jean, 35, writer

Race

Ethnic background can be a highly volatile subject when a child is bringing a potential spouse into the home. The child who mistakenly thinks that his or her parents are liberal and understanding may be quite surprised at the reaction his or her choice of spouse might bring. For example, when confronted with a Native American, Susan's mother screamed at him, told him to get out of the house and said that if she ever saw him on the property, she would shoot him with a shotgun. This made a very difficult choice for Susan, who had come to the house with Walter to tell her parents that she was pregnant. Susan ended up not marrying Walter. Instead, she made a marriage of convenience, which soon ended in divorce.

Although interracial marriage has become more common in the past few decades, it is often quite difficult for in-laws to adapt to the interracial couple. The Oscar-winning film *Guess Who's Coming to Dinner* opened society's eyes a few decades ago; however, the old racial stereotypes continue to set families ablaze with conflict.

Ted and I met at the hospital where I was a nursing student and Ted was a medical resident. The folks were thrilled when I told them I was dating a doctor, but then they found out from my sister that Ted is African American. This was 30 years ago, when interracial marriage was taboo. Mother said that she liked Ted, and could see that we were in love, but if we wanted their approval, we must promise that we would not have children. Needless to say, we wouldn't make that promise. A month later, we were married by a justice of the peace, with only Ted's parents in attendance. Mother didn't speak to us for two years. After our first child was born, she started to warm up to Ted, and after 30 years and five children, she actually recently said that Ted had been a good son-in-law. I give Ted credit for really putting up with a lot.—Barbara, 58, retired nurse

I recently saw June, a mother of six grown children, in therapy. She was devastated that her youngest daughter Amy (age 23) had just had a child out of wedlock. The biggest problem for June was that the father of her new granddaughter was African American. Initially, she had put pressure on Amy to give up the child for adoption, only to find that the father was anxious to marry Amy, and that he would never allow an adoption, but would gladly raise the child himself. June saw this as a real possibility, because, she said, "the father is a college graduate and his parents are professional people." When I suggested that June might want to meet the father of her granddaughter, she was irate, and said that it would never happen. I pointed out that the reality was that her granddaughter is part African American, and that if she did not accept this fact, in the end she would be the loser through bitter feelings, and would risk alienation from her daughter, granddaughter, and prospective son-in-law. June continues to refuse to meet her granddaughter, the maternal grandparents, or the father. Although her daughter Amy does not live with the child's father, she does receive financial support and dates him, against the families' wishes. After several months of therapy, June decided to reconnect with her daughter and granddaughter, but she still refuses to meet her granddaughter's father. June continues to hold out the hope that Amy will give up the relationship. (Cultural and ethnic influences on the in-law system are dealt with in greater depth in Chapter 10.)

COMING TO ACCEPTANCE

The roles and responsibilities of parents-in-law in helping a new union get off to its best start can be challenging. Duvall (1954, p. 78) notes that at least seven roles are well represented in the behavior of mothers-in-law; in my experience these descriptions can be extended to all in-laws:

Roles in which rejection is the primary factor:

1. *Aggressive opposition = mother-in-law refuses to speak to daughter's husband.*

2. *Active proselytizing = father-in-law makes constant negative comments about son-in-law's work prospects.*

3. *Persistent resistance—a formal politeness = daughter-in-law calls in-laws by formal titles (Mr. Rogers and Mrs. Rogers).*

4. *Initial resistance gradually lessening as the marriage continues = "I thought it would be horrible for my daughter to marry a plumber, but now he's starting to grow on me—I'm impressed with how he treats her."*

Roles in which acceptance is the primary factor:

1. *Resigned acceptance = "I knew they would get married anyway, so I may as well try to like her."*

2. *Readiness to explore and accept = "It's so interesting to learn about his Pakistani culture."*

3. *Active aid in assimilation* = *"Let us help you with the down payment on your home."*

According to Duvall (1954, p. 71), "Every marriage is a mixed marriage, bringing together a man and woman from different walks of life." Duvall finds that the greater the social distance between the pair, the more mixed the marriage is thought to be, and the more difficult the marriage adjustment. However, I have found that no matter how mixed the marriage, the initial acceptance into the in-laws' family is a primary factor in how successful the marriage will be. Duvall found (and I have amply witnessed) that fear of not being welcomed as a new member of her husband's family is widespread among women.

In-Law Issues for Second Marriages

A frequently observed cause of stress in marriages and in the extended family of in-laws is the perception of violation of acceptable social standards of conduct and behavior. This is especially true when a marriage follows a trying divorce. The divorce of the partners often leads to the estrangement of former close relationships between the in-laws. All relationships take time and effort to develop into friendships. This is particularly true where a new marriage relationship is seen to be based on the rendering apart of former relationships, as occurs in bitter divorce proceedings. It is difficult under those circumstances for the new relations to establish bonds of close friendship with the newly married couple.

For example, Sam and Ruth divorced, and immediately thereafter, Ruth married Bob. It was general knowledge among their friends and relatives that Ruth and Bob had been intimately involved prior to the divorce. Their intimate relationship was generally viewed, by Bob's and Ruth's families, associates, and friends, as a breach of acceptable standards of conduct. Both Ruth and Bob foresaw a major problem in establishing a new relationship with Ruth's extended family, who, they expected, would be resentful of Bob because of his perceived role in ending Ruth's marriage to Sam. Ruth felt resentful toward her extended family because of her perception of their lack of welcome of Bob. Bob became stressed when he saw how Ruth was dealing with his in-laws' reception of him. Thus, Bob and Ruth found that despite the proliferation of divorces and the relaxed standards of society in relation to marriage, their premarital behavior presented a major in-law problem.

The couple sought therapy in an attempt to smooth the transition and remedy the situation. After the couple's first session, I suggested that we invite the in-laws to the next session. Both Ruth's and Bob's parents and a few of their siblings attended the session. I related the idea behind an old legal axiom, *Matrimonium subsequens tollit peccatum praecedens* ("Subsequent marriage obliterates precedent sin"), which expresses society's means of permitting all of the parties, and society as a whole, to rationalize away the uncomfortable situation. In other words, if the individuals making up the new couple—and those who comprise the extended family—could work to build new relationships without reference to former breaches of conduct, they could move forward to meaningful relationships, absent the specter of past perceptions or judgments. An understanding of the old legal axiom permitted them to do this. There then developed an extended discussion about the changes brought by the new relationship. An agreement was reached that Ruth and Bob would be accorded the respect the deserved as newlyweds, without reference to their previous conduct. There was a feeling of relief in the group that it was indeed acceptable to forgive the past and welcome the new relationship.

Disclosure of Past Romantic Associations

Along with problems relating to prior marriages and breaches of conduct, some newlyweds feel threatened by the discovery of the existence of one or more undisclosed former romantic associations. This can be especially difficult if in-laws, friends, and family are aware of these relationships. Prior to marriage, the therapist might recommend that the couple frankly and completely disclose to each other all former romantic associations and give a positive assurance that those relationships are completely ended. Generally, such a discussion takes place privately between the couple, however, in some instances, the in-laws may be involved or a therapist is sought to help one or the other work through the intense feelings such disclosures engender.

Stress is placed on the marriage relationship when one of the partners discovers that the other partner has had a theretofore undisclosed significant romantic association with someone who is, or might still be, involved in the couple's life. For example, it is stressful for a wife to learn that her husband's new secretary is someone with whom he has been romantically involved. The failure of the husband to disclose the former relationship raises questions regarding his integrity. Similarly, if the husband discovers that his wife's new tennis instructor is a former romantic interest, he might justifiably feel insecure. Prior disclosure, which include in-laws, of former romantic alliances can eliminate later doubts and stressful feelings.

What about Children?

Between the partners in a marriage, there should be a clear understanding regarding each person's intentions of having children. It is easy to assume that a future spouse intends to participate in the birthing and rearing of children; unfortunately, this assumption is often ungrounded. It is best to have a clear agreement regarding parenthood. Parents-in-law also enter the equation with their expectations of becoming grandparents, and this should also be addressed before a couple marries.

For example, Barbara and Gary were engaged. Barbara was the youngest in a family of seven children and had long vowed that she would never have any children. Gary, an only child, had always dreamed of raising his own large brood, and he also carried with him his mother's regret that she couldn't have more babies. The couple sought therapy to help them come to an agreement they could both be happy with. I encouraged them to discuss their dreams and reasons for and against children. Gary admitted that he'd always felt lonely. Barbara had felt surrounded all her life and, because she had invested so much in her career, did not want to sidetrack it on the *mommy track*. We discussed ways that Gary could feel part of the large extended family of Barbara's nieces and nephews, and Gary acknowledged that he had never been comfortable in close relationships with children. He decided to try to be the best brother-in-law and uncle possible, and the couple agreed to try to include his mother in joint family activities that would include all the children. Barbara agreed to consider the possibility of having children in the future. Seven years later, when Barbara felt secure in her career, the couple decided to have a child, and Gary admits that the reality of caring for just one child has significantly altered his plans for a large family.

Because second and multiple marriages are such a significant factor in our society, it is appropriate to consider the subject of in-law issues related to the rearing of the existing children of a new spouse. No assumptions relative to this subject should be made by either partner. The couple should reach a clear understanding with each other, and with the offspring concerned, regarding duties, responsibilities, and standards of conduct of the existing children and all family members. Concerned in-laws should be advised of this accord, to avoid misunderstandings. Persuading the offspring to accept and abide by the agreed-upon standards of conduct may be difficult. The challenge of accomplishing this persuasion can become a strengthening and bonding exercise for the newly formed family group and its extended family. The importance of including the offspring in the decision-making process within the family cannot be overemphasized. Children who are a part of the decision-making process are more easily incorporated into a new family unit, and cohesion is more quickly achieved. When both parents present a united front that is based in love and acceptance, the family goals become attainable. If a child believes he or she can divide and conquer the parents, it is difficult to reach consensus and to create a new family bond.

Because of the many complexities that the addition of children brings to the in-law relationship, this topic is further covered in Chapter 5.

BEYOND "FALLING IN LOVE": THE REAL REASONS PEOPLE MARRY THE FAMILIES THEY DO

Given the myriad factors that can cause marital and in-law discord, it is amazing any of us marry at all. How is the choice of spouse made? Although some writers declare that choice of mate is random, authors such as Leader (1975) and Boszormenyi-Nagy and Spark (1973) make the observation that mate selection is most often made for a very strong reason, although the motivation may not be on a conscious or overt level. The partner may have been looking for what Leader terms *proper in-laws,* that is, those who meet the person's expectations of what an in-law should be, or he or she might be trying to replicate or contrast the original family.

Leader lists these possible reasons for in-law selection:

1. **Compatible with a past happy family life:** "I feel lucky finding someone who also has a wonderful family."
2. **Provides love and support not found in the original childhood home:** "My mother died when I was three—it's nice to be part of a warm family."
3. **Increases social status and receives financial support (marrying up):** "Mom always told me 'It's as easy to marry a rich man as a poor man.'"
4. **Supports prior beliefs regarding a cold and rejecting world—repetitious patterns:** "What's the difference—one family's as good as another and people are all out for themselves." (1975, pp. 486–491)

I have also noted that many people marry to recreate the birth family or to replace lost loved ones. The feeling of community or the need for a connection with forces larger than oneself to provide continuity and belonging is also a push toward marrying. Adding to this might be the fact that marrying in-law families with problems and then helping the partner work out or act out the family-of-origin issues may make one feel strong and needed. Marriage to the right mate may let one feel powerful in the family arena, whereas in the past that same person may have felt powerless.

In addition to having a powerful influence on choice of mate, in-laws can determine the subsequent relationship after the marriage. The in-laws may desire a substitute son or daughter, perhaps a child they can mold or one they never had. According to Leader (1975), it is not unusual for couples to get caught in a never-ending cycle of emotional and financial dependency. These influences are subtle and revolve around such issues as social events, proximity, where the parents take vacations, or financial assistance for graduate school. And although parents-in-law may not approve of their child's choice of mate, they may find grandchildren very acceptable, thus creating additional feelings of rejection and hurt.

Boszormenyi-Nagy and Spark (1973) talk about families who adopt in-laws as substitute sons or daughters. Leader has also observed in his clinical work that spouses can be blamed for not meeting their partner's unconscious nurturing needs. Such was the case with a couple who came to therapy because the wife was filled with anger and the husband was depressed. A few days prior to their marriage, the husband's parents had been killed in an auto accident. Fran had unconsciously been in the position of marrying Blake's parents, because she found in them the love and financial support she had never received from her own family. Blake's mother had reassured her that because Blake had an artistic temperament, he would probably never make a good living, but that she and her husband would be there to help out. Now that they were dead, Fran felt cheated and Blake felt depressed. In therapy, we first dealt with grief issues and attempted to support Blake in beginning to deal with his loss. Because financial pressures were causing stress, I also suggested that they see an employment counselor. Fran and Blake continue to make progress with their issues.

Sometimes, where parents die, divorce or move from the childhood home, neighborhood, or state, rather than the child leaving home, the home leaves the child. Older children, particularly, may not put down roots or feel a part of their new home. Where parents remarry, the children may never feel they are part of the newly constituted family. At times, homes become chaotic because of crises such as a death in the family, divorce, or alcoholism. The future spouse may find the security he or she seeks with the significant other or with the other's family. Indeed, it is not unusual for a person to speak of *falling in love* with the family. Sometimes a good match is made between a rescuing family and a person who needs to be rescued.

I was from a physically abusive family. After graduation from college, I confronted my stepfather. I couldn't believe it. My mother sided with him and they told me to get my things and move out. Ramon's family took me in and we were married a year later. We now have two children and are happily married. I don't know who I love more, Ramon or his family.—Amy, 37-year-old photographer

Some marriages take place because people want to fit into a big in-law family that resembles their own birth families. When I saw Pam, she was very clear as to why she had married. She was the youngest in her family and her parents had moved to another state. As she said, "Home left me, and I had to build my own nest." She married into a family with younger children, and now feels like she belongs.

Another reason that a particular in-law may join a family may have to do with birth order. (More on this in Chapter 5.) For example, after the older brothers and sisters of a family's youngest child have married, the youngest is left basically as an only child. As with the following couple, these children may marry the senior children from other families, thus helping them recreate their original families.

I fell in love at first sight with Patricia, who happened to be the oldest of nine children. When her dad met me for the first time, he said, "So you must be the youngest in a large family." Surprised, I asked him how he knew, and he laughed and said she always chose the youngest in a family so that she could "feel at home."—Glenn, 28, consultant

In-laws can also become a replacement for family members who have been lost through divorce or death.

When I went to my future in-laws' home with Rudolf and met his mother, I knew immediately that I wanted to be a part of that family. My mother-in-law reminded me so much of my own mother, who had died when I was a teenager.—Lisa, 43, designer

It is not unusual for a person who has suffered the death of a family member to marry into a nurturing family.

WEDDINGS AND MARRIAGE

The day finally comes when a couple decides to marry. It is hoped that, by this point, the future in-law relationship has been successfully negotiated, because chances are high that the engagement and wedding-planning stage will again move the family system toward a destabilization. Weddings are the basis of myriad in-law problems and misunderstandings. Miss Manners, Elizabeth Post, and Amy Vanderbilt have tried to deal with these problems by issuing strict edicts of protocol. There appear to be good reasons for these rules; they can circumvent many problems with future in-laws.

Tensions run high at the time of weddings. Many decisions must be made and numerous factors need to be considered: flowers, cake, dresses, location, and type of ceremony. There are tuxedos to be rented, a honeymoon to be planned, limousines to be reserved—a multitude of details must be addressed according to the means and desires of those involved. The wedding is often a major social and financial event for the family, especially the bride's parents. More than any other occasion, weddings seem to dredge up in-law jokes and one-liners, such as: "What is the mother-in-law's place in the wedding? To wear beige and keep her mouth shut." Comments like these can be painful for a mother-in-law who likes to be involved, especially if the bride or groom is an only child, or she has only sons. Because responsibility for the planning of the wedding is closely connected to financial issues, we often find that the person who is paying has the ultimate say.

According to most etiquette guidelines, the wedding is the bride's; hence, the family of the bride is in charge of the wedding. However, if the family of the bride is not paying for the entire wedding, they often lose control of the event. In any case, there can be many hard feelings, people slighted, protocols overlooked, and deadlines missed. Little annoyances can turn into major problems, particularly if one or both of the families are not pleased with the choice of spouse.

Despite what many members of the wedding industry recite as absolute requirements for a well-organized and smoothly executed marriage ceremony and reception, the bride-to-be and the groom-to-be should have the ultimate responsibility for deciding what type of a wedding celebration they are going to have. Accordingly, they should reach an agreement as to precisely how the marriage is to be celebrated and precisely who is to pay for each of the expenses incurred. Problems arise when assumptions are made that are based solely on the practices of those who are involved in the wedding industry. The recommendations dictated by those practitioners are often more concerned with the enhancement of their profits than with a response to the desires and needs of the bride and groom and their parents. It is far wiser for the bride and groom to decide what type of a party they wish to have and to reach a clear agreement regarding the budget and who is going to pay specific expenses, rather than waiting until the expenses have been incurred and then "splitting" them. The same considerations apply to the honeymoon. Many newlyweds find that, because of misunderstandings, their expectations regarding payment for the wedding, reception, and honeymoon have not been met. As a result, stress that could have been avoided afflicts the new marriage. The bride-to-be and groom-to-be might find it wise to co-sign a written agreement regarding the expenses of the wedding, reception, and honeymoon. If part of the expenses are to be borne by others (in most cases, the parents-in-law), the couple should have their agreement as well.

Some of the early displays of disagreement may surround who attends the wedding—guest lists can become a real bone of contention. The wishes of six people—the bride, the groom, and each of their parents (future in-laws)—must be considered regarding who should be invited. Often, there is an additional decision as to whether everyone on the guest list should be invited to both the wedding and the reception or to just one or the other. Again, protocol can help: if it is agreed that this is the bride's wedding, hard feelings can be avoided if the bride's wishes are considered first. However, the bride may want to start the relationship off on a peaceful note by honoring her future in-laws' requests whenever reasonable.

Julie and Phil, two professionals who had been living together for two years, decided they would pay for their own wedding, with each taking equal responsibility. Julie found a problem developing between Phil and her mother, when she and her mother started to plan the wedding. Phil felt that he, rather than Julie's mother, should be involved in making the arrangements with Julie because his financial contribution allowed him to have equal input into the wedding plans. During a therapy session with the couple, it became clear that Phil wanted to have control, but also wanted to delegate all the work of the wedding to the women. Julie pointed out that with decision making goes responsibility. Phil quickly decided to take a lesser role.

Even with everyone trying their best, there will be slip-ups and major misunderstandings. Recently, I received a call from a woman I had seen in family therapy five years earlier. She asked if she and her husband could come in for a cooling-off session around her son's impending wedding. I said I would be delighted to see them again. As I hung up the telephone, I thought that her use of the word *impending* had an ominous quality.

It turned out that Dr. and Mrs. Reed were especially angry when their son, Tom, showed them the printed wedding invitation. Having decided on a formal invitation, Meg, the bride, and her father had not included the groom's parents' names on the invitation. Because Tom was their first son, the Reeds felt slighted and upset. During the session, we discussed life cycle issues and I introduced the forming, storming, norming, conforming paradigm to the Reeds (see Chapter 2). The Reeds could definitely identify the wedding invitation as a storming-phase issue and could see that their reaction (even though it might indeed have been justified) was putting undue pressure on Tom and putting them in an adversarial position with Meg. Dr. Reed also talked about his wanting the fact that he was a doctor to be reflected on the invitation, as well as his sense of a lack of control regarding his son. He expressed loyalty to his wife's parents, saying that they had done a far better job of dealing with him 33 years earlier at his own wedding. By the end of the session, Dr. Reed had calmed down considerably and left the session with the comment, "This too shall pass."

A week later, I got a call from Mrs. Reed. She said she wanted to let me in on a good laugh. Apparently, when the couple had arrived home after the session, Dr. Reed pulled out their 33-year-old wedding book to show Tom how an invitation *should* look, and, to his surprise, found that his parents' names were not on the invitation. Mrs. Reed said they had had a good laugh with Tom, and a potential in-law misunderstanding was avoided.

. . . You Marry the Entire Family

Individuals have the potential to react with an unlimited variety of responses in life. Paradoxically, they also tend to limit the number of responses they normally use and hence create similar relationships wherever they go. If a person has a negative relationship with his or her parents, there is no reason to believe that, as that person becomes more familiar with his or her in-laws, the response will be any more positive than to his or her birth parents (Boszormenyi-Nagy & Spark, 1973). The same can be said for the parents-in-law: there is no reason to believe that they will treat a son- or daughter-in-law any more positively than they do their biological children. It does happen, but the exception proves the rule. For example, in response to Lester's offer to be *put to work,* Jeannette, his mother-in-law, asked Lester to do some yard work and was told that he would be glad to do it *later on.* After making this suggestion several times, it became clear to Jeannette that her son-in-law had no intention of mowing the in-laws' lawn on his day off.

There is an old saying that if one looks at the wife's mother, one will see what the wife is going to look like in 20 years. This adage is equally true in reference to fathers and husbands. Many people also believe that partners will probably treat new spouses in the same way they treat their own mothers or fathers. A potential spouse may want to look to those relationships as forecasts of how he or she will be treated. To take the point further, it could easily be assumed that a married couple will treat the in-laws the way the in-laws treated *their* in-laws. Thus, if grandparents-in-law were warehoused in anonymous nursing homes or were not visited over the years, parents-in-law might assume they will receive the same treatment unless some steps are taken to develop a more compatible relationship or make some systemic changes.

WHAT WILL WE CALL YOU? REDEFINING ROLES

In our society, there is no change in name to designate the change in a child's relationship to his or her parents after the child has married. This may result from the changed relationship's not being acknowledged as one of the significant forces in peoples' lives.

> *For the first year, I avoided calling my mother- and father-in-law any name, because I was unclear as to what they would prefer and didn't want to offend anyone.*—Tracy, 35, editor

> *My father died when I was a young kid and I really admire my father-in-law and would like to call him Dad. When I asked my wife how long she thought it would be before I could call him Dad, she just laughed.*—Marcus, 24, law student

When a new person is introduced into the family, it becomes necessary for the family to redefine roles. This redefinition is fraught with discomfort, including the loss of the familiar and a movement into the world of uncertainty.

The son is no longer *our little boy,* but takes on adult responsibilities as a husband, a lover, and perhaps a soon-to-be-father. The daughter is no longer *the little princess* but is now a wife, a lover, and perhaps a future mother. An early issue adding to the ambiguity of many in-law relationships is "What will we call each other?" This is especially true—and potentially explosive—with the parents-in-law.

My mother-in-law just couldn't accept me and made a point of telling me how much she cared for my husband's first wife. I kept hearing "She was just like a daughter to me." There is no way I ever could call her "Mom," and I didn't think she would like it if I called her Shelly, so for the first two years, I just referred to her as "Hey, you." Now that we have a son, I call her Grandma.—Crystal, 41, teacher

When I asked for his daughter's hand, my father-in-law gave me the third degree and scared me to death. He wanted to know what I had done to deserve his little girl and how I planned to support her—he really grilled me. After we got married, I called him Sir for the first year, until he took me aside and said, "The name is Bill." I really thought I had arrived.—Jason, 30, computer programmer

These comments illustrate the problematic nature of what one should call the new in-law. If you think I'm making mountains out of molehills, think again. These seemingly minor issues are often ignored but have been known to cause some major difficulties and discomfort.

Are they called Melvin and Tillie? Mom and Dad? Mr. and Mrs. Jenkins? The question of "What do we call you?" is usually not a problem for the parents-in-law (since it is customary to call the daughter- or son-in-law by the first name), but many new children-in-law find it very difficult to approach the subject of names.

Therapists can often ease the situation by suggesting that the parents-in-law address these issues directly, ending the difficulty a new child-in-law has with the subject of names. Taking the lead with the child-in-law on these predictable issues can help set a precedent for open discussion on the more difficult issues of family roles, life-cycle changes, grandchildren, and financial matters. According to Radcliffe-Brown (1952), we value independence and psychological distance in our culture. There is a mandate of privacy for the nuclear unit. There is the belief that there should be a sharp break between parents and adult children. The therapist can help clients make this transition less stressful.

In a survey conducted by Popenoe (1945) of the American Institute of Family Relations, the following terms of address were used by persons toward their parents-in-law:

Father & Mother/Dad & Mom	66%
John & Mary (first names)	15%

Mr. & Mrs.	12%
Grandpa and Grandma	3%
Direct address (avoiding name)	2%
Pet names	2%

Since the study was done 50 years ago, it would be of interest to know how parents-in-law are addressed today. One would imagine that in our less formal society, the percentage of first names would have increased.

My daughter-in-law insisted on calling me "Mrs. Hobson," even after they were married. It's always made me feel like a stranger to her.—Doris, 56, housewife

I asked my fiancé's parents what I should call them, and they said, "We always thought our first names were just fine." I'd always hoped to be able to call them "Mom" and "Dad," like my parents referred to their in-laws. But when they asked me to use their first names, I got the feeling they would never think of me as a daughter or a member of their family.—Jean, 35, writer

One might ask, "What about the wedding rings? Don't wedding rings adequately reflect the changed familial relationship?" Wedding rings are a symbol of a couple's fidelity to one another, but they don't necessarily signify the immense change in parent, child, and sibling relationships. Name changes denoting marital status might be more significant. In a playful moment, I formulated the following name alternatives for the father-in-law, mother-in-law, and child-in-law, by dropping the first letter of each: *ather* for father, *other* for mother, and *hild* for child. Using new names would reinforce the change of status on a daily basis, and, more importantly, would symbolically indicate a new dynamic in the relationship—something that doesn't really happen following a one-hour ceremony. For those who find *other* offensive as a name for mother, consider these alternatives: *ad* for dad, *om* for mom, and *id* for kid! While my options may be facetious, the reality of what to call future in-laws—or indeed how to note the married status of a child—is either nonexistent or bleak. In the early stages, both future parents-in-law and children-in-law must address the situation with a long-term view and, when possible, be accommodating to the desires of others. A little warmth here will go a long way toward a loving relationship.

WORKSHEET

For Children-in-Law

Can families help each other before they become in-laws? How does one go about sorting out all the many dimensions of in-law relationship expectations? One can become intimidated by the whole prospect before a formal in-law relationship is ever even contemplated. Following are some questions the therapist may wish to discuss with clients during premarital family counseling:

1. What are the family's perceptions and expectations about in-laws?

2. Do you like the way your father-in-law treats your mother-in-law (and vice versa)?

3. What kind of an in-law do you want to be?

4. Have you recognized that you are not just marrying your spouse, but are marrying the entire family?

5. What types of in-law relationships did you have with your family of origin?

6. What systemic changes in the family will the addition of an in-law make?

7. What would show the family that the married child is loyal?

8. Do either the parents-in-law or children-in-law consider premarital sexual activity or cohabitation an issue?

9. Are the in-laws giving permission (both verbal and nonverbal) to marry? If permission to marry is not being given, is the decision based on any of the following factors?
   a. Age
   b. Race
   c. Education
   d. Religion
   e. Socioeconomic status

10. Have the future in-laws taken on the role of rejection through any of the following?
   a. Aggressive opposition
   b. Active proselytizing/looking for gloom and doom
   c. Persistent resistance—a formal politeness
   d. Initial resistance gradually lessening as the marriage continues

11. Have the clients explored what it will mean in the long run if they don't accept the in-law?

12. Have expectations regarding future or existing children been addressed, including the roles of in-laws and prior in-laws?

13. Are there unresolved issues around past romantic associations?

14. Have family members decided what the new parents-in-law will be called?

CHECKLIST

For Parents-in-Law

The following comments were made by children regarding negative attributes of parents-in-law. (See Figure 3.1.) Although all of these comments could be flipped to the children-in-law, it is my experience that these are more fundamental to the children-in-law's conflicts with parents.

Loving. *I couldn't have asked for a better daughter- or son-in-law. I'm glad you married my child.*

Generous. *We know that these early years are tough, and want you to know that we've set aside some money for each of our children to help out when you buy your first house.*

Accepting. *I'm so pleased that my child found such a wonderful person. I'm sure they will be very happy and the new spouse will be a nice addition to our family.*

Tight in-laws. *I want to spend time with the kids as long as they contribute what I consider is their fair share. I put in a lot of hard work to make myself financially secure. Now they should do the same thing.*

Demanding. *I feel that children and grandchildren should spend holidays and vacations with us. I also expect weekly letters and daily phone check-ins.*

Complaining. *I want the children to come but I don't care for the extra work and noise . . . if only they would pitch in.*

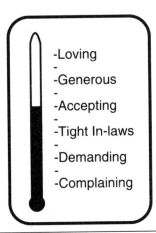

Figure 3.1   A Thermometer of In-Law Style

CHAPTER 4

Understanding Family Loyalties

FAMILY LOYALTIES: UNSETTLED ACCOUNTS

To some degree, all marriages are burdened with each spouse's unsettled accounts of loyalty to his or her family of origin. Loyalty to one's birth family is an often unrecognized force impacting in-law relationships. This is discussed extensively by Boszormenyi-Nagy and Spark (1973) in *Invisible Loyalties.* Their thesis, as the title of their book implies, is that loyalty cannot be measured, weighed, or seen. Invisible loyalty, a feeling that one has for those who are important in one's life, can cause people to behave toward in-laws in ways that may seem irrational to the casual observer. Looked at in the context of a loyalty issue, the irrational behavior toward nonbiological family members begins to make sense.

Loyalty to the birth family is a natural feeling; it gives us a sense of closeness and affiliation toward those with whom we were raised and toward those who raised us. Boszormenyi-Nagy and Spark discuss the fact that in order to love ourselves, we must at least make peace and, ideally, find connections of love with the birth family. If we do not love and respect those on whom we were dependent in early life, we will find it difficult (if not impossible) to love ourselves as adults. This lack of love for the internalized parent would explain the inability of a client to love himself or herself. How does this relate to in-laws? I have found, through clinical experience, that a spouse who develops increasing guilt over disloyalty to his or her parents may deal with the guilt by rejecting the mate or the mate's family.

To be able to grow, one must recognize and deal with the invisible bonds originating from one's formative period of growth. Otherwise, one is apt to live them out as repetitious patterns in all future relationships. Growth and change on the part of one family member can mean personal loss and relationship imbalance for another. The question then becomes: Where do these issues belong in the early part of a new relationship? Parents and siblings can acknowledge the change of relationship with their family members as they integrate a new in-law into the family system, all the while honoring the fact that loyalty to the birth family is a powerful influence. Over time, positive in-law loyalties can also develop.

This change–integration–loyalty sequence transition can happen fairly quickly if clients can develop the expectation that they might love or honor their in-laws as they were loved by their *grandparents*. This shift might be made mentally and not made through verbal comments, as new in-laws may be young and not appreciate being prematurely cast in a grandparenting role. This approach is based on the idea that most grandparents have a much looser set of expectations of the children than parents do, and have often honed an indulgent and benevolent repertoire of styles. Making this generational shift can move loyalty issues into a less competitive arena.

THE IMPACT OF MARRIAGE ON FAMILY LOYALTY

We have explored marriage and weddings in depth in Chapter 3, but the impact of this occasion on family loyalties is relevant here. The marriage of a son or daughter in our society is a high-stress occurrence. The parent–child triad is like no other relationship. The biological and emotional ties predate the child's birth. A choice makes itself manifest: The marriage of the adult child can be viewed as a loss for the family, or the in-law can be integrated into the family and new relationships can be formed. "Marriage often provokes confrontations between two original family loyalty systems, in addition to its demands on both spouses to balance their marital loyalty against their loyalties to their families of origin." (Boszormenyi-Nagy & Spark, 1973, p. 103)

When a man and woman contemplate marriage, their loyalty to the anticipated nuclear family unit must grow to such a pervasive importance that it overcomes original loyalties. In some cultures, the loyalties have been overcome by geographical moves. Witness the old Chinese system of moving the bride into her husband's family home. Because the parents chose the mate, arranged marriages theoretically left children less vulnerable to the feelings of guilt related to disloyalty.

Once a man and woman marry, they are faced with the challenge of identifying with each other. This means making new loyalties in which they both come first in each other's eyes, according to Duvall (1954). They must necessarily redefine loyalties to both sets of parents. Old identifications with the members of both families now must undergo a change: "Everybody is an in-law when you are married." But old loyalties and responsibilities carry on in the lives of both the husband and the wife. They still are adult children of the parents who knew them when . . . ; they still are and want to be part of the families they came from and married into. At the same time, their own new family unit must be strengthened and honored as a new bond to be nurtured by the individuals as well as their families. The basic task of the early years of marriage, according to Duvall (1954), is to cement the marriage bonds to the place where the two feel, behave, and fundamentally want to be as one.

Wallerstein and Blakeslee (1995) see one of the major tasks of building a good marriage is to invest fully in the new marriage and to redefine the connection with the birth families. In interviewing couples with "good" marriages, Wallerstein and Blakeslee found that "The Marriage" was of more importance than the individual partners and that personal sacrifices were often made for the good of "The Marriage."

INTERPERSONAL FAMILY LOYALTY ISSUES

In addition to global issues of family loyalties that impact in-law relationships, there are interpersonal issues between family members. Siblings, according to McGoldrick (1980), can also blame long-standing problems on the intrusion of a spouse into the family. McGoldrick identifies three dysfunctional ways in which a couple may deal with their extended family's in-laws: (a) conflict, (b) enmeshment, and (c) distance or cutoff. McGoldrick explains that the ideal for a couple is to become independent of their families while maintaining close and caring ties. I would suggest that the couple become *inter*dependent of their birth families while setting boundaries as well as maintaining close and caring ties. (More on siblings in Chapter 6.)

Major reasons for lack of integration are often related to in-law disagreements involving differing styles of parenting. For example, one mother-in-law became extremely agitated with her daughter-in-law because she expected her to be the *family correspondent,* and she had not heard from the couple for several months. To deal with her anger, she sent a postcard to her daughter-in-law with the message, "I have polio." A week later she received a postcard in reply from her daughter-in-law asking, "Are you on a respirator?" Although these kinds of in-law struggles for recognition can seem amusing, they are at worst destructive and at best highly unproductive.

TYPICAL LOYALTY AND POWER ARRANGEMENTS

There are powerful gender connections between mothers and sons and between fathers and daughters (Goulter & Minninger, 1993). These connections can be determining factors in the health of an in-law relationship when the son or daughter eventually marries. Typical of in-law relationships are some unwritten but extremely resolute loyalty rules.

The first (and perhaps stronger) rule is "Nobody can take care of a son better than his mother." Its corollary is "For some women, nobody can be better than daddy." Komarovsky's (1962) study of blue collar marriages found that not only are wives closer to their own mothers, but husbands are often closer to their mothers than to their fathers. Of the men, 43% reported a close relationship with their mother and 27% with their father. In a number of families in this study, Komarovsky found that a dependent wife tended to create a situation where the husband's will would be pitted against his mother-in-law's, making the couple allies. Wives who had not resolved conflicts with their own mothers tended to accentuate this type of in-law conflict. On the other hand, Komarovsky found that some wives would mute in-law conflict by suppressing facts. The study found that the extended family was important to the young couples and, although the direction of change may be toward a nuclear unit of parents and children, the blue collar couples studied in the early 1960s had strong kinship ties. My experience with clients some 30 years later confirms the existence of these ties.

The Predominance of the Mother-in-Law in Family Loyalty Issues

Why is the mother-in-law often seen as the most problematic in-law? Caplan (1981) sees *mother blaming* as a way to keep the status quo and to avoid power shifts from men to women. I believe it is because of what mothers symbolize to each of us: caring, loving, sacrificing; always putting children and their needs first; the ones who take care of others. The concept of mother is larger than any one person; to some, mother love is modeled in Mary, mother of Jesus (Friday, 1987). Benjamin Franklin's old saying, "My son is my son 'till he takes a wife, but my daughter's my daughter all the days of my life," has been around a long time for good reason. I like to tell my clients that "a daughter's a daughter all of her life" because women traditionally have been in charge of the home, and therefore, many wives take over responsibility for the relationship with their husband's family as well as their own.

A few years ago, during the height of the women's movement, an article was given to me by my supervisor at the University of Rochester School of Nursing. The gist was that everyone—including mothers—needs a mother, and that the expectations we have of a mother are not possible to meet. Thus, being the ideal mother-in-law is also an impossible goal. I have long noticed that Mother's Day, for many women, is not a happy day. The work of being a good sport and enjoying the day stands alongside the guilt from not meeting all of the inflated expectations. There is also the issue that, until the past few years, when men have begun to change messy diapers and wipe runny noses, the major share of hands-on parenting was done by mothers. The bond between child and mother was the primary bond.

Under those circumstances, it seems obvious that the mother will have a stronger attachment for the children than the father will. When the children leave home, Mom is often out of a job, while Dad continues with his job and is still surrounded by his workplace pseudo-family. Although the mother's connection with the children is a natural result of the social structure, the mother–child bond, rather than being understood, has been criticized and pathologized by the mental health community, as well as by the public. Mothers-in-law have been made the brunt of jokes and cruel comments. Despite the inevitable dynamics of the mother–child relationship, in-laws, and especially mothers-in-law, have been criticized and avoided. (More on rewriting in-law jokes in Chapter 7.)

The mother–child bond can cause a great deal of in-law strain. An example is the case of Jane, whose mother-in-law had a large house with several empty bedrooms. Even though Jane's mother lived nearby in a small house with no unoccupied bedrooms, Jane insisted that she stay with her own mother while the couple visited their hometown. She stated during therapy that taking her child to her mother's home was much less stressful than going to her mother-in-law's house. This was hard for her husband to deal with; his mother was constantly putting pressure on him to have Jane stay at her home. This is only one type of tension between mothers-in-law and wives. Another issue is that the mother and daughter may have similar child-rearing patterns, making it easier for the daughter to be in her mother's home.

In the study of blue collar marriages mentioned earlier, Komarovsky (1962) found that the in-laws mentioned in unhappy relationships were predominantly the mothers-in-law; in only one-fifth of the cases did major conflict involve another in-law. The study also found that, in the less-educated-husband group, one-third of both males and females experienced grievances with mothers-in-law. Komarovsky identified the following four conditions as being associated with an unsatisfactory relationship between husbands and mothers-in-law:

1. Marriage to a better-educated wife.
2. Wife's hostility toward her own mother.
3. Wife's emotional dependence on her own mother.
4. Economic and social interdependence, including joint households with in-laws.

Again, this study is dated, and it would be of interest to see whether these variables still hold true in today's world.

Because women more than men are responsible for interpersonal and intrafamily relations, sisters-in-law as well as mothers-in-law are frequently criticized for failures in achieving harmony with the extended family. The multiple bases for sister-in-law difficulties are expected because the term sister-in-law refers to several relationships: wife's brother's wife, wife's sister, husband's sister, husband's brother's wife, and others more remotely related. Duvall's (1954) survey found that, of these, the wife's sister is least often a problem, and the husband's sister is the most often difficult.

Brothers- and fathers-in-law are seen as less problematic than the females in comparable roles because they are rarely involved in the interactions that cause problems. Duvall found that the most common complaints about brothers-in-law were incompetency, immaturity, and irresponsibility. The most common complaints lodged against fathers-in-law were meddling, nagging, and criticism. The father-in-law syndrome appears to be ineffectuality and resistance to change; the mother-in-law is seen as interfering and demanding.

Housekeeping, as well as child-raising methods, can present a big loyalty issue for a couple. The husband and the in-laws are usually cited for putting pressure on the wife to keep to the family standard.

My husband Russell's mother was shocked and dismayed when it came to light that I, his new wife, had not been hand-washing her son's socks or ironing his shorts. I couldn't believe it. I told her I had heard that Japanese women won't even touch their husbands' underwear or socks. They use chopsticks to put them in the washer.—Crystal, 41, teacher

Housekeeping issues provide an example of what Boszormenyi-Nagy and Spark (1973) term *overcoming original loyalties.* These authors see mothers- and fathers-in-laws as being in quasi-blood relationships, and these relationships are heightened with the birth of grandchildren, who may have the physical characteristics of the in-laws. According to Boszormenyi-Nagy and Spark, every individual move toward maturation threatens disloyalty to the family system. Loyalty is grounded in biological survival, and original loyalty issues cannot be ignored. They must be dealt with (worked through) or they will undermine new relationships. Problems arise when a husband and wife feel that they must overcome their own or their spouse's original loyalty to the birth family. Ideally, they can resolve some of their dependency issues without overcoming their parents and in-laws, and the resolution can be accomplished with honesty, goodwill, and, often, humor.

REALIGNING LOYALTIES

Families describe themselves as being self-sufficient. In my experience, this is not a true description. Family members rely on each other and they have an interdependence with their community. The network of friends and family impacts highly on in-law relationships. Families who adapt to new members are those who have a history of being accessible and open to neighbors, friends, and family.

Every newly married couple belongs to at least three families—their own (each other), and those of both sets of parents. When their parents-in-law have divorced and remarried, the number of family units to which this new marriage must establish loyalty hierarchies expands dramatically. If the newlyweds are to establish a strong family unit of their own, they must inevitably realign their loyalties, placing their own newly established family before their parents. "Unless the cohesive force in the new family unit is stronger than that which ties either of the couple to the parental home, the founding family is threatened" (Duvall, 1954).

Fay had always been close to her father, who was also her swimming coach and attended all her meets. When Fay met Bert, she gave up her hopes of being an Olympic champion and dropped off the swim team. "Daddy" became irate. He was the power in the family, to whom everyone deferred. Daddy could do no wrong, even when he later walked out on the family for another woman. The entire extended family attended a family-of-origin session to help Fay and Burt deal with marital problems. As we looked at the family history, Fay's father admitted it was no coincidence that he walked out on the family when Fay left. "Without my little girl to take care of, there was no reason to hang around."

Many couples do not start out with a balance of family loyalty. Instead, they discard their original loyalties, to the long-term detriment of all concerned. Many soon-to-be in-laws are put in the position of dealing with their future spouse's unresolved issues of loyalty to the birth family. Rather than deal with those primary intergenerational issues of loyalty to one's parents and to one's child, it may be easier for the family to scapegoat the outsider. This remedy becomes difficult when the outsider marries into the family, becomes an in-law, and then closes the loop by parenting a child and biologically joining the two families. Such was the case with Sascha and Doug, who, after the birth of their first child, had a financial setback and returned home to stay with Doug's father and stepmother, with whom Doug had many unresolved issues. Feeling the tension between Doug and his father, Sascha took every opportunity possible to become annoyed with Doug's father. Rather than suggesting that they talk it out, Doug agreed with her and said that he felt that his parents were slighting them both. The climax occurred when the stepmother-in-law asked Sascha if she would take the baby's diaper out to the containers at the side of the house rather than leaving it in the kitchen garbage can. At that point, Sascha rushed up to her room, packed up their clothes, and the couple and baby stormed out of the house. They then went to Doug's mother's house, where they were warmly greeted.

Doug did not feel that this was an issue of disloyalty to his father. Instead, he saw it as a simple in-law dispute involving Sascha and his father and stepmother. That view let Doug off the hook and made him feel justified in expressing his years of hostility and anger at his father. His mother was very happy to see the couple and her grandchild, and all three adults could understand Doug's anger at his father, and Sascha's anger at her father-in-law and his wife. In this way, an in-law was used as a scapegoat to disguise the real issues and to take responsibility for the long-term hostility between the father–stepmother unit and the son.

At a large extended network session that included all the parties involved, along with Doug's brother and sister, we created a genogram and discussed the family's history with in-laws. We then did a family sculpture that mirrored Doug's hostility toward his father for leaving his mother to remarry. It became obvious from the sculpture that there was a great deal of contention between generations. Using structural and strategic techniques, I situated Doug and Sascha in the center of the room with their age-peers, and then had the next generation sit outside the inner circle, and gave them the role of trusted advisers. These trusted advisers discussed how difficult it was to be married, and talked about their hopes and dreams for the younger generation. We then had the younger generation discuss their problems, hopes, and dreams. It became clear that each generation had its own problems and this helped all parties see their role in solving them.

A Balancing Act

Another unwritten loyalty rule that impacts the in-law relationship is: "Over the long term, your son- or daughter-in-law will likely treat you no better than your child treats his or her in-laws." Thus, parents who desire to have a good relationship with their biological children will encourage the married children to have good relationships with their in-laws. Like many maxims, this is easier said than done. As a therapist, I know intellectually that I should encourage my children to have close relationships with their parents-in-law. However, as a parent and a grandparent, I've been guilty of seeking the position of *most favored in-law,* in the sense that I will feel valued and will have the highest number of contact hours with my children and grandchildren.

Leader (1975) says that new family relationships are determined partially by family-of-origin relationships. Taking on new relationships can be seen as an additional step toward maturity. One's own family of origin plays a significant role with in-law inclusion issues, because some couples and individuals need strong ties with family and some desire a more distant connection. These ties and connections become evident when, during the course of therapy, young couples discuss their parents' reaction toward closeness or distance and then discuss their in-law needs, which are often similar to the biological family's needs. Such was the case with the following family, in which the son and father had strong inclusion needs, while the mother desired a more distant connection.

Daddy's Boy

A young professional couple, Ted and Mindy, came to therapy after a disastrous week-long visit from the young man's parents. As Ted drove his parents to the airport, his mother stated that the next time they came, they would stay in a motel and would rent a car, because she felt that staying with Ted, Mindy, and their young son was just too confusing. Ted was hurt and Mindy was angry. In discussing the history of the family with the young couple, Ted said that he had always been very close to his father. Often, that closeness excluded his mother. His mother initially welcomed Mindy into the family, because she felt that with Mindy taking her son's attentions, she would have more time to spend with her husband—time that he was now devoting to his relationship with their son. Mindy, however, did not see Ted's father as a threat. She encouraged Ted to spend as much time with his father as possible while she kept busy with her own activities. Mindy saw her mother-in-law as a couch potato who lacked initiative and ambition. Mindy's attitude helped to position Ted's mother as the nagging mother-in-law.

In dealing with this in-law issue, I felt it important to stay problem-oriented and to frame it as an in-law problem, although it was obvious that there were problems between Ted's mother and father, and that Ted had been triangled in to ease the tension. (It is important when conducting in-law therapy for the therapist to avoid being too ambitious and hunting for other problems, such as a faulty relationship between the parents.)

The problem I formulated with Ted and Mindy was: How to have an enjoyable visit with both of Ted's parents. We sought to determine what an enjoyable visit would look like, and Ted said he was willing to give up some time with his father in order to include his mother. Mindy felt she could give up some of her community activities and spend time with Ted's parents during the next planned visit. We then discussed some of the goals for the visit. One was to keep the age hierarchy straight: To keep both Mom and Dad in the trusted adviser role, as grandparents and parents-in-law. We discussed elevating Mom by asking her opinions and getting her involved in planning joint activities. We also sought to avoid loyalty struggles by refraining from comparisons between Ted's mother and Mindy's mother, who is more active and lives in the same neighborhood. The couple was encouraged to accept Ted's mother as an individual and not look at her as strictly a mother-in-law or grandmother. We then discussed some behavioral objectives that might help to ease the tension. One was to plan activities each day as couples. Another was to get a babysitter for a weekend or overnight so the couples could take a trip together. All of these strategies helped Ted and Mindy see his parents—especially his mother—in a new light and made for a more successful in-law relationship on subsequent visits.

Mama's Boy

The relationship between sons and mothers can also be fraught with potential for problems. One young woman stated that her mother-in-law had a stranglehold over her husband. The husband laughed and said the idea of a stranglehold was ridiculous. He simply enjoyed being included in his mother's life. The wife added that she could see little need to spend time with her own family, now that she was married and had a family of her own. In discussing her family of origin, the wife stated that her father had never been home and had always done anything he wanted to do, while her mother was a slave to the family. She had decided not to follow in her mother's footsteps, and feared that with her husband visiting his family all the time, she was becoming like her mother. She felt that the time the husband was spending with his mother and siblings forced her to be alone to run the house, as her mother had. Further discussion revealed that her father, since divorcing her mother, had moved back in with his own mother. This couple has a husband and father-in-law with strong inclusion needs and a wife with lesser inclusion needs. The couple resolved this issue by deciding to respect each other's needs. The husband agreed to help more around the house so his wife could have some free time, and to schedule some couple time. The wife agreed not to get upset about time he spent with his family, as free time was at the discretion of the user.

These issues can be especially problematic when married children decide to live with the parents-in-law. For example, when 26-year-old Lara and her husband Steve had been married for a year, their lease expired but they hadn't yet found a place to live, so they moved in with Steve's parents for a month while they looked for new quarters. Steve is the oldest of five—he has three brothers and one sister. Although Lara claimed she didn't have a problem with her in-laws, she disliked the way they treated her husband. The family interaction made her angry, and then it made her husband angry enough to want to leave. Lara was especially upset because his mother always sought Steve's advice about her problems with his father and the younger brothers and sisters, with issues like, "Your brother wants to get an earring in his ear," or "What do you think about these two dating?" Lara didn't think it was Steve's responsibility to give advice about his younger brothers and sisters or about his mother's love life. The couple ended up renting the first house where tenants were allowed to have dogs.

Daddy's Girl

Fathers can often wield too much power in their daughter's life (Goulter & Minninger, 1993), pressuring the husband to live up to a feeling that his father-in-law is always right. This relationship can skip a generation, alternating between a successful father-in-law and father-in-law-as-failure. Or, complementary roles can exist: father is hero, husband is failure; husband is hero, father is failure.

Although Patty's husband, Nathan, worked hard as a high-tech executive, he was often told by Patty that he was an ignorant man who could never live up to her father. Nathan, who was a teetotaler, could never figure out what his alcoholic father-in-law had achieved that he must *live up to*. Patty and Nathan's daughter Amanda, who saw her father as a failure, picked an over-achieving husband, Ronald, as a spouse in order to meet what she saw as her mother's expectations of a man. Although Ronald was a highly successful executive, Patty resented her son-in-law, partly because of her continued loyalty to her father. Patty even predicted that when Ronald had children he would realize that no one is ever good enough for one's own children.

This brings us to another loyalty rule: In-law bashing may affirm one's own parents in the short term, but it is destructive over the long term. In therapy, many clients engage in projecting onto the in-laws the anger they bear toward their own parents. For example, Nick and Tammy came to see me in order to discuss their increased hostility toward one another. The fights had escalated to the point where they were pushing and slapping one another. Frequently, their fights were fueled by Tammy's close relationship with her mother and the fact that Nick's parents were never allowed to tend the couple's three-year-old daughter Heidi. Nick and Tammy spent the majority of their family time, including holidays and vacations, with Tammy's parents and virtually ignored Nick's parents. For the first few years of their marriage, this arrangement had been fine with Nick. He had had a great deal of resentment toward his parents, traceable to what he described as an overly restrictive and sometimes physically abusive childhood. Cutting his parents out of his life was, in his mind, nothing more than they deserved.

As Heidi got older, Nick began to see his little daughter's love for Tammy's parents and the delight it brought to Tammy. As the years went on, Nick began to think of his own childhood and longed for a relationship with his parents that included Tammy and Heidi. When he approached Tammy with the idea of mending fences with his parents, Tammy was surprised and resistant. How did Nick know that Heidi would be safe with Nick's parents after what they had done to him? Nick quickly found himself defending his parents and talking up their good qualities. Tammy continued to be resistant and, in retaliation, Nick began to criticize her parents and became more resistant to his in-laws. Unfortunately in this circumstance, Tammy's in-law bashing had negative consequences in Nick's relationship with her parents.

In a second case, a couple in therapy for marital problems came to a session highly upset with their 22-year-old son, Jed, who had informed them that he was getting married the next weekend to his 18-year-old girlfriend, whom the couple had never met. Jed said that their future daughter-in-law, Kay, had run away from home and that the wedding would occur without the knowledge of her parents, who did not approve of the relationship. At the insistence of my clients, the girl's parents were told of the event but Jed and Kay refused to give the date. The wedding took place without the girl's family. This was particularly sad for Kay's mother: the bride was the only girl in a family of four boys.

Six months after the wedding, Kay was pregnant and desired to make amends. Her parents were excited about their first grandchild and were willing to work things out. Jed felt left out. He saw Kay's parents as being against him. With support from his parents (who were my original clients), Jed agreed to a session that included Jed, Kay, and both sets of parents. During the first two-hour session, we had a getting-to-know-you time, and looked at family history by doing a genogram. After doing the genogram, I observed that the family had not gone through the proper process of giving their daughter away and becoming in-laws. We discussed the process of forming, storming, norming, conforming. I suggested that we have four two-hour sessions in order to go through the courtship and marriage process and complete these stages of group development.

At the first session, which we called the forming session, the family formally introduced themselves to one another and then we did individual family histories and genograms, focusing on how the people in the genogram had left home. We also put together a history of marriages in the family.

At the second session, the storming session, we discussed what had transpired when the couple got married, how individuals felt about the couple's elopement, and what dreams, hopes, and frustrations everyone harbored. We explored what Kay and Jed's marriage would mean when children entered the family. After the discussion, we did family sculptures. They unanimously reflected the fact that all of the family members desired to have a more harmonious relationship. Toward the end of the session, I asked the couple if they would mind giving up their rings to their parents, with Jed's family taking Kay's ring, and Kay's family taking Jed's ring. This activity was a symbolic preparation for the next session, planned as a norming session in which such issues as permission to marry would be addressed. The couple agreed to give up their rings until permission to marry could be granted by their parents.

At the third, or norming, session, we did a family sculpture to explore how the family would be situated after permission had been given for the couple to marry. I helped them to sculpture the family with Kay and Jed in the center and the parents seated behind them as trusted advisers. At this point, the parents discussed the issue of permission to marry and talked about their children's childhood and their expectations of the children. Kay and Jed then went to their future in-laws and each asked for permission to marry their child. These moves were made with great enjoyment and fun. Permission to marry was granted, rings were exchanged, and the groom and bride kissed.

At the fourth or conforming session, we discussed the hopes, dreams, and expectations of the in-laws. We discussed what it meant to be an in-law, and explored some of the typical issues that might arise, such as how holidays and vacations would be handled. We also discussed control needs, inclusion needs, intimacy needs, and problem-solving needs. (These come from the work of Berg-Cross and Jackson and are further covered in Chapter 7.) We talked about helping behaviors and the expectations of the parents-in-law and the children-in-law regarding appropriate behaviors for each generation. We talked about family celebrations and explored the nature and extent of activity and the observation of rituals, including holidays and religious events. We talked about the role models that were given in relationship to in-laws, how the in-laws had been treated in each family, and how the couples would like to be treated.

At the end of the session, the two sets of parents decided that they would have a renewal of their marriage vows. This would not only recognize the young couple's marriage, but also reaffirm the vows of the older couples. When I spoke to Kay and Jed several months later, they told me they, too, had been through a reaffirmation marriage ceremony, and were very pleased with the results of the in-law focused therapy sessions.

DEALING WITH FAMILY SECRETS AND MYTHS

All families have skeletons in the closet. In the not-too-distant past, these secrets primarily revolved around illegitimate children, adoption, past marriages, and sexual peccadillos (Framo, 1965). Today, those categories of family secrets are viewed as relatively mild, due, I believe, to the desensitizing of the topics through exposure ad nauseam on the many television talk shows. Currently, such topics as former drug abuse, alcoholism, imprisonment, incest, and rape are the taboo subjects that form the base of the secrets held by families. "The keeping of family secrets is a form of collective denial that is not necessarily pathological. Most families have a skeleton or two in the closet, and keeping them there is, within limits, functional. Family secrets can serve to protect the self-esteem of the family members. Family secrets become a problem when they undermine mutual trust, inhibit dialogue, and distort reality in such a way that family adapt ability and development become restricted" (Simon, Stierlin, & Wynne, 1985, p. 136).

Although some therapists (Simon et al., 1985) believe family secrets should not be unearthed, it is my experience that the majority of family members often either already know the secret or know that there is a skeleton in the closet. Keeping the secret under wraps only diminishes the self-esteem of the entire family. According to Imber-Black (1993), "Opening certain secrets may be profoundly healing for individuals and relationships, while opening other secrets may put people in jeopardy, particularly where issues of physical safety are concerned. And then there are secrets that hold the potential of both reconciliation and division, with no guarantees of which will pertain" (p. 4).

The therapist can help normalize family secrets by letting clients know that secrets are not unique to their family and that many families have similar bones in their closets. However, a caveat is required here: in some instances, it may not be appropriate for other members of the family or in-laws to press for family secrets. Some secrets can be developed only in more structured settings such as therapy sessions. This was the case with John and Alison. John had just completed medical school and planned to move back to Texas to join his father's medical practice. When the couple had visited Texas for a weekend, the wife came home with many complaints about how she and her mother-in-law got along. Her mother-in-law expected them to become best friends, and wanted to have long chats with her, to talk about all of Alison's personal problems. Alison had recently ended an affair, which was the reason the couple was in therapy. She and John had agreed that they would try to work out the issue themselves and would not share the information with the family. John had told his mother that Alison had been having some problems, and his mother was determined to understand the basis of her daughter-in-law's problems. Alison likened her mother-in-law to a bird dog who would sniff out a problem and never let it go. Intrusive, but well-intentioned, the mother-in-law had no idea she was treading on thin ice, and John finally had to tell his mother to mind her own business.

We discussed what had happened in therapy, and I asked the couple if the secret was worth the price they were paying—total alienation of a beloved family member. The couple agreed that their marriage was, at that point, stable enough to talk about the problem with selected others. Several months later, when John's parents were in town, we had a joint session and started by talking about the reasons secrets are kept, and the fears that underlie them. Alison and John then discussed the affair and what they felt led up to it. They also reaffirmed their love for each other. At that point, John's mother said she had sensed this was the problem. She had wanted to draw her daughter-in-law out, because she and John's father had experienced a similar incident. They had been able to overcome and resolve it to build a strong 40-year marriage, and she wanted to let Alison and John know that she empathized with them and that their marriage could go on.

In-laws might want to reconsider prying into changes in moods or problems that might have arisen for the couple. Pressing these symptoms may alienate the in-law rather than resolve problems.

FAMILY EVENTS THAT STRESS THE BONDS OF LOYALTY

Although they offer the potential for a lot of fun, family gatherings such as vacations, holiday celebrations, and family reunions can also place an enormous stress on the family's loyalty issues. Duvall's (1954) research confirms the potency of these situations. Conflicts around these issues can often be seen during family gatherings, perhaps because, in most families, the females are the coordinators of such social events, and are responsible for arranging the family's social calendar.

When Franz asked for Judith's hand in marriage, I agreed that he could move her 1,000 miles away, but with the proviso that he would bring my daughter home for Christmas. We even agreed that I would pay the airfare. Only two years later, she is telling me that they have to be fair and spend every other Christmas with Franz's parents. I feel like Franz has betrayed me. After all, a promise between men is a promise.—Dayton, 63, stockbroker

Other people go to Disneyland for vacation; we get to go to my in-laws' housing tract in Ames, Iowa, where it's always hotter than hell and the kids always come down with colds. My wife says the kids have to get to know their grandparents. I'll wager they would be a lot happier visiting Donald Duck than seeing grouchy grandpa.—Thomas, 40, utility repair person

I recently saw Mort and Megan, a young couple with two children who were having friction because of Megan's plans for a family trip to the Bahamas. Mort had trouble accepting the idea that his in-laws were going to pay for the trip. He said that it made him feel like he wasn't paying his own way and that he was taking from others. I discussed with Mort the idea that his feelings were rational and valid—it can be difficult to take things from others and still feel a strong sense of self-esteem. However, I pointed out that, given his feelings, taking the trip and being pleasant to his in-laws could be viewed as a sacrifice on behalf of Megan, because even though he had strong feelings in this regard, he was willing to subjugate these feelings to her needs. We also discussed the idea that taking from his in-laws may also raise some loyalty issues regarding his own family. To deal with these loyalty issues, I suggested that he discuss with his own family his feelings about taking things from others. I asked him to tell them that I had congratulated him on the fact that they had raised him with such excellent values, and also suggested that taking the trip with the family would be highly unselfish.

Mort discussed these issues with his own family and, to his delight, his parents were sympathetic with his discomfort at taking from his in-laws. They then reassured him of their support and suggested that he and his family take a camping trip with them the following summer. This balanced out the loyalty issues.

Family Reunions (from Hell)

Events with the biological family can bring up loyalty conflicts. In many families' *Book of Fun Things to Do,* family reunions often come in dead last, competing only with an IRS audit. Why? Because family reunions represent a large gathering of diverse people who happen to have a biological connection and little else in common. There are often too many new faces (many of which you will never see again), too much forced joviality, and too much bad food. Blood kin may enjoy the experience, but why subject a poor unsuspecting in-law to such an outing? Bilofsky and Sacharow (1991) in their book on in-laws refer to family gatherings as "time bombs."

> To this day I resent the fact that every year as my children were growing up we had to go to Texas for a family reunion with my wife's family. Because they all lived there already, her family members could just take a few hours off from work and be at the reunion, saving their vacation time for trips to Yellowstone or Hawaii. We on the other hand had to skip any form of exotica and spend our scarce vacation week (usually in the dead heat of summer) in that blast furnace. Now that all my own children have families of their own, I never subject them to that awful obligation. I feel truly delighted when they want to attend family gatherings, but I never put the pressure on them.—Forrest, 65, retired securities analyst

One wife, whose spouse did not enjoy mixing with the in-laws at these forced occasions, came up with the following solutions:

1. Only the family member goes to the reunion, thus letting the spouse off the hook.
2. The in-law puts in an appearance for only a portion of the reunion, and then conveniently has to "rush back to work to take care of an emergency."
3. The spouse agrees to attend the family reunions only every other year, enabling the family to enjoy its vacation in a new environment.

Although family reunions deservedly may have a bad reputation among in-laws, they do present opportunities to strengthen family ties and to enable children to become acquainted with their relatives. Should the entire family decide to attend and make the best of it, the therapist might offer the following advice to the spouse whose family is hosting the gathering: "Prior to the reunion, reaffirm with your spouse that your loyalty is with him or her, and that no matter how silly you begin to act with your long-lost cousins, you will transform yourself back into a sane creature before your return home."

Parents-in-law can help make the reunion smooth for children-in-law by acting as hosts to the newcomers, so that at no time do they feel abandoned or at the mercy of the mob.

WORKSHEET

Client Family Loyalty Issues

1. Do you feel tension regarding the loyalty you have for your biological family versus your in-laws?

2. What kinds of loyalty issues do you think you might encounter in relationship to the following?

   a. Biological family

   b. In-laws

   c. Nuclear family

3. Do you deal with your own family issues or have you inadvertently let your spouse deal with them, reframed as in-law issues?

4. Have you dealt with in-law loyalty issues regarding family events such as reunions and holidays?

5. What kind of in-law boundaries do you maintain? (Can your spouse talk to the in-laws about your marital arguments?)

6. Does your spouse understand and accept your loyalty to your family of origin (his or her in-laws)?

7. Are you engaged in in-law bashing? Are you aware of the long-term risks of this behavior in terms of biological loyalty? (Your spouse may turn on you and yours.)

8. Have you considered what kind of in-law you want to be?

9. Have you thought about family secrets regarding in-laws and how you will handle them and still maintain family loyalty?

10. Is there a *most favored in-law* race going on in the family and are you involved?

11. Have you worked out holiday and family reunion strategies to make the most of the in-law relationship?

CHAPTER 5

Life-Cycle Changes: How In-Law Relationships Change through the Aging Process

Limited attention has been devoted to in-law relationships during the later part of the life cycle. Most writers refer only to in-law adjustment problems of young married couples (Troll, Miller, & Atchley, 1979). Many seemingly typical events can disrupt and define the expectations of in-law relationships. Such milestones as the addition of children to the relationship, divorce, illness, grandparenthood, the natural aging process, the need to be cared for, death, and other expected and unexpected events will certainly impact the in-law relationship.

To be healthy and to survive, the in-law system must be flexible enough to allow for change and growth. One young man in therapy told me that his parents had taken care of him all his life and so now, at 30 years of age, he felt that it was time to be the man of the house and to start taking care of his parents and parents-in-law. I pointed out that caring is mutual and empowers all people involved in giving to others. At different ages, however, we have different needs and responses—advancing age does not mean that in-laws or parents desire or need to be *taken care of*. The opposite also applies: Just because one is 30 years of age does not mean that one cannot accept some caring from in-laws and/or parents. There are time when we can give support and times when we need support.

Many family issues are highly predictable, in terms of changes for the family and in-laws. In their ground-breaking book on the family life cycle, Carter and McGoldrick (1980) formulated a six-stage family life cycle. These six stages include:

1. Between families: The unattached young adult.
2. The joining of families through marriage: The newly married couple.
3. The family with young children.
4. The family with adolescents.

5. Launching children and moving on.

6. The family in later life.

The previous chapters, in addressing such issues as marriage (Chapter 3) and permission to marry (Chapter 2), included specific issues related to the Carter and McGoldrick stages in terms of an in-law perspective. The stages mention families joining through marriage, but they mention in-laws specifically only in the fifth and sixth stages. Figure 5.1 is a brief overview of the six stages and the in-law tasks related to those stages.

VERTICAL AND HORIZONTAL LIFE-CYCLE CHANGES

Carter and McGoldrick (1980) have looked at the flow of what they call the family anxiety on both a vertical and a horizontal level. The vertical flow includes interactions such as relating and functioning, family patterns and attitudes, expectations, labels, myths, and other issues that are carried from one generation to another. Carter and McGoldrick liken the vertical axis to playing the hand of cards that you are dealt. The horizontal flow (stressors) includes predictable developmental stressors as well as unpredictable events,

STAGES	IN-LAW TASK
1. Between families: The unattached young adult	
2. The joining of families through marriage: The newly married couple	Realignment of relationships with extended families, including in-laws
3. The family with young children	Realignment of relationships with the extended family, including in-law, parenting, and grandparenting roles
4. The family with adolescents	Beginning to shift concerns toward older generation, including in-laws
5. Launching children and moving on	Realignment of relationships to include grandchildren and grandparenting roles
6. The family later in life	Making room in the system for the wisdom and experience of elderly in-laws and supporting the older generation without overfunctioning for them

Figure 5.1   Life-Cycle Stages and Related In-Law Tasks

including life-cycle transitions such as birth and death. External issues such as war, untimely death, and chronic illness are also considered horizontal stressors. Carter and McGoldrick state that other horizontal life-cycle issues are related to the stress of living in this place at this time: women's liberation, the increasing divorce rate, pollution, the energy shortage, and global unrest. Using their model, Carter and McGoldrick say that the most stressful times for families occur when they are involved with horizontal stressors such as retirement, birth of a child, or illness, and, at the same time, may be experiencing vertical stressors, such as their attitudes toward in-laws.

Carter and McGoldrick examine these stressors in terms of three systems: (a) the social system, (b) the extended family system (which we will call the in-law system), and (c) the nuclear family system. For example, although retirement could be considered a horizontal stressor, the mother-in-law's retiring and coming to live with her son would interact with the vertical stressor of the daughter-in-law's attitude toward the in-law, which might have been impacted by her relationship with her own mother.

In Carter and McGoldrick's view, "the degree of anxiety engendered by the stress on the vertical and horizontal axis at the points where they converge is the key determinant of how well the family will manage its transitions through life" (1980, p. 10). Figure 5.2 illustrates some of the horizontal

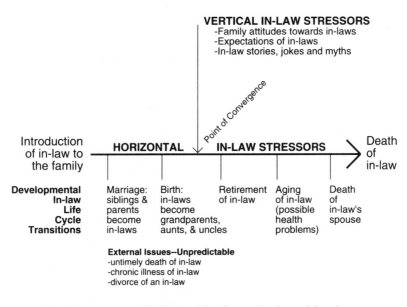

Figure 5.2   In-Law Life-Cycle Stressors

and vertical issues facing in-laws. The diagram is designed to give the therapist and the family a feel for in-law stressors and for how the concepts can be utilized to further understand the dynamics of the extended family and help in-laws to conceptualize where they have been and where they are headed.

The horizontal stressors often do not occur in the order portrayed, but Figure 5.2 will nevertheless give the reader some understanding of the concept. In the following sections are brief comments on several of the in-law stressors.

Empty Nest

An important and often understated horizontal stressor is the empty nest, when the children leave home. The empty nest is very much impacted by the family patterns and myths regarding the children's leaving home, as well as by the commitment and involvement of the parents-in-law in their children's life. Many parents (especially mothers) feel left in a vacuum once their children are grown and have left home, because until that point their lives have been full of their children's concerns. Many have feelings like "Who really needs me now?" These parents, with time on their hands and a perceived empty life, often are the most interfering in the lives of their children-in-law. Duvall (1954) asks: Is it any wonder that mothers continue to absorb themselves in those whose lives have been their business all along? "Until communities find real status for the middle-aged, middle-class woman, we may expect to find many a mother interfering in her children's courtship, marriage, and family life, for nature abhors a vacuum, and so does Mom" (p. 63). There have been some social changes since Duvall's work of 1954, with an increase of women finding fulfillment in areas outside the domestic realm.

How the family adjusts to the marriage of a child and the introduction of an in-law may depend on the role that the family member held within the family and how much the fulfillment of that role is missed. Is there a strong attachment with other family members and will the frequent contacts be missed? Is this an only child? What kind of space and time did the child fill? Is the family in a life-cycle change (such as moving toward an empty nest)? If there is a dramatic role change in the family during the shaking-out phase, the members of the family may have to go through a grieving process for the old role in order to integrate a new member into the family. As with any loss, it may be necessary for family members to go through the loss stages, which Kubler-Ross (1969) identified as denial, anger, bargaining, depression, and acceptance. This is how these stages might be expressed in in-law client systems:

Denial: *The second night of our honeymoon, who should appear at our beachfront hotel but my mother-in-law. She wanted to see for herself that I was being good to her daughter, and said it wasn't too late for an annulment. And on the* *night we got back from our honeymoon, my mother-in-law called to tell my wife that her old boyfriend was back in town, and that she might want to call him. Talk about denial.*—Marvin, 48, attorney

Anger: *I told my son that getting married was just plain stupid. He had just started medical school. We had big plans for him. My daughter-in-law was just going to be a ball and chain around his neck. He told me, his own mother, to mind my own business. All of the communication we have had for the last year has been through his father and that's fine with me.*—Rita, 50, doctor

Bargaining: *Jessica was my last child to leave home. I liked Ned my new son-in-law, but I just couldn't stand the idea that Mom and I were going to be in the house alone. I remember the first day she left, I went in the bathroom and cried like a baby. I had told her I would buy her a car and send her to Europe, but she got married anyway. What can I say?*—Crede, 57, banker

Depression/Acceptance: *It wasn't that I didn't like my daughter-in-law Katrina. We had lost a son ten years ago in an automobile accident. I just wasn't ready to lose another son, even to marriage. It took me a couple of years to accept the fact that David and Katrina were a couple. I feel good about their marriage now; it's like I've gained a daughter, not lost a son.*—Crystal, 41, teacher

Clues about how the family might deal with the role changes and the acceptance of the in-law can be found in the past as well as in the present. The therapist might want to ask the client how the family has dealt with past marriages and unresolved issues related to those marriages. Have circumstances surrounding the marriages been explored, and have in-laws been given the opportunity for unresolved anger, blame, or guilt to be resolved? Has the family been able to move on after resolving those issues? Relationships of the child with the family of origin—parents and siblings—may come into play at this point. This is especially true if the chosen spouse has been selected to act out unresolved anger on behalf of the partner. In some cases, the spouse or live-in may be given unspoken or spoken encouragement to support the partner in achieving distance from the family.

In-Laws as Grandparents

Inclusion of a new member into the family with the birth of a child increases the number of interactions and changes the dynamics of in-law relationships. Even before the grandchild is born, the in-law relationship may revert to a storming stage, starting with such issues as illness, morning sickness or miscarriage, and the possibility of increased need of resources such as money and help with baby-sitting the existing children.

Rubin and Rhonda, whom I saw in therapy, were extremely angry with their extended family. Rhonda had been bedridden for much of her pregnancy and was highly upset that she did not receive more attention from her mother-in-law. This also caused a rift between Rubin and his parents; he carried the message from his wife that his parents were not helpful or sympathetic enough. When the baby was six months old, Rhonda felt the need to punish the in-laws by not letting them see the child on a regular basis. During therapy, Rhonda was able to express her anger and hurt and to realize that withholding access to the child was counterproductive. As Rubin pointed out to Rhonda, "The least they can do to make it up is to give us some free baby-sitting." Rhonda laughed and said she would ease up. When I last spoke to them, the couple said things were better and that the baby loved his grandparents. Because grandparenthood represents a significant factor in the in-law life cycle, it is covered in greater depth later in this chapter.

Retirement

I was recently at a meeting where a male friend said, "When you finish your in-law book, send me a copy. My mother-in-law is coming to our house next week, because she recently retired. She informed me that she needs rest in order to calm her frayed nerves. I don't know what will be expected of me, and I'm nervous about her visit. I don't even see eye-to-eye with my own mother, which makes me feel doubly tense with the thought of being available for my mother-in-law."

Aging and Menopause in the In-Law Life Cycle

The birth of the first grandchild can be an unexpected life-cycle adjustment for the grandmothers because at the same time that the daughter (or daughter-in-law) is in her reproductive years, the grandmothers are dealing with menopause and the end of their childbearing years. Some women and men may also have become mothers-in-law or fathers-in-law through marriage or adoption and may never have had children of their own. There may be deep-seated pain or biological denial and resentment at seeing the daughter-in-law or son-in-law have children. This can cause an initial bout of envy or even jealousy, which is heightened by our youth-centered culture. Some in-laws keep these feelings to themselves; for others, the anger or jealousy, if not dealt with, can spill over into the in-law relationship. This happens in situations where in-laws make comments like "I'm not ready to be a grandmother/grandfather," or "I don't want to be called grandma/grandpa."

Our society has problems with women being grandmothers; when I go out with my grandchildren, I always call myself grandma or make a comment about being a grandma, and find that the response elicited isn't curiosity about how I like being a grandmother but embarrassment or comments like "You look too young to be a grandma."

Curbing In-Law Criticism

Depending on the geographic proximity, experience, and attachment to children of the parents-in-law, they may be more or less involved with the discipline or nurturing of the grandchildren. Several factors come into play with in-law grandchildren. One can be the *too good* in-law grandparent, who criticizes the new parent for not taking good enough care of the child—not feeding the baby enough or feeding it too much, diapering too tightly or not changing the baby often enough and causing diaper rash. Comments about whether to let the baby cry or to pick up the baby too often can cause a long-term rift between parents and in-laws. Any in-law would be well advised to curb negative casual comments where children are concerned.

Some parents-in-law are highly critical of their children's parenting skills and are in competition with the parents. Especially where the first grandchild is concerned, these in-laws often may not understand the developmental stages of children and become critical of the parents' discipline, especially in the "terrible twos." In-laws may not be willing to childproof their house by removing breakables, and may get upset with occasional feet on the furniture or fingerprints on the walls. When such incidents occur, these critical in-laws blame parents for failing to train their children correctly. They then wonder why they seldom see the grandchildren. On the other hand, some inconsiderate children-in-law allow their young children to get out of control and destroy the parents-in-laws' possessions or to eat in nondesignated areas. These issues need to be dealt with carefully and with tact. Seemingly insignificant comments can have long-lasting consequences.

Divorce

Brenda, a recently divorced social worker, came into therapy complaining that her daughter, Maryanne, did not include her in events with her son-in-law's family. In anger, her daughter had told her, "Get a life of your own." Brenda was hurt and depressed. As she processed the situation in therapy, she realized that her daughter had a point. To be a successful in-law, she would have to begin to develop a friendship network outside of the family. (Because of the enormous impact divorce brings to the in-law system, this topic is covered in much greater detail in Chapter 9.)

Aging and Widowed In-Laws

In a similar situation, a young couple came into therapy to discuss the wife's frustration with her father-in-law.

Mike's 78-year-old dad was recently widowed, and now he expects to spend every minute of every weekend with us. I don't even get to sleep in—he calls at 7:00 A.M.

every Saturday to find out what we're doing. When we do anything with him, it's like we're going in slow motion—he has phlebitis and can't move very quickly. I thought I was marrying Mike, not his dad!—Gigi, 28, photographer

When the couple mentioned this in a therapy session, I pointed out that the father-in-law is in the early stages of grief. He was probably feeling very vulnerable and needed predictability. The couple decided to plan events on the calendar with him for three months in advance. They hoped this would take away his panic at being abandoned and let him know they wanted to include him in their lives. It also took the couple off the hook from feeling they had to include him in everything they did. Gigi suggested that they give her father-in-law the option to cancel at the last minute; she knew that it must be difficult for him to make plans. Her father-in-law needed closeness, but he also needed freedom to do the work of grieving. The couple and I discussed the implications of the primary question for a newly widowed in-law: "Where do I fit in?" We further explored how the father-in-law could be included in the family by setting limits but still keeping him empowered and elevated (more on this later in this chapter). With the ongoing advances in medical science, the aging segment of the population can be expected to increase with each succeeding decade. This forms immediate social and personal problems: "What about grandma (or grandpa)?" Parents can ease the transition by promoting an attitude of respect in their homes toward their elders. Being careful not to disparage their parents and parents-in-law in the presence of their children is certainly an important way to start. Respecting the contributions of the elderly in-laws, and not taking for granted their many kindnesses is another. According to Duvall (1954), "As parents inculcate patterns of thankfulness for the richness that grandparents add to the life of the young family, they go out of their way to preserve the family traditions and to honor the older family members who represent the family heritage. Respect for elders characterizes stable family life" (p. 155).

Death and Grief

Demographic data regarding in-laws show that most older men are married, and most older women are widowed. In 1979, 67% of all men over the age of 75 were living with a wife, while only 21% of women in this age bracket were living with a husband (Uhlenberg & Myers, 1981). These statistics indicate that most households will in time be called on to help a mother-in-law (or father-in-law) through the grieving process. Unfortunately for some families, the grieving process will also come into play with the untimely death of an adult child or a grandchild.

Horizontal untoward events, such as the death or illness of a family member, can maximally test the strength and flexibility of an extended family system and can be highly disruptive to in-law relationships. For example, Sarah felt that her mother-in-law, Jeanine, had been very angry at her for many years, blaming her granddaughter's drowning in the family pool on Sarah's negligence. Comments to this effect had been made shortly after the child's death five years earlier, and had driven a wedge between the two women. They remained cool and distant with one another until Jeanine suffered a heart attack. At that point, Sarah's husband, Rod, who loved both his mother and his wife, felt that the women must change their relationship. No longer willing to stand the tension, Sarah and Rod entered therapy to discuss the issues. Rod was torn with a loyalty to his mother as well as to Sarah, and he was ridden with his own guilt around their child's death. The in-laws were included in a subsequent session, during the course of which Rod's mother claimed that she did not even remember making the remark about negligence. After a tense discussion of the grief cycle and the meaning of the loss of a child in the life of a family, both the mother-in-law and the daughter-in-law agreed that life was too short and that their love for Rod was more important than holding onto a grudge.

In some cases, the in-laws, rather than one's own parents, will give support after the death of a child. Such was the case with Lou, a father whom I saw for a few sessions while he grieved the loss of his son to congenital heart failure.

When my two-year-old son died, my own parents just weren't there for me. To my surprise, it was my father-in-law who came forward. He sat down with me and said that he wanted to pay any hospital costs and for the headstone. This is not easy for a guy to say, but at that moment, I really loved him.—Lou, 37, dentist

The role of the grandparents is essential when a parent, especially the mother, dies. The mother- or father-in-law often steps in and helps bring up the children, to the lasting gratitude of the surviving spouse. But one in-law issue that can be particularly tricky relates to the choice of guardianship responsibility for the children if both parents should die before the children are grown. The chance of this happening is remote, but it still begs consideration because, in the absence of a guardianship agreement, the courts often ask the wife's parents to designate a family member to raise the children. When parents try to decide whom to designate, many in-law issues arise, especially when the in-laws are not living in the same geographic region. Even if the grandparents are not the designated guardians, the chances of their being in contact with the children and the quality of that contact will be related to whether the children are raised by the maternal or the paternal family members. (More on this in Chapter 10.)

Death of a parent-in-law, the last stage in the individual life cycle, can also be a devastating event. Death, whether expected or unexpected, can bring about grief issues that carry enormous impact through many subsequent years in the lives of survivors, especially if not resolved in a healthy way. The resulting "baggage from the past" can sidetrack survivors in every aspect of their lives (Horsley, 1989). Present grief can combine with unresolved grief from past losses to exacerbate already painful situations. When clients are carefully guided through a resolution of past grief, they can better deal with the feelings of grief from present losses.

Grieving the Death of a Spouse

Death of a spouse is a devastating event. This represents an end to the long-term relationship for both the spouse and the children in the family. It would seem that a death at the end of a long life is not as tragic as an early death (Worden, 1982), and sometimes the sadness is minimized by family members when the person is an older family member. Nevertheless, my experience shows that age and the expectation that a person is near the end of his or her life does not minimize the grief felt by survivors who have been in close contact with the deceased. There seems to be, over the long term, little understanding of the full impact on an elderly person of loss of a spouse. Because death of a spouse is such an important in-law life-cycle event, I want to cover some of the major areas connected with the loss of a spouse so that therapists can bring an understanding of the grieving process to those in-laws and family members who are affected by the repercussions.

It is important to remember that the active grieving for a spouse is a four-year process. Not all events will take four years, but it takes four years to come to some comfort level (Parkes & Weiss, 1983), especially with once-a-year occasions such as Christmas, anniversaries, and holidays, which are very difficult times for in-laws who have lost a spouse. Some activities are done on a daily basis, such as grocery shopping and the tasks of the daily routine, and after doing these things four times, people usually become more comfortable doing them without a lost family member. With the annual events—anniversaries and holidays—the survivor does not have as much "practice" in getting through them alone. It thus takes four years before the widow or widower learns how to get through these events without the loved one present.

It is also helpful for clients to be aware that depression reaches its peak six months after the death. American society is death-denying. Often, we feel that mourners should be *getting over it* in six months, rather than realizing that the height of depression caused by the loss of a spouse occurs after six months. Another important issue is that the second year after the loss of a spouse can often be more difficult than the first year (Parkes & Weiss, 1983). During the first year, the surviving in-law receives a lot of attention. By the second year, the supporting others have gotten into their own routines, and the surviving spouse is left alone to try to adjust to the fact that the rest of his or her life will be lived without a significant other.

It is helpful to let clients know that grieving is a normal process and that drugs and alcohol can be very detrimental in proceeding through the normal grieving process. Another issue the therapist may wish to suggest to clients is that *just listening* is important. They don't always have to *do*. They can listen. Not all problems are solvable, and sometimes people just have to be heard.

One of the biggest in-law problems I have seen during the grieving process is when another family member—a son or daughter—is pulled into the empty spot to replace the person who has been lost. This can be very difficult on relationships. Spouses can feel quite angry about the demands that their in-laws are making. Pressure in this area can be eased by having a number of family members try to meet the unfilled roles and expectations left by the deceased in-law. Framo (1992) mentions that, like any other system, the family system does not like a void, and married children will often have their loyalty tested when they are asked in subtle and not so subtle ways to help Mother or Dad by doing some work around the house, driving to the doctor, or helping to get finances in order.

Surviving in-laws might be encouraged to stay in their present residence for a year before they make any decisions about selling their furniture or moving. They can then go through the early stages of grief in a familiar setting. Indeed, it would probably be better for them to stay for at least two years so they can make reasonable decisions about their future. Sometimes it is difficult for clients to see their loved ones go through this sadness or discouragement. However, it should be remembered by in-laws that surviving family members need to be *supported,* not *rescued.*

One daughter-in-law, Peggy, said that she was angry with her husband, James, because ever since her father-in-law died, James seemed to be at his mother's beck and call, driving her everywhere, making repairs, running errands. This became a loyalty issue. "Who is more important, your wife or your mother?" After brief therapy, this family came to understand the dynamics of the loyalty pull back into the system and this helped James and Peggy recruit other family members to fill some of the roles of the lost family member. However, they also had to recognize that some roles, such as friend, lover, and companion may never be filled again for the mother.

According to Anderson (1984), upon reaching widowhood, primary and secondary ties with siblings and children are cultivated, while primary and secondary ties with other kin are allowed to disintegrate. However, widows were shown to have more primary ties with all kin than did widowers. Often however, being widowed does not negatively impact close family ties; in fact, it strengthens ties with siblings, particularly sisters. Thus, a greater variety of kin are reported to be a part of a woman's primary kinships network after the loss of a spouse. On the other side of the spectrum, younger widows whose marriages have been broken by death find that their mothers-in-law continue to make them feel a part of the family (Duvall, 1954).

SUCCESSFULLY TRANSITING THE HORIZONTAL IN-LAW STRESSORS

As McGoldrick's vertical and horizontal life-cycle model illustrates (Figure 5.2), the success of the in-law in navigating each horizontal event is largely dependent on the vertical repertoire of coping mechanisms and in-law "baggage" the family member brings to the situation. Although the timing of the horizontal stressors most often is outside the control of any individual, the vertical stressors—the individual's attitudes, expectations, and labels—can be somewhat modified to make the in-law transits less difficult. Kushner (1981) suggests that clients move from the "Why me?" stance into acceptance and even into openness—letting a horizontal life-cycle event become life-transforming. Byng-Hall (1991) suggests that families can write new scripts in order to help them deal with the horizontal stress brought on by loss. Rolland (1991) states that much of family stress and, therefore, in-law vertical stress is caused by overemphasis on the anticipation of loss by family members. Rolland advises that this negative view of life must be counterbalanced by using stressful experiences to ultimately improve the client's quality of life, thereby proactively modifying the vertical in-law anxiety flow. Because this vertical axis represents the modus operandi for coping that in-laws carry through the generations, one individual's shift in adapting positive ways of dealing with life events can have positive consequences in subsequent generations.

TASKS RELATED TO THE IN-LAW LIFE CYCLE

Empowering Family Members

According to Duvall (1954), multigenerational compatibility was simpler in earlier times when there was a place in the family for aging relatives, but those conditions are relatively rare today. Now, an older relative who must make his or her home with the family feels, in many cases, only in the way. There is so little to do, so little room, and so little inclination to double-up in a culture that says, "No roof is big enough for two families." On the other hand, many children-in-law honor their parents-in-law because "they reared the wonderful person I married." These children-in-law, according to Duvall

(1954), see the spouse not so much as mirroring his or her mother, as having become what he or she is as a result of the mother's active application of the best she knew in human development, in other words, the recognition that in the majority of cases parents do the best they can with the emotional and physical resources they have at the time. Duvall further postulates that "many women express themselves as appreciating their mothers-in-law especially because they both (mother and wife) love the same man" (p. 120). One out of every four men and women in Duvall's study reported that they liked their mother-in-law as a person.

Duvall goes on to explain that there is often no place in the family for aging family members unless the older relatives can make a contribution to the on-going life of the family as participating members. Babies still need to be cared for, meals cooked, shopping accomplished, clothes laundered. In many homes where the wife and mother works outside the home, an older relative can be (and often is) a stabilizer for the whole family. However, unless the older relative recognizes the autonomy of the members of the younger generation and has a life that is satisfying enough in itself, there is the ever-present danger of intruding and living *for* the younger family members rather than *with* them. Unless the young family is sound enough in its own foundations to benefit from the experience of a person of different age and background, the structure may be weakened.

Building on Strengths

As parents live longer, it is important for clients to recognize their in-laws' strengths and encourage them to continue to be independent and functional. It is sometimes difficult for the new couple or family to realize that the older in-laws also have their hopes, dreams, desires, and indeed, plans for the future. Constantly focusing on the health of older family members, or encouraging them to cut down on activity or consider retirement, gives no affirming messages to older in-laws. The parents who effectively encourage their children's autonomy are rarely if ever the ones who "live for their children." They are almost always persons in their own right; they have interesting lives of their own, and they do not require their children's attention and achievements to fill their aching voids. Duvall's (1954) research findings led her to encourage aging parents to find fullness in their own lives so that they will not cling to their children for their own emotional needs. This advice is as sound today as it was in 1954.

When older in-laws are encouraged to realize their potential, they are safeguarded from the temptations to be meddlesome and possessive of their children's families. Education has a contribution to make throughout a lifetime of readjustment, reevaluation, and reassessment of oneself in relationship to those held near and dear. This sort of education doesn't have to wait until all the answers to life's riddles are in. "It can begin with the present, with the readiness of individuals to improve and to grow . . . for to live is to grow, and to stop growing is to die" (Duvall, 1954, pp. 319–320).

Keeping Family Members Competent

I was recently visiting my daughter and son in-law. It was evening and I had a 40-mile drive ahead of me. My son in-law gave me directions on getting to the freeway. A few minutes later I heard him whisper to my daughter, "Do you think she will make it to the highway all right?" My daughter assured him that I would. My reaction at the time was one of humor, but I wonder how it will be when a similar comment is made in 20 years? Will my confidence be eroded by declining faculties and similar comments? Will it start by them questioning my competence, then proceed to drawing me a map, then they'll want me to drive behind my son-in-law to the highway entrance, and finally I'll just be driven home? Questioning in-laws regarding their competence can be a dangerous game and can erode confidence and get a child-in-law into a caretaking role that he or she may come to resent.—Olivia, 60, teacher

Empowering oneself as more competent than others may feel good in the short run but, in the long run, it necessitates taking on increasing responsibility for others. It is important that we build on the strengths of our in-laws, rather than focus on their negative characteristics or attributes.

One young man felt that, because his father-in-law had been in an automobile accident, it was an indication that he should be driving only when there was a necessity and then only for short distances. When questioned about the accident, the young man conceded that his father-in-law had actually been rear-ended by another car and bore no responsibility for the accident. This shows some stereotypical thinking on the young man's part, that older people should not be driving. In this case, *older* was 62.

While visiting a friend in another city, 50-year-old Ruby received a phone call from her 68-year-old mother-in-law, who had fallen and broken her arm during her daily six-mile run. Ruby replied that she and her husband were concerned about her mother-in-law's depth perception and her brittle bones, and wondered if she should be running at *her age*. In contrast, the day after I heard this story, an article caught my eye in the *New York Times Magazine,* "A Tale of Two Swimmers" (Lear, 1992), about 15-year-old swimmer Anita Nall, an Olympic hopeful, who was then the world's fastest 200-meter breaststroke champion. Earlier in the year, Anita had injured her knee in an early morning run with friends. Anita brushed off the accident with the clever retort that she had probably fallen over some air. At 15, it is highly doubtful that her parents or other family members questioned her *depth perception.*

THE NOT-SO-EMPTY NEST: WHEN GRANDCHILDREN
ENTER THE IN-LAW EQUATION

Babies make mothers- and fathers-in-law into grandparents. But grandchildren rarely clarify the role played by the parents-in-law. On the contrary, claims Duvall (1954), who says the expectations about what it means to be a good grandparent are many and varied. She points out that parents' mixed feelings range from fear that the grandparents will be bad for the children to warmest appreciation for their rich contribution to the family members' lives (p. 141).

In looking at McGoldrick's (1980) life-cycle formulation of the family (Figure 5.1), it would seem that two stages are at high risk for destabilization of the family. One is the second stage, the joining of families through marriage, with its task of realignment of relationships with the extended family and friends in order to include a spouse. McGoldrick asserts that the third stage, in which the family adds young children, requires realignment of relationships with the extended family to encompass the grandparenting role. The birth can also put a strain on the relationship between the in-laws. The daughter-in-law can be put on the defensive very easily when the new grandmother intrudes on her territory (Duvall, 1954). In the Duvall study, daughters-in-law suggested that mothers-in-law exclude themselves from discipline of the grandchild, and that such seemingly helpful suggestions as offering to clean the daughter-in-law's house could be seen as criticism of the new mother's housekeeping abilities.

Troll et al. (1979) points out that, with the trends for earlier marriage, earlier childbirth, and longer life expectancy, grandparents are younger and more numerous than ever before. About three-fourths of older people in the United States have living grandchildren. Of this number, nearly half see a grandchild almost every day—an indication that a great deal of in-law interactions also take place. To my knowledge, no studies have been done on the quality of the in-law contact through grandparenting, yet this represents an important role for in-laws, and grandparenting activities and expectations are often a source of in-law problems.

We know that the grandparenting roles of in-laws are important issues even in divorcing families. Johnson's (1989) research showed that in divorcing families it was not uncommon to find young children rotating among four homes: their mother's, father's, maternal grandparents', and paternal grandparents'. Johnson found that some paternal grandmothers formed coalitions with former daughters-in-law and assisted them in caring for grandchildren, even when sons voiced objections to these coalitions. (For more on divorce and in-laws, see Chapter 9.)

Although he does not mention in-laws specifically, Bradt (1980) states that contact with the extended family can have a stabilizing influence on the nuclear family, particularly where there are problems with children. Bradt sees the birth of a child as a time when the new parents' mothers-in-law, as well as aunts and uncles, may be mobilized in order to support the nuclear family. He also states that older members of the extended family can provide missing authority and leadership. The addition of a child can increase the strength of the kinship bond, but can also cause asymmetry.

Gluck, Dannefer, and Milea (1980) state that at the time of the birth of the first child, unresolved conflicts with parents—especially the woman's mother—will often come forth, and the birth of the grandchild will often signify active reentry of the extended family into the couple's system. Stern and Ross (1952) say that most aging men and women find it fairly easy to be ideal grandparents when they see their grandchildren only occasionally. But when three generations live under the same roof, the charm of the youngest for the oldest is liable to wear off very soon—often, indeed, within days.

Beyond the care and nurturing of grandchildren, parents-in-law may also get involved in the actual timing of the grandchildren's birth. One young couple, Lizabelle and Garth, came to my office especially frustrated because Garth's mother clearly stated that she felt her son should quit school and that her daughter-in-law, Lizabelle (26), should get pregnant right away while her biological clock was still ticking. Garth's parents were divorced and Garth's father, who was paying his son's tuition, felt that his daughter-in-law should not get pregnant until his son had graduated from college. The two conflicting messages from his parents confused the son and infuriated his wife, who was from France and desired to recreate her own family within the United States. The couple's solution was to stop using birth control and to "let nature take its course." I last spoke to Lizabelle several months ago and she was not yet pregnant.

Perceptions and Styles of Grandparenting

Because in-laws as grandparents are an important part of the extended family, understanding and clarifying the agenda and roles of grandparents can help to avoid problems. Where there are preexisting problems, this examination can promote dialogue. Fortunately, we know more about the in-laws' grandparenting styles and roles than we do about the in-law relationship. Following are several studies the therapist might find useful in helping both children-in-law and parents-in-law discuss their expectations and desires regarding grandparenting. Discussion of grandparenting can promote understanding and empower both children- and parents-in-law.

In an analysis of life-history interviews and questionnaire surveys with 268 grandparents, Kivnick (1982) found that people's thoughts about being grandparents fell into the following five categories:

1. **Centrality:** For these individuals, grandparenthood activities and feelings become more important as other activities and close friends and relatives become less important.

2. **Valued elder:** These grandparents focus on passing skills and traditions on to the grandchildren, and having the grandchildren think kindly of them and regard them as wise.

3. **Immortality through the clan:** These individuals focus on grandparenthood in terms of personal immortality, and this is achieved through the continuity of their families into the indefinite future.

4. **Reinvolvement with personal past:** Being a grandparent lets these people remember when they were grandchildren, or to when they were parents with children the same ages as their grandchildren are today.

5. **Indulgence:** These grandparents treasure the opportunity to *spoil* their grandchildren and to be more lenient and less critical than they were with their own children.

Kivnick points out that although all of the grandparents interviewed seemed to think about grandparenthood in all five categories, different people gave different emphases. Kivnick feels that grandparenthood plays a more important role than is generally recognized. This may also be the case with in-law roles (pp. 143, 144).

I suggest that there may also be a sixth category related to in-laws being grandparents: the *reluctant grandparent* who is not ready to make the transition from parent or in-law to grandparent. Stories are frequently told by befuddled and bemused children regarding their mother-in-law's or father-in-law's reluctance to acknowledge being old enough to be a *grandparent*. This reluctance often shows up in what the in-law chooses to be called by her or his grandchildren. It may be a first name, such as Grandma Susan or Grandpa Chad or just Susan or Chad, or a pet name, such as Papa, Ba, or Juju.

One client, Victoria, was agitated when she came into individual therapy. When she had recently announced that she was pregnant, her mother-in-law, Mercedes, commented, "This is a cruel world and you shouldn't bring a child into it." This was the first grandchild and Mercedes was not happy that Victoria was pregnant because she felt too young to be viewed as a grandmother. Victoria was dismayed about her attitude and lack of support.

Prior to the next session, Victoria invited Mercedes and Mercedes' mother, Matilda, to join us in an effort to support Victoria and to discuss matters with trusted advisers who were experienced in child birth and rearing. Mercedes and Matilda, although reluctant, agreed to attend the session. To move the issue away from the emotionality of the direct tension between Victoria and Mercedes, I drew a horizontal line on my easel pad, put *birth* on one end and *death* on the other, and we discussed the family life cycle with particular emphasis on the hopes, dreams, and fears of women. It was a very rich session. The three women represented three stages in the family life cycle, and at one point, Mercedes voiced her concern about being a grandmother. Matilda talked about how she felt when she became a grandmother. Victoria then spoke about her hopes and dreams for her baby and her desire to have Mercedes and Matilda involved with her child. We then discussed Kivnick's five categories of grandparental involvement. Mercedes and Matilda liked the idea of being seen as valued elders and having immortality through the birth of a grandchild and great-grandchild.

Several months after the session, Victoria told me that Mercedes and Matilda continue to build on the session with support and advice regarding the upcoming birth. In fact, Victoria has some concern that they will be too involved, so it will be important for us to continue to frame them as the *trusted advisers* rather than as the *decision makers* in Victoria's life.

Moving the parent-in-law into what Whitaker and Keith (1981) conceptualized as the trusted adviser role at the birth of a grandchild can often be tricky, and can bring up loyalty questions. According to Fischer (1983), in cross-sectional data that included interviews with 33 daughters-in-law, 30 mothers, and 24 mothers-in-law, all the daughters in the study who lived near their husband's parents were concerned that their own parents have equal time with the grandchildren. This concern seems to illustrate Fischer's findings that the birth of a child increases the contact with maternal grandmothers more than with paternal grandmothers. While each group is equally likely to be called on to baby-sit as well as give gifts, Fischer found that paternal grandmothers were more likely to *give* things, and maternal grandmothers were more likely to *do* things. Daughters more willingly ask their own mothers, rather than their mothers-in-law, about child rearing and the addition of a child is likely to emphasize the differentiation between the young woman's mother and her mother-in-law.

As the daughter-in-law moves toward her role as a new mother, the son could also move toward his mother around issues of child raising. A wise wife might encourage the husband to have a dialogue around child rearing with his mother, for as one young mother stated, "I encourage my husband to have a relationship with my mother-in-law because one baby is enough. I don't want to end up mothering my husband and I want him to take equal responsibility with our kids." If the wife is uncomfortable about having her husband discuss child rearing with his mother, the couple can reach agreement in advance about which issues will be discussed. For example, Morris continually called his mother for advice about toilet training their three-year-old son, Ernest. Lindsay viewed it as a betrayal of confidence in her own parenting skills, and as opening their family to criticism because they had waited so long to begin the transition with Ernest. A daughter-in-law might help to move the mother- and father-in-law into the trusted adviser role by getting advice on parenting issues or other issues related to their grandchildren. In the study of Montana ranch families, Komarovsky (1962) found that mothers-in-law did not initiate discussion of issues with daughters-in-law as often as daughters-in-law did. It seems that if paternal mothers-in-law or fathers-in-law want to connect with their daughters-in-law more frequently, they may have to take the first step. Questions of how things are going or offering a helping hand are good ways to open communication. Criticism or unsolicited advice will be a quick turn-off.

The fifth focus of grandparenthood, identified by Kivnick as "indulgence and treasuring the opportunity to spoil the grandchildren," illuminates a familiar in-law loyalty problem that is often dealt with in couples and family therapy. One young man stated during therapy, "Her parents give the children so much. How can my parents possibly compete?" Inherent in this indulgence paradigm is the fact that children who live closer or who are seen more are naturally given more emotional and perhaps financial support. While in the short run indulgence may feel satisfying, in-laws may want to balance this style with some of the other grandparenting roles, such as passing down skills.

Styles of Grandparenting

In addition to discussing with families their perception of the grandparenting role, therapists might find it useful to discuss styles of grandparenting with the in-laws. In their study of grandparents of teenage children, Cherlin and Furstenberg (1985) identified the following four styles of grandparenting:

1. **Detached grandparent:** A distant figure not involved with the grandchildren.
2. **Passive grandparent:** Inactive but functions by being around. This grandparent may be filling the role that Troll (1983) terms "the family watchdog."
3. **Influential grandparent:** Sees children often and is a major figure in the grandchildren's day-to-day life.
4. **Selective investment grandparent:** Turns his or her attention to a selected grandchild in order to make up for a poor relationship with other grandchildren.

In my clinical experience, in-laws who express selective investment in their grandparenting style are especially frustrating and place a strain on in-law relationships. I remember at my own family get togethers my cousin often bragging that grandfather had told him that he was, "the smartest grandchild."

Us Against Them

Families who are functioning well most often have a hierarchical structure: the parents having more power than their underage children, and the parents-in-law being treated as respected advisers. However, therapists will often find children in trouble at school and at home when they live within a fragmented parental system, and the child joins allegiance with one of his or her grandparents. This is illustrated in humorist Sam Levinson's comment, "The reason grandparents and grandchildren get along so well is that they have a common enemy" (Boyd, 1995). There can be a real risk of "parentified in-laws" where child care is turned over to in-laws by working parents. The parents and in-laws may have different parenting styles and philosophies that stem from their family backgrounds. Either or both parents can wind up with insufficient power to parent their children, and the parents may then feel incompetent, unappreciated, frustrated, anxious, and stressed. The grandparents may enjoy having the child as their ally against the *bad parent,* who is often the son- or daughter-in-law, but in the long run the entire family suffers. This outcome can represent a self-fulfilling prophecy: the in-laws may not have sanctioned the marriage, and failure of the parental system may prove that their opinions were correct. All people enjoy being right, but it is sometimes more important to be supportive than to be right, as in the end it is the children who suffer most.

Duvall's (1954) research shows that enlightened grandparents (in-laws) are sensitive to the importance of the parent–child relationship and will consult with the parents before making proposals for their grandchildren. By actively including the mother and father in planning, the threats of envy and jealousy are largely avoided. Duvall goes on to say that a family conspiracy between grandparent and grandchild in which parents are left out is safe only when the basic relationship between the adults is fundamentally secure. Otherwise, the grandparent runs the danger of alienating the parents and losing contact with the young family.

Duvall (1954) found in her research that grandparents get themselves into emotional hot water with the family for the following primary reasons: they don't keep up-to-date, they interfere in the disciplining of the children, and they become a threat to the mother when she perceives that her children love the grandparents too much.

In one young family, the grandmother had become ill and moved in with her son, his wife, and their two daughters, Jesse (10) and Kristy (14). Jesse loved the grandmother very much and felt very close to her. Being a typical adolescent, Kristy resented the grandmother's intrusion in the home and felt that sharing the house with the grandmother was a real imposition on the family. She constantly bad-mouthed her grandmother, and a great deal of tension and friction was created in the home. Kristy may have mirrored some of the attitudes of the mother, who was not happy about having her mother-in-law in the home. No doubt, Kristy was allowed to express her anger because it mirrored the anger of her mother. During the course of therapy, it became evident that the mother-in-law was seen as an intrusion in the home. The intervention was to involve the husband in the process, because the conflict revolved around his mother. We also sought to bring in his three other siblings. The family determined that she would rotate among her four children, moving from one home to the next on a quarterly basis. This is not an ideal situation for an older person. However, the mother-in-law was willing to do this in order to maintain the goodwill of her granddaughter and daughter-in-law.

Children need grandparents to add richness, perspective, and fullness to life. According to Duvall (1954), in societies where grandparents are normally close to the children, there is much more of the relaxed, leisurely teaching of the culture than in today's family structure, where mother and father are busy and grandparents are often too far away to serve these functions. Duvall says, "Much has been said about the relief from their children that grandparents provide for parents. Little is said of the need children may have for some relief from their parents. It is quite possible that grandparents serve a real purpose in providing for children a different touch, another approach, a new setting and emotional climate that is not possible in the day-in-day-out contact with parents alone" (p. 147).

It is important to realize that grandparents have a unique freedom to enjoy their grandchildren. When they brought up their own children, they were bound by the expectations and demands of parenthood. But now, in their relationships with their grandchildren, they are free to enjoy the children as persons.

What Will We Name the Baby?

With the addition of a new baby in the family, in-law loyalty issues begin to emerge with the choice of a name for the baby. Again, as with what to call the parents-in-law, many questions emerge about the baby's name. Will the parents-in-law or siblings-in-law be slighted if the baby is not given their name? Which (if any) in-laws will the baby be named after? Will the couple strike out on their own and give the baby a name of their own choosing?

One couple came to therapy for help in settling a family dispute. After learning through amniocentesis that their expected child would be a boy, and announcing this to the parents-in-law, Sharon was incensed when her father-in-law emphatically demanded, "Of course, you will name him Clifford Henry Rutherford IV." Sharon's husband, who was the III and tired of being referred to as *Little Cliff* (or worse), was adamantly opposed, and the incident took away from the new parents' excitement and joy about an event that wouldn't even take place for another five months. Sharon also feared that this signified future meddling and control by her father-in-law.

The entire family agreed to attend a session to discuss what children meant in the family life cycle and the changes the birth would bring. A genogram of the family history identified an earlier power struggle between the father-in-law and his own father, which was being mirrored in his demands regarding his coming grandson. The mother-in-law interjected here that she had been reluctant to bestow on her son a III appellation, but had been conned into submission by her father-in-law, and resented it ever since. The family decided that the time had come to break with tradition. This allowed Sharon to graciously offer to give the baby the father-in-law's first name as his middle name.

The family was pleased that they had made the effort to resolve this issue, because the baby was born with major birth defects and died shortly after birth. When I called to offer my condolences, Sharon reflected with bittersweet irony that the conflict over the name actually brought her closer than ever to her parents-in-law and that this helped enormously in the grieving process.

Who Will Come to Visit and Help after the Birth?

This can be a difficult in-law issue, especially when it is the first grandchild on both sides of the family. Often, women want their own mothers to be with them when they go home from the hospital after the birth. Because this may seem exclusionary to the new father's family and cause hurt feelings, it might be wise to invite the paternal family to help out during the second week at home, or to plan a special event with the new baby and the paternal grandparents.

Attending the actual delivery and birth of the child may also be an issue for in-laws. The mother may desire her own family to attend the birth, but she may not want the paternal side of the family to be there. These issues should be worked out with special respect and consideration for the new mother, who will be going through a major physical and emotional experience.

CHECKLIST

In-Law Issues Related to Life-Cycle Changes

1. Where is the in-law relationship in terms of the family life cycle?

    a. Between families: The unattached young adult

b. The joining of families through marriage: The newly married couple

c. The family with young children

d. The family with adolescents

e. Launching children and moving on

f. The family in later life

2. What are the horizontal stressors in the relationship with the in-laws regarding life-cycle transitions—retirement, empty nest, death, or divorce of an in-law?

3. What are the vertical stressors that impact in-laws—myths, attitudes toward in-laws, family history, or past relationships with in-laws?

4. How can the vertical messages change to enable growth when transiting the horizontal stressors?

5. Are family members having difficulty with accepting new roles, as shown by any of the following?

a. Denial

b. Anger

c. Bargaining

d. Depression

In-Law Death and Grief

Are you aware:

1. That active grieving for a spouse is a four-year process?

2. That the height of depression occurs six months after the loss?

3. That the second year can often be more difficult than the first year?

4. That grieving is a normal process?

5. That grieving in-laws may pull an adult child in to fill the void?

6. That pressure may be eased by having a number of family members meet unfilled roles left by the dead in-law?

7. That it is suggested that the surviving partner stay in the same living conditions for one year or more after the death of the spouse?

8. That special holidays and anniversaries can be depressing periods?

Tasks Related to the In-Law Life Cycle

1. Does the family respect the contributions of the aging in-laws?
2. Has the family developed a clear idea of where older in-laws fit in?
3. Do the older in-laws have a life and interests of their own?
4. How do the in-laws and children feel about living together?
5. Have other alternatives been considered if living together is not feasible?
6. Does the family encourage in-laws to be independent and functional?
7. Does the family try to focus on in-law areas of competency by making affirming statements?

In-Laws as Grandparents

1. How do various general characteristics of a grandparent fit with the in-laws' conduct as grandparents? Are changes or modifications in these roles or styles desired?
   a. Grandparent role perceptions:
      (1) Centrality
      (2) Valued elder
      (3) Immortality through the clan
      (4) Reinvolvement with personal past
      (5) Indulgence
   b. Grandparenting styles:
      (1) Detached grandparent
      (2) Passive grandparent
      (3) Influential grandparent
      (4) Selective investment grandparent

CHAPTER 6

Siblings-in-Law

We get so caught up in the parent-in-law situation that sibling-in-law relationships are often overlooked, although these relationships can range from being rewarding to being highly problematic. Individuals or couples seldom come to therapy to deal directly with sibling-in-law problems; however, therapists hear of them often, especially where financial issues and family businesses are concerned. Sibling-in-law problems are most likely not major issues in therapy because these problems are generally overshadowed by the more dramatic parent-in-law problems. However, if sibling-in-law problems are present but are never addressed, family members are unable to draw strength and resources from sibling-in-law relationships as the parents age or when family crises occur.

PAST HISTORY

A sibling relationship can be termed a referent relationship because, in most cases, a relationship with one's in-laws exists only in relationship to one's spouse. However, sometimes in-laws have been members of the same social group or have introduced their sibling to the future spouse. Hence, siblings-in-law sometimes enter the relationship with a past history that may or may not be amicable.

> *When I was in high school, I was visiting my sister at college. I knew she had a new boyfriend, but I had not met him. As we drove into a service station to get gas, I saw a guy I had known in high school. I said to my sister, "That guy is a real jerk." My sister turned to me with a very hurt look and said, "That's my boyfriend." They are now married and guess what—I still think he is a jerk but now he is my brother-in-law and I make it my business to get along with him.—*
> Wendy, 23, graphic artist

SIBLING-IN-LAW EXPECTATIONS

Kaslow and Schwartz (1987) state that with the expansion of the family and the entrance of in-laws, there is a possibility that new friendships can be established between birth siblings and in-law siblings. If expectations for these relationships are too high or unrealistic demands are made, these sibling-in-law relationships can be a great disappointment, especially if the new in-law is expected to fill a lost role in the family.

> When my oldest sister married Stan, I was happy that he was coming into our family because he was going to be another son for my parents and a brother for me—we lost our brother, and I thought Stan was going to take the place of Alan for my dad to have another male around. It turned out that Stan was an abusive husband and father and after three children and seven years of marriage, Sis finally got up the courage to divorce him.—Jean, 35, teacher

Another setup for in-law disappointment is when a new in-law is expected to be the brother that the siblings never had.

> When I got engaged to my husband, there were just two children in his family, my husband and his sister. His sister is nine years older than he is and is very motherly. She seemed to feel when we got engaged that she was part of the process, and she got very involved in everything we did. She sent me a card about how exciting it was for her brother to be engaged because she felt I would be the sister that she never had. Boy, was she in for a big surprise. I already had four other sisters and two brothers, and I was very close to my family and didn't need another sister who had so many expectations of me.—Lisa, 43, designer

> When I married Mimi, I looked forward to spending time with her brother Cleave. I knew he was a good golfer and tennis player and, although I was a bit of a duffer, I knew we would have fun together. Well, forget that. I quickly found out that par golfers and A tennis players will give you a couple of courtesy games but, after that, you are on your own. Nothing, my brother-in-law informed me, can ruin a good tennis game like playing with a partner who hits a soft serve. So much for brother-in-lawly love.—Albert, 27, nurse

Expectations can run high for a new brother- or sister-in-law, who may be held to a family norm that he or she has never agreed to accept.

> I feel like I've been a bit of a disappointment to my sisters-in-law because Dave's sisters, one in particular, are very good at remembering birthdays, keeping in touch, writing letters, sending little gifts, and doing all these things that Dave never does, and that I don't do either. I feel like they were expecting me to do these things in return, because I am the female in the family, and because they do them and they're the females. But I don't do them, and if they get done I expect Dave to do them because it's his family.—Jane, 27, secretary

AGE AND BIRTH ORDER

In addition to unrealistic expectations of siblings-in-law, age and birth order may play a part in sibling-in-law dissonance. The spouse may be of the same or a different generation than his or her siblings-in-law, as illustrated in the following case.

Alison, a client in individual therapy, was a *bonus child*—she arrived long after her parents had given up on having more children. Her brother Larry was 12 years older, and Alison saw him as being a real pain in the neck, because he treated Alison and her husband John as though they were kids. Larry constantly gave John unsolicited advice, and things finally came to a head when John, the son-in-law, graduated from medical school, because Alison's father thought it was great to have a doctor in the family. Larry could not handle not being number one, and soon moved to another city.

Birth order issues come into focus in sibling-in-law relationships. Leman (1985) states that some of the most compatible marriages are made when the oldest child from one family marries the youngest child from another. If one marries the most compatible child in the family in terms of birth order, logic says that one may not be as compatible with the spouse's siblings. Following are some examples of in-law birth order situations that create conflict.

Youngest Sibling/Youngest In-Law

The youngest child (who is often the family pet or family clown and loves the limelight) (Leman, 1985) now comes into close contact with a sibling-in-law who is also the last born and who also likes being the star. In his extensive sibling research, Toman (1993) found the last children to be submissive dependent. They also tend to be more impulsive and carefree, and have a higher tolerance for frustration. The last born can also be opposing toward peers, thus causing in-law conflict.

> *I was the youngest of three children and married the oldest of four. My sister-in-law was also the youngest in her family. When I was pregnant with our first child, my sister-in-law was going to school to become a psychologist. She was learning how to do testing and evaluation so she asked me if I would take a psychological test. I agreed, to help her out. I was very naive and happy and didn't realize that my sister-in-law had some in-law rivalry issues. So, I remember one day we were at her house on Sunday, and I was very pregnant and was just getting ready to put the rolls in the oven, and she said, "Well, I got your psychological testing evaluated and he said you're either pregnant or a lesbian." Well, from that day on, I have been extremely guarded with my sister-in-law.*—Barbara, 58, retired nurse

Oldest Sibling/Oldest In-Law

The oldest children in families often take charge and enjoy being senior. They may have experience at leading boys and girls alike (Toman, 1993). They are often serious, don't like surprises, and like people to be on time

(Leman, 1985). In the following case example, Ben, the youngest child, married Crystal, the oldest in her family, who then came to loggerheads with her brother-in-law, Ben's oldest sibling.

> *Both my brother-in-law and I are the oldest in the family. He has always tried to tell his younger brother (my husband) what to do and now he is trying to run our lives as a couple. As the oldest daughter in the family, I am also used to being in charge. My brother-in-law has picked the wrong person to do battle with!*—Crystal, 41, teacher

Middle Children as In-Laws

What of the middle children? Leman (1985) states that middle children often don't have the hang-ups of only children or oldest children, and although they did not have the breaks or privileges of older children or only children, they may have less fear or anxiety than firstborns. Middle children have often learned to be more flexible and easy to get along with, and may turn out to be the more adaptable of brothers- or sisters-in-law. By being in the middle, this in-law is prepared for all types of relationships (Toman, 1993).

> *As the middle child of three girls, I have little or no conflict with any of my in-laws. I have noticed that my oldest sister is sometimes bothered with comments made by my husband, who is the youngest child, or by my younger sister's husband, who is the oldest child; however, I have never been bothered by any of them. I think that sometimes my brothers-in-law do weird things but I never get mad. I just think, oh, that is their "education phase" or their "hey dude" phase. I figure that people need the time to adjust to new situations. As a middle child, I am used to being in the push–pull between the oldest and the youngest.*—Eliza, 33, bond portfolio manager

A Matter of Culture

As an in-law, it is important to be aware that culture as well as upbringing can play a large role in creating in-law problems. The following case was referred to me several years ago by the child protective agency.

A judge had mandated that two couples who were in-laws come in for three sessions of family therapy. The sister-in-law, Jean, had reported her brother Fred and sister-in-law Gretta for child abuse because the couple continually left Frederick, age one, in the crib each morning while they went swimming at the beach. The two couples had not spoken since the family court session.

At our first session, the two couples discussed the reason they were in therapy. Gretta, who was from Germany, was very angry at Jean, for reporting them. Jean stated that she was concerned for Frederick and only reported after telling Gretta numerous times that it was not correct for her to leave the baby alone at home. Jean stated that Gretta did not believe her when she said that it is against the law in the United States to leave a child unattended. As the session went on, it became clear that this was not a case of intentional child neglect. Gretta felt that Frederick would be traumatized if he had a baby-sitter he did not know, and hence, felt that it was safer to leave Frederick alone. Gretta pointed out that this was common practice in Germany, and Jean stated that this is not the way things are done in the United States. The women became quite angry with each other, and at that point, I encouraged the males in the family to form a dyad to discuss the problem while the women listened to the discussion.

The men took the issue to a more global level by discussing the child protection law and what was required in the United States, and the consequences of breaking the law. They also talked about the downside—the intrusion of government into people's lives and how families should settle their own in-law disputes.

Gretta told about how German people pride themselves on their independence and are very child-oriented. Jean admitted that Frederick was very independent for a one-year-old. The problem then became not neglect, but how family members (including the in-laws) could help raise the next generation to be independent while keeping them safe and protected.

With the problem redefined, the entire second session was spent constructing family genograms and listening to in-law stories. The major topic remained how in-laws and others can help to keep children safe and protected. Gretta had some especially touching stories of in-law courage and strength exhibited by her family during World War II.

In the last session, we discussed the in-law relationship and talked about siblings-in-law and such issues as birth order, personality traits, different personality types, and how people behave with and respond to their in-laws. The couples left the session with a view of the broader picture but concurred that there were still some hard feelings, that would diminish with time. The issue permanently resolved itself when Gretta and her family moved back to Germany where she said her mother would tend Frederick during their couples outings.

SIBLING-IN-LAW PERSONALITY TYPES

As we have often heard, not everyone marches to the same drummer or hears the same music. Indeed, some people seem to have *tunnel hearing* and are oblivious to the wildly divergent viewpoints of others. When there are conflicts between siblings-in-law, it can be beneficial for the therapist to help the client understand the different and unique way that each person views the world. Some therapists use the 16 Myers–Briggs types (Hirsh & Kummerow, 1989; Keirsey & Bates, 1978; Myers & Myers, 1980) to illustrate diverse viewpoints. I have found it helpful to use a model of siblings-in-law person-alities, based on nine personality types (Baron & Wagele, 1994; Palmer, 1995; Riso, 1990):

1. Giving in-law.
2. Conflict-avoidance in-law.
3. Take-charge in-law.
4. Critical in-law.
5. Observant in-law.
6. Gadabout in-law.
7. Opposing-view in-law.
8. Emotionally intense in-law.
9. Superachieving in-law.

Descriptions of sibling-in-law types and survival strategies for clients.

1. Giving In-Law

This is often a sibling-in-law who speaks from the heart. Early in the in-law re-lationship, giving in-laws will listen to what the new spouse says and give a great deal to both the sibling and the new in-law. However, if they give too much and don't feel that they have been given enough in return, they may cut off the offending party and become somewhat cold. This treatment may aggravate the person who has been cut, because the giving in-laws will exhibit close and cozy relationships with other in-laws or family members. Giving in-laws gravitate to-ward powerful people and enjoy sharing the spotlight; they are prideful and re-quire a great deal of attention. They can look provocative, flirtatious, and dependent; however, they are very independent, high-energy people who can be creative and playful and know how to have a good time.

Sibling-in-Law Survival Tactics

1. Hang in there if the giving in-laws have cut you off. They are loving and want to be liked. Make every effort (especially if it seems like a gargan-tuan effort) to reconnect and make amends. You will be rewarded.
2. To return to their good graces, do some nice things for them but don't expect great returns.
3. Don't be frightened away by their quick temper outbursts. These quick outbursts are like hot brushfires, and once passed, leave more fertile soil—and a more loving relationship, because these people seldom carry a grudge.

4. Spend time having fun and laughing—but take an interest in their problems, to give them a break from focusing on yours.

5. These in-laws are not good at keeping secrets. If you don't want something known, don't tell them.

2. Conflict-Avoidance In-Law

This sibling in-law can see both sides of an argument, is great to talk to, and gives good advice regarding problems with other in-laws or spouses, while all the time overlooking his or her own needs. Conflict-avoidance in-laws can be trusted to keep a secret. They appear to be very good-natured and seem to have all the time in the world for other people's problems, when actually their own problems are churning inside. They will put the petty concerns of others above their own, which often may not be so petty—finding a job or following through on their child's request. They can lose focus and let nonessentials crowd out essentials, and may space out on food, TV, books, or alcohol. These are wonderful in-laws, but if they let their anger go to sleep and avoid dealing with problems, they may unleash their anger and resentment when least expected. Remember, they are much deeper and more intelligent than they may seem. Underneath an easygoing facade is a highly competitive and very stubborn in-law.

Sibling-in-Law Survival Tactics

1. Recognize their need to be praised and acknowledged.

2. Be aware that their easygoing attitude is only a facade and that there is a great deal going on inside—"Still waters run deep."

3. Support them in staying focused on the tasks they choose.

4. Don't try to tell them what to do or where to go. To avoid conflict, they will simply comply with the desires of others. To empower these in-laws, give them choices.

5. Don't pry—give them time alone. They need *down time.*

3. Take-Charge In-Law

This sibling-in-law always needs to be in charge of every situation, is easily *angered,* and at times seems like a bully. Take-charge in-laws don't mind a good argument and are often surprised when an in-law has been offended by the energy of their response. Alcohol and take-charge in-laws often don't mix. These in-laws can not only take charge, but completely run over everybody else, causing in-law rifts that are difficult to mend. Although at times they seem frightening, their assertiveness is excellent for moving people and groups forward. These are the in-laws who pull together huge family reunions and are so energetic they make sure everyone has fun (along with a few arguments along the way). These courageous leaders inspire others to speak their own mind, and can be very loyal and generous.

Sibling-in-Law Survival Tactics

1. Recognize this in-law's need to be heard and acknowledged early in the conversation.

2. Encourage noncompetitive family activities such as park or zoo outings.

3. Avoid confrontations.

4. Make *I'm feeling uncomfortable* statements when the argument or discussion is getting too heated. When things become too uncomfortable, excuse yourself. There is no point in trying to talk down an angry take-charge in-law.

5. Try family gatherings without alcohol.

6. If they ask to be forgiven, believe them; these in-laws do have a soft spot in their hearts.

4. Critical In-Law

A hypercritical sibling-in-law knows how all of the adults and children in the family (as well as the universe) should behave. Miss Manners and Emily Post are these in-laws' gurus. They love to be right, and often are. They can be great in-laws: they are excellent at things that require precision, such as sewing, decorating birthday cakes, editing, and helping with homework. Everything they do is perfection, which means that one shouldn't ask them to help if one doesn't want them to take the time to get things right. A milk carton on their dinner table will not do and will be replaced by a ceramic pitcher. They hold themselves (as well as their in-laws and their siblings) to a high standard. They hate being late and expect family gatherings to be at the right place and the right time. They can become quite angry, especially if they feel that they are right and others are not meeting their standards. Critical in-laws can be very direct in their anger; they speak from the gut, but often will not remember what they have said to offend others. These in-laws like predictability and do not enjoy a big surprise family bash for their birthday or being imposed on to baby-sit at the last minute. They are critical of others but often have difficulty taking criticism. One client described her critical brother-in-law: "He can dish it out, but he sure can't take it."

Sibling-in-Law Survival Tactics

1. Be on time, especially for the events planned by these in-laws, and bring the food or items that you agreed to bring.

2. If you don't have the time, inclination, or energy to do what the critical in-laws ask you to do, decline. These in-laws understand lack of time and know that doing things their way takes time.

3. Don't be surprised if they don't remember things they have said that offended you. They will remember your slights, but seldom remember their own. If you want to talk about how they have offended you, confront them in private. Set up a time, get permission to talk about the issue, and then tell them how you felt when they said that you don't know how to discipline your kids.

4. Don't point out their faults or inconsistencies in public. Exposing the faults of critical in-laws in front of others is very hurtful. They are hard enough on themselves without having others expose their errors to the world.

5. Enjoy the fact that someone has the energy and guts to envision a perfect world.

5. Observant In-Law

This sibling-in-law tends to be a real loner and thinker. Observant in-laws enjoy sitting back and watching the family, rather than engaging in the activities. Although they are often seen as shy and withdrawn, they really like living in their world of ideas. To explore these ideas, they require time to think about and process family events. For example, they will enjoy their sister-in-law's concert far more after the event, when they have gone home and have had time to contemplate and replay the event in their heads. These in-laws carefully guard their time and energy, and often their money, because they fear that these resources are in short supply. Because of their tendency to withdraw, they can become isolated and overlooked by the more active in-laws. They expect that other family members also enjoy being left alone; however, this respect for others' privacy can be mistaken for a lack of interest in family issues. They are often highly dependent on the family network because they do not interact with many people and often work in jobs that are isolated, such as computer programming or accounting practices. When approached, their sensitivity and caring make them good people to go to with problems. They tend to be logical, knowledgeable, and original thinkers.

Sibling-in-Law Survival Tactics

1. Believe these in-laws when they say they would rather watch the family play games than participate. Don't push.

2. Give them time to process family events and don't ask them to come up with knee-jerk responses.

3. Include them as idea people in the planning of family activities and events.

4. If you want an objective opinion about an event, ask their advice, but don't ask them to take sides—they don't deal well with conflict.

5. Don't be afraid to give them a hug. They need to be encouraged to express emotion.

6. Be sensitive to the fact that even though they might not be the life of the party, family and in-laws are an important part of their lives.

6. Gadabout In-Law

Some have called this sibling-in-law the human hummingbird. Gadabouts are in-laws who are always on the go—in constant search for all of the experiences that life has to offer. This running around is based in a fear that they will be stuck in depression or despair if they stop, and thus their modus operandi is constant activity. These in-laws invite you to stay for a week but don't cancel any of their usual activities. They invite you along or leave you at home with the kids "so they can get to know Auntie." Gadabouts can be fun to have for in-laws, but they can also be frustrating, because they are always looking for the best option. Late on Saturday night, they may decide that Sunday dinner with you is not high on their agenda. They always have a lot of tasks going and may need to complete only a few. This can be frustrating: it may be *your* job they don't get done. They are masters at getting others to do their work.

Sibling-in-Law Survival Tactics

1. Have compassion; realize that fear of stopping is at the base of their constant motion.

2. Be clear about dates and times you need them to be available. They are loyal family members.

3. Don't push them to get together. If you don't happen to be a top priority for them, it is their loss.

4. If you don't want to feel used, tell them you won't hold their purse while they go on the water slide. Just say no.

5. Play with them. They will get you to do things you never thought were possible.

7. Opposing-View In-Law

Some siblings-in-law can make you crazy. This one always takes the opposite view of every statement that an in-law makes. Often caught up in causes, opposing-view in-laws are a bit paranoid about those who do not agree with their opinions. Because they are self-doubting and take the devil's advocate role, they may have trouble staying with a tough situation or making a decision. They expect to be slighted and will lie in wait for an in-law to make a mistake or to slight them. When that happens, they have a feeling of satisfaction because it is the proof that they have been looking for: they *knew* that in-law doesn't like or respect them. They are constantly scanning the in-law environment for dangerous, sabotaging in-laws. They are hypersensitive to slights—"Yes, my brother-in-law didn't ask me to usher at his wedding"—and they relish holding a grudge, as it saves them from being hurt again. These in-laws can be powerhouses in the family, and are often the people who can be relied on to carry out difficult and time-consuming projects.

Sibling-in-Law Survival Tactics

1. If you enjoy being a devil's advocate, argue with them. They love it and are good at it.
2. Don't buy into their habit of looking for personal slights. Be honest by telling them why you are handling things the way you are.
3. Don't make fun of their passion for causes; their causes are real to them.
4. Don't overpromise; they expect people to come through and want more than good intentions.
5. Don't be put off by their habit of acting superior; it often covers a good deal of self-doubt.

8. Emotionally Intense In-Law

The emotionally intense sibling-in-law often has a comfortable and unique home environment: the towels are coordinated with the slipcovers. These in-laws often have distinctive ways of dressing and enjoy being a little off-beat, with eclectic clothing or an unusual style of haircut. They are intense people and like to think and talk about the tragedies of the world. They feel special because they can experience a depth of feeling that others do not. They understand and know loss. They are aware that the world is not complete, and they long for what is missing. These in-laws can be jealous of siblings as well as other in-laws, but will often express this in passive–aggressive ways—being late for events or complaining about the work created by the family reunion, which they planned. They may not delegate, because they constantly *do* in order to be praised for the special people they are. Emotionally intense in-laws may be problematic for brothers-in-law and sisters-in-law. They want to have deep emotional relationships; however, there is ambivalence because they also envy the close relationship the in-law (husband, wife) has with their sibling. These in-laws are constantly getting into trouble by telling people their *real* feelings. They can be difficult to live with: they get too deeply into their emotions, thus going at times too high, too low, too deep, or too far out. When they go too deep, the result can be severe depression.

Sibling-in-Law Survival Tactics

1. Appreciate these in-laws' intensity and need to feel unique.
2. Be tolerant if these siblings-in-law bring in more intensity and drama than you would choose to have in your life.
3. Accept their propensity toward depression; however, if you think they are going too deep into the dark side of their life, point it out and encourage them to get professional help.
4. Put up with their envy; they are basically loving in-laws.
5. Don't try to avoid them; rather, tell them when they are coming on too strong.

9. Superachieving In-Law

This is the American prototype of the successful sibling-in-law, who is always working on projects, whether at the office or at home. This in-law takes a to-do list on vacation, or, if at home, takes on major projects such as building fences or hooking room-sized rugs. This in-law is always trying to show how successful he or she is by impressing the parents-in-law. After Thanksgiving dinner, super sibling is the one in the kitchen doing dishes or finishing the carving of the turkey to make sandwiches. Superachieving in-laws irritate take-charge siblings-in-law by bossing them around. This constant drive for competition and pats on the back can drive the other siblings and in-laws crazy, because they are always compared with the superachiever by their parents. These are the Type A personality people who often end up with health problems or in family crisis as a result of never having any down time.

Sibling-in-Law Survival Tactics

1. Tell them how it makes you feel when they take over the task because they think they can do it faster.
2. Let them know that they don't have to perform in order for you to like them, but that you like them for who they are.
3. Encourage the parents to avoid comparisons between you or your spouse or other children-in-law and the superachieving in-law.
4. Show concern when they are going too strong and are not taking care of their health.

5. Remember that they really do care about having good sibling-in-law relationships.

THE SPICE IN LIFE

As these nine very different in-law types illustrate, sibling-in-law relationships are highly complex. Clients may want to look at their own personality
variables, and then compare them with the siblings-in-law, to determine where
there might be compatibility or direct conflicts. Would they have chosen that
sibling-in-law for a friend, were they not connected through marriage? Sur-
prisingly, the answer might be yes. Marriage may force some sibling-in-law
relationships that turn out to be among the richest in peoples' lives. They are
the variety that bring spice to life. They introduce people who might otherwise never have been known.

TRIANGLES

Some of the most problematic sibling-in-law relationships are those where the
in-law is triangled into a problematic relationship between spouses. The classic situation is where the husband has been abusing the wife and the brother-
in-law is called in to settle the rift. In the film, *The Godfather,* for example,
Sonny is called in to settle a domestic fight between his sister and her husband.
It turns out to be a setup. After he leaves, Sonny is murdered at a freeway toll
booth by a rival "family." Most domestic triangles involving in-laws don't end
so badly; however, in cases of physical abuse, it is often wiser to let police or
clergy attempt to untangle domestic problems, rather than bringing in siblings-
in-law. (Triangles are dealt with in more depth in Chapter 8.)

SIBLING-IN-LAW CRISIS

A great deal has been written regarding the family of origin's and the individual's responses to crisis, but few sources explore the impact of these events
on the sibling-in-law relationship. Sibling-in-law stories portraying deep disappointments or anger often revolve around issues of loss, including divorce
and death. It is not unusual to hear family stories of how siblings-in-law be-
haved at the time of crisis.

Divorce

Numerous studies have been done regarding divorce and its impact on individuals and families; however, the sibling-in-law response to divorce has, to

my knowledge, not been studied. As is mentioned in Chapter 2, people often *marry the family*. When there is a divorce, they may end up divorcing the whole extended family, including their siblings-in-law. Often, biological ties are honored above friendship, but curiously at times, the sibling in-law shows more loyalty to the ex-spouse than to his or her biological sibling. Such was the case with Milford, who was going through a divorce.

> *I had always done a lot of things with my brother-in-law, Derik; however, after Patti and I separated, things started to fall apart. It wasn't that Derik didn't support me, it was that he was too supportive. Patti and Derik had always been highly competitive and so when I called to tell Derik that I was going to file for divorce, he said that he didn't blame me and thought that I should have done it years ago. He then spent the next 10 minutes basically trashing Patti. At first the comments felt good; however, as I thought about it, they also made me feel uncomfortable. Patti and I had two kids and I didn't think it was good for Derik to be bad-mouthing the mother of my kids. I told him so, and he said, "Well, that is the last time I will come to your aid." We have not talked since and that was a year ago. I guess in-law relationships are over with the marriage.* —Milford, 38, contractor

Death of a Spouse

Death or illness of a spouse can dramatically change the dynamics of the sibling-in-law relation. An in-law can feel that he or she was a big part of the family only to find that when the spouse is ill or dead, the spouse's siblings are no longer supportive. There are no more invitations to dinners or outings. This is especially true after the children are grown. The children may be invited to family parties and events to which the sibling-in-law has not been invited. Is it any wonder that widows often complain of being invisible? These formerly beloved aunts or uncles often become nonpersons once the sibling-in-law who connected them to the family has passed away.

Death of a Child

When a death occurs in a family, siblings-in-law can play supportive roles with the extended family. However, when tensions and jealousies exist, the sibling-in-law relationship can be destructive.

> *When my son was killed in an airplane accident, we arrived at the airport in another city, and were met there by my sister-in-law, who said to my husband, "You're going to my house right now." Well, we had planned to go to my husband's stepmother's house, and I said, "No, he is not going with you. He's going with me to your stepmother's house." We literally got into a pulling match about where he was going. So I turned to my brother-in-law and said, "Can't you do*

something about your wife?" And my husband and I got in the car and left. My sister-in-law and I have never discussed this event, but it still makes me angry to think about her insensitivity.—Emma, 31, social worker

When families break apart, either through natural causes such as death or illness, or through divorce, attention should be given to the new roles the siblings-in-law will play. (More on these issues in Chapters 5 and 9.)

Inheritance/Family Business

Money issues involving family businesses and inheritances are often the most wrenching problems that siblings-in-law encounter. These issues often travel through biological, not marital, lines. Efforts to control family businesses, and bickering over shares of inheritance often break out when the biological child is pushed by his or her own ambition (or that of a spouse) to get his or her share. Trying to get their fair share can drive placid persons to become assertive and often aggressive.

A couple nearing retirement age came for therapy. Marina, was very concerned about her husband, George, because he had just learned his blood pressure was dangerously high. She attributed this to anxiety over his business, a chain of movie theaters. George had inherited the business from his father and was planning to pass it down to his own son. The son refused to take over the reins; he was not interested. The couple's daughter, Marguritte, and son-in-law, Clem, had been managing the theaters for many years and had their own ideas about running them. Their opinions, always articulated by Clem, the son-in-law, provoked constant arguments with George. Marina was afraid that unless they resolved the disagreements, George would have a stroke.

I suggested an extended family session that included all the siblings and their spouses. The session was emotional, especially when the oldest son, Harold, told his father how much he appreciated his desire to keep the business in the family name, but pointed out that although he was loyal to the family, one of the family values he appreciated was independence, and thus he wanted to pursue his chosen career.

Once George understood that his biological son, Harold, would never be interested in the business, he was able to see that his daughter Marguritte was also part of the family line and that if his son-in-law and daughter took over, the business could continue in the family and be passed to his grandchildren. This session gave George permission to retire and also reaffirmed the standing of Marguritte and her husband Clem in the family.

Finance and inheritance issues are all too common among siblings-in-law, and countless families have broken apart because of unresolved issues. Chapter 11 deals with considerations to help families avoid such difficulties.

SEXUAL ATTRACTION BETWEEN SIBLINGS-IN-LAW

Sexual attraction between siblings-in-law can create very uncomfortable relationships, both between spouses and between their own brothers and sisters. An example of this was seen in the Woody Allen film, *Hannah and Her
Sisters,* where the character portrayed by Michael Caine fell in love with his
ex-sister-in-law. When siblings-in-law have affairs with each other, while they
cannot be construed as incest because there are no biological ties, intense
problems are created because once the affair breaks off, the in-law relationship remains. One cannot be a dance-away lover when one has to sit next to the
ex-paramour at Thanksgiving dinner. Such was the dilemma expressed by the
following client:

> *I cannot believe to this day that I had an affair with my brother-in-law. It all
> started with my daughter's bout with leukemia. At the time, my brother-in-law
> was working at the hospital as an anesthesiologist. The hospital was putting
> Britney through some unbelievable tests, literally hanging her by her toes. It was
> only natural that I would look to a family member for support. Bradley was al-
> ways there at the hospital, while my husband, Lucas, was for the most part at
> the office. Somehow we were just thrown together in our grief and fear. When
> her blood count was up, I would hug my brother-in-law with joy, and when it
> was down, I would hug him for support. All of a sudden, we started thinking we
> were in love and since life was so short, we should do something about it. You
> know, live before you die. We met at a hotel a couple of times but it didn't work
> out. I just felt like a real cheat. The funny thing was that Britney had a bone
> marrow transplant and is doing fine and Lucas has forgiven me and Bradley.
> The problem is that I cannot forgive myself and that is why I am in therapy. I
> have betrayed my family.—Natasha, 32, attorney*

It would seem natural that an in-law would look to another in-law or family member for support. However, in intense situations, the best advice still
seems to be: Avoid sexual relationships with siblings-in-law at all costs.

But what if a female client is being harassed by her sexually aggressive
brother-in-law or vice versa? She is caught in a double bind: loyalty to her
spouse's family prevents her from revealing the unwanted advances, and her
own self-respect makes her reluctant to be seen as a victim. If she lets her in-
laws know what is going on, she may be viewed as an instigator. Biological kin
boundaries may be drawn. The sister-in-law might even be made to feel responsible for breaking up the aggressive brother-in-law's marriage. However,
if the perpetrator is not stopped immediately, the situation can often esca-
late into rape or other assault. Sometimes, the incidents will stop when the
client avoids being alone with the sexually aggressive sibling-in-law; however,
it has been my experience that the only way to end the unwanted advances is
to let the aggressor know early on that he or she will be exposed to the entire

family if the advances continue. This behavior cannot be tolerated and should not be kept as a family secret, because other members of the family are likely to be experiencing the same behavior.

RESENTMENT AMONG SIBLINGS-IN-LAW

Competition between in-laws can impact the biological connection between siblings. Siblings-in-law sometimes become jealous or resent the loyalties of the biological siblings. Competition can arise regarding accomplishments of offspring, or lifestyle issues. Are the in-law's children better educated than their cousins? Are they better mannered? How do they treat their elders? Who helps the grandparents more? Are the siblings-in-law children kind, considerate, and honest? The children, often the pride of the in-law system, are a measure of failure or success for all the world to see. The grandparents may unwittingly be pulled into the system as quasi-judges, being encouraged by in-laws to play favorites with their grandchildren, thus supporting the idea that one sibling-in-law's child is better than another's. There may also be envy over family size or even the ability to have children.

Socioeconomic status can have a strong impact among siblings-in-law, with education as well as financial well-being playing into this effect. How is money spent? On material items, such as cars and boats, or on more culturally broadening activities such as travel, concerts, or workshops? Are the in-laws paying for one family's clothes or entertainment and not the other's? Often, the in-laws who live closest to the parents get the most attention and resources. However, on the downside, when there are problems, they are also expected to give the most support.

These represent just a few of the many areas for sibling-in-law conflict. Each family can make up its own list during therapy, as a way to identify problems and externalize issues of conflict.

Sibling Competition

Competition between siblings can look like an in-law–in-law conflict. A client, Bethann, told me that her son-in-law Clarence and her son Lance did not get along. They seemed to compete with each other. When I asked Bethann how this was manifested, she said that her daughter Hilary always spoke about how rude and inconsiderate her husband Clarence felt his brother-in-law Lance was. It turned out that Clarence and Lance never had direct sibling-in-law conflict; it always came through Hilary. After further discussion, it came to light that the father in the family had always favored Lance and, while growing up, Hilary constantly created crisis situations in order to get attention. The conflict expressed in my office was really one of sibling rivalry, and Clarence, the son-in-law, had unwittingly been brought in to allow Hilary to indirectly express her anger.

In a group session with the entire family, including the father, I asked each member to do a family sculpture of how he or she saw the situation at present. When Hilary sculptured the family, she placed her brother and father side-by-side, separated from her by her mother. She had her hand reaching out toward her father, and her father was focusing his smile on the brother. When I asked her to do a sculpture of how she would like it to be, Hilary decided to stand with her husband and place her brother across the room with his wife. The parents, together, moved back and forth to each group, giving each of their children equal time. Interestingly, none of the sculptures done by family members included altercations between Hilary's husband and her brother.

CHECKLIST

Working Out Sibling-in-Law Relationships

In the long run, it is in everyone's best interest to work out the sibling-in-law relationships. But how is this done? How does the client work on getting along with his or her siblings-in-law? Does one ignore all the conflicts, and hope that maturity will prevail? Does one take up the subject with his or her spouse or parents-in-law, thus creating a conflict in the larger system? Or does one confront the sibling-in-law directly? The tools of transactional analysis might be helpful in changing the cycle of sibling interactions (see Chapter 8 for more on this), or the client in-law might try to understand their own as well as their sibling-in-law's worldview.

The questions below will help clients to distinguish their own characteristics as well as those of their siblings-in-law, giving better insight into themselves and others. After the clients have looked at their own in-law type, they can discuss how they might come into conflict with their sibling-in-law's point of view. Clients who have problems defining their characteristics may want to review the in-law personality types as described earlier in this chapter. (Personality variables are described in Chapter 7.)

Point-of-View Questions for Siblings-in-Law

Giving in-law: Was your acceptance in the family based on your ability to please others? Are you drawn to "important" people?

Conflict-avoidance in-law: Did you have to hide your anger in order to be heard or accepted by your parents? Were your feelings and priorities discounted, causing you to abandon your own point of view and take on the opinions of others?

Take-charge in-law: Did you feel dominated by bigger, stronger people who wanted to control your life? As a child, did your survival depend on being strong and taking a tough personal stand in any confrontation?

Critical in-law: Were your early behaviors primarily targeted to avoid criticism and punishment through correct behavior? Are you convinced there is only one right way to do any task?

Observant in-law: Was it necessary to develop a rich inner world to protect your personal self and feelings from attack, in order to have your individual opinions and values respected? Are time and energy your most important assets, which you must guard from others?

Gadabout in-law: Do you have a positive memory of your childhood, even though you objectively had somewhat less than happy experiences? Do you move toward pleasure and away from pain?

Opposing-view in-law: As a child, was your home life and the discipline you received unpredictable? To avoid being hurt or embarrassed, was it important to check out danger signals in your home, and change your behavior accordingly?

Emotionally intense in-law: Did you feel abandoned or suffer a real or imagined loss in your early years from which you have never fully recovered? Does *melancholy* describe your inner emotions? Do you have a sense that things could and should be better than they are here and now?

Superachieving in-law: Was your value in the family predicated on your performance? Do you think that it is more important to be rewarded for a job well done than for being a nice person?

WORKSHEET

Issues Regarding Siblings-in-Law

1. Do you recognize that in order to have good sibling-in-law relationships you have to be a good in-law?

2. Are you living out old anger or fantasies from your sibling relationships and projecting them onto your siblings-in-law?

3. Do you respect your siblings-in-law's way of viewing the world or value the differences they bring to the family?

4. Can you integrate the survival tactics suggested in this chapter into your siblings-in-law relationships?

5. Do you avoid triangling your siblings-in-law into stressful situations? Are your siblings triangling in siblings-in-law to deal with past conflicts and competition?

6. Have conflicts around money or inheritance related to siblings-in-law been resolved?

7. Have you figured out where divorced or widowed siblings-in-law fit into the family system?

CHAPTER 7

Promoting In-Law Growth and Reauthoring to Mend In-Law Relationships

Providing therapy to families with a history of in-law problems requires the employment of a variety of theories and techniques. As mentioned in Chapter 1, I have found that a number of approaches are needed to accommodate the variety of in-law problems encountered in my practice. I tend to use a problem-oriented approach because it is less threatening and blaming, and it stands a better chance of keeping in-laws engaged in therapy. If clients have had an emotional or physical cutoff from their in-laws, it may take time for them to explore the cost and benefits of having in-laws included in the family sessions. It is helpful to point out to family members that feelings of anger are extremely strong connections with in-laws and, in the long term, the resolution of problems requires less energy than enduring a lifetime with a host of problems. In the worst-case scenario, identifying and dealing with these problems can bring an end to the in-law relationship, but it has been my experience that, in these situations, the definite termination reflects the verity of the saying, "Better a horrible ending than a horror without end." In most cases, however, the steps taken to resolve in-law problems serve to strengthen the entire family system.

PERSONALITY VARIABLES

Individuals who have long-standing in-law problems might be encouraged by the therapist to step back and look at their own personalities and then overlay their characteristics onto the in-law system. When looking at personality variables, the therapist may find the following approach helpful. The In-law Growth and Adjustment Program (ILGA), designed by Berg-Cross and Jackson (1986), is a social-cognitive program geared at working with in-law families in private practice. The program has the potential of being preventive as well as diagnostic, as it helps individuals delineate their personality differences. It is a two-day program that includes questionnaires and discussion. From the published literature and their clinical experience, Berg-Cross and

Jackson identified five personality variables and two systems variables that they felt greatly influence in-law relationships.

I have never employed the complete ILGA program, but I find discussion of differing personality variables especially helpful when dealing with clients and their families. The cognitive approach enables the individual family members to gain distance from the problem, helps them to consider their personal contribution to it, and generates perspective on their in-law relationships. When using the program, I start by introducing the family or individual to the five personality variables: (a) control, (b) inclusion, (c) intimacy, (d) problem solving, and (e) helping behaviors, which Berg-Cross and Jackson have identified as the variables that most affect in-law relationships. Before discussing the needs variables as representing differences, I point out to in-laws that there is nothing inherently right or wrong about behaving in these ways—they only give insight into our own and others' point of view. In the sections that follow, each needs variable is accompanied by in-law comments.

Control Needs

Some individuals have a high need to control (as opposed to a couple's need to control, as opposed to a parent's need to control) decisions and activities in their lives. This need for control defends individuals against the fear of being out of control.

FATHER-IN-LAW: "It drives me nuts when people don't make plans. I like to have everything nailed down, including what and where we will eat."

These are also the people who, in order to feel in control of an event will have the need to change at least some small piece of the plan.

DAUGHTER-IN-LAW: "Why don't we meet at 10:00 rather than 10:30? I'll drive. Let's take a lunch rather than buy."

Inclusion Needs

In-laws vary in their need for inclusion; they represent a high (vs. low) need to be included in shared times and important events. Those who have a high inclusion need (need to be strongly involved) have great difficulty understanding those with a low inclusion need.

SISTER-IN-LAW (HIGH INCLUSION):   "She didn't ask me to be her bridesmaid. They went on vacation without us. They never invite us to dinner."

SON-IN-LAW (LOW INCLUSION):   "I don't want to play games with my in-laws. Why do we have to go to dinner every Sunday anyway? In the evening, I need some down time."

Intimacy Needs

In-laws also vary in their needs for physical contact such as touching, hugging, kissing, and intense relationships.

BROTHER-IN-LAW (LOW INTIMACY NEEDS):   "My in-laws are always kissing, pinching, tickling, and hugging. A handshake is just fine with me."

MOTHER-IN-LAW (HIGH INTIMACY NEEDS):   "He seems so distant. He never wants to touch."

Problem-Solving Needs

In-laws have their own styles of compliance, including assertive, aggressive, withdrawal, or compliant behaviors.

FATHER-IN-LAW (ASSERTIVE):   "I wish he would speak up. I never know what he is thinking."

SISTER-IN-LAW (AGGRESSIVE):   "I'm taking my children to the wedding reception whether they were invited or not."

SON-IN-LAW (WITHDRAWAL):   "When he talks in that loud voice, I just space out."

MOTHER-IN-LAW (COMPLIANT):   "I don't mind if you use my ticket to see *Phantom of the Opera* without me. I'll stay home and baby-sit."

Helping Behaviors

In-laws have their own ideas and expectations of appropriate helping behaviors.

DAUGHTER-IN-LAW: "I wish she wouldn't clean my refrigerator out and offer to dust every time she visits. I wish she would just relax."

MOTHER-IN-LAW: "I think it is important to pitch in and help. I don't want to be seen as a slacker."

The expectation that these needs will be recognized and met can be a constant source of irritation among in-laws. Meeting one person's needs often negates another's. Some in-laws will feel that they are not being considered when, in fact, their needs are in direct conflict. For example, whether the daughter-in-law or mother-in-law wanted inclusion was a significant predictor of mother-in-law adjustment in a study (Berg-Cross & Jackson, 1986) that found women were more compliant with their own mothers, and more assertive with their mothers-in-law. Frequent phone contact and compliant problem solving helped with mother-in-law adjustment. Where the daughters-in-law had a strong need for inclusion, they felt they needed to be asked to do things by their mothers-in-law. Clients need to assess their own need for inclusion and then ask significant in-laws how they view being included in family activities. It is too easy to assume that others carry our same needs and opinions. If there is a need for inclusion, the therapist might suggest such simple interventions as having the client call his or her mother-in-law. In-laws need to realize that if one wants space or inclusion, one must let others know.

As the therapist introduces and discusses the personality variables with the family, it is important to point out that the variables are being brought into the picture to help the client identify, observe, and differentiate his or her own individual styles of behavior, rather than for judgment purposes. Therapists may discuss individual personality needs and encourage observations and comments on how meeting one's own needs can infringe on the needs of other family members.

After the nuclear family members have made some consideration of personality differences (which may take several sessions or several months, depending on the severity of the problem and length of therapy), the therapist might encourage individual clients to bring in their families of origin for a family history session. These two-hour sessions usually include only one side of the family at a time—there is usually too much history to involve the entire network at this point. During the family history session, it is helpful to use an easel to draw a genogram (McGoldrick & Gerson, 1985) of the family. Along with the general family information, the therapist can help the family to list family strengths, family values, and family mottoes. (For more on the structure of these sessions and getting families into therapy, see Horsley (1988) and Landau-Stanton et al. (1994).)

Identifying systems variables can also be useful for extended families in therapy. Along with personality variables, Berg-Cross and Jackson (1986) have identified two categories of family systems variables—family rituals and relationship variables—which impact the in-law relationship.

Family Rituals

Berg-Cross and Jackson (1986) ask in-laws to consider the nature, extent of activity, and observation of rituals, including holidays and religious events, in the families of origin and the in-law families, and to explore how they are dealt with in the nuclear family. They offer a list of family rituals that can be used to elicit family discussion, or, if the therapist prefers, the family can make its own list. These events can cause division or can be a strength to family relationships if the previously discussed personality variables such as inclusion are not understood and agreed upon. This year my family, next year yours, and some events will be limited to the nuclear family. Some holiday rituals mentioned in their training program include the following:

1. **Christmas:** Selecting Christmas tree, having Christmas dinner together, Christmas caroling.

2. **Easter:** Attending church, hunting for eggs.

3. **Thanksgiving:** Thanksgiving dinner, following the same menu each year, going on a hunt for nuts, and carolling after dinner.

4. **Fourth of July:** Cooking out together, making ice cream, reading patriotic essays, watching fireworks together.

5. **Mother's Day:** Dinner or picnic with mother and/or mother-in-law.

6. **Father's Day:** Exchanging gifts with father and/or father-in-law.

7. **New Year's celebrations:** Drinking a toast at midnight.

8. **Passover:** Seder gatherings.

9. **Chanukah:** Exchanging gifts, songs, and stories.

Relationship Variables

Relationships of the biological child and their siblings to their parents, as well as the relationship between their parents and their parents-in-law, according to Berg-Cross and Jackson (1986), will be a strong predictor in the success of the new in-law relationship. The tone of the relationship often orbits around the mother-in-law. Other relationship variables identified by Berg-Cross and Jackson (1986) include the connection between the prospective parents-in-law and their own parents-in-law, where it was found that parents will often become role models of the relationships they had with their in-laws.

Duvall (1954) found that, after the mother-in-law, the next most difficult in-law was the sister-in-law. According to comments from respondents, many problems arise out of the sister-in-law's inability to realize that her married brother is a grown man capable of managing his own affairs. Her interfering can be seen as a continuation of patterns of quibbling and bickering that had their origins in sibling rivalry early in the childhood of the brother and sister. Interestingly, 25.8% of the respondents claimed to have no difficult in-laws.

The relationship between the parents-in-law and their other children is another variable. Parents may have to juggle or balance the needs of the biological children against the needs of sons- or daughters-in-law.

The relationship variable discussion lends itself to bringing in several systemic theories. Among them is the issue of family loyalty (Boszormenyi-Nagy & Spark, 1973), covered in Chapter 4. A second issue centers on the work of White (1989) and White and Epston (1989) regarding externalization of the problem and the reauthoring of lives and relationships.

Reauthoring work is especially interesting with in-law problems and is accessible, fun, and creative. This method is detailed later in this chapter. When discussing clients' attitudes regarding in-law inclusion, helping, holiday rituals, and problem solving, the therapist may also want to refer to the questionnaires found in the appendix of the Berg-Cross and Jackson (1986) article.

COMING TO TERMS WITH REALITY

Even after a couple has been married for several years, new sets of in-law problems can crop up. A client told me about a schism and emotional cutoff with her children revolving around plans for her daughter and son-in-law to live with her and her husband after the son-in-law graduated from medical school. The plan was that the young couple would live with them while the son-in-law studied for the licensing exam. The schism occurred when my client received a very formal letter from her daughter, which stated that the son-in-law had been accepted into graduate school to earn a master's degree in public health. Thus, after he finished medical school, instead of moving to New York, they would go to Chicago. It made the mother-in-law extremely angry that her son-in-law had not provided any information to the family regarding his alternative plan of attending graduate school. I recommended that rather than being angry at the son-in-law, my client might confront her daughter with the issues.

In the next session, my client said that she had confronted her daughter about what she felt was lying. Her daughter stated that the son-in-law had wanted to tell the family all along, but that she was the one who did not want the family to know, because she was afraid that her husband would not be accepted into the graduate program. We then discussed the frustration that this woman felt toward her son-in-law and how the daughter's attitude affected the attitude of the parents toward the son-in-law. This example illustrates how in-laws (in this case, the son-in-law) can become unwary victims of unresolved issues between the parent and child.

When In-Laws Live Together

There is an old saying, "Fish and family stink after three days." This homily refers to the fact that having family members living in close proximity, especially for an extended period, can be extremely difficult. In today's world, many young couples are returning home to live with the parents until they can financially get back on their feet or can find employment. If parents-in-law and children-in-law plan to live together for an extended period, they might be able to avoid problems by discussing the personality variables identified by

Berg-Cross and Jackson (1986), mentioned earlier in this chapter, and by being aware of their own personal biases. Clarifying these needs can help to avoid some of the friction inherent in close living conditions.

According to Duvall (1954), in any close relationship there is a need for distance from time to time. Only those we love can hurt us deeply. Because we love them, we expose ourselves to the pain and the problems of involvement. Strangers and those outside the family generally do and say things that can be shrugged off as only minor annoyances. Things done and said in the family are felt much more sharply.

In Komarovsky's (1962) nonrandom cross-sectional study of 58 White, native-born Protestant families, with parents under age 40 and the highest level of education 4 years of high school, 92% of the wives who were married less than 7 years and whose mothers lived in the community, saw their mothers several times a week or daily. There was a decline during the duration of the marriage: after 7 years of marriage, only 59% saw their mothers daily or several times a week. Of the men, 60% saw their mothers weekly or daily; as they aged, 48% saw their mothers as frequently. Komarovsky found that fewer men had contacts with their mothers, yet a number of those interviewed mentioned the husband's relationship with his mother as a problem. Apparently, economic and social interdependence with in-laws makes it difficult for uncongenial persons to go their separate ways.

THE MOTHER-IN-LAW JOKES: REWRITING STORIES AND SCRIPTS

The in-law jokes and stories we all tell say a great deal about what our culture thinks about in-laws. Nearly all of the classic comedians have harvested countless guffaws at the expense of the in-law relationship. For example, it isn't surprising when perusing Milton Berle's *Private Joke File* (1989) to find that the only in-law mentioned is the mother-in-law, with the majority of jokes aimed at either getting rid of her or limiting her interference in the family's life. Here are a few examples: "I bought my mother-in-law a nice new chair—she won't plug it in." "Some airlines have a mother-in-law flight. It's non-stop." According to research by Duvall (1954), American mother-in-law jokes carry variations on a few familiar themes:

1. Mother-in-law talks too much.
2. Mother-in-law knows all the answers—the wrong ones.
3. Mother-in-law is a meddlesome troublemaker.
4. Mother-in-law is ego-deflating.
5. Mother-in-law is mean.

6. Mother-in-law is a loathsome object of aggression.
7. Mother-in-law comes too often and stays too long.
8. Mother-in-law is to be avoided.

These derogatory jokes directed toward the mother-in-law reflect the fact that as *keepers of the kin* (Chapter 2), mothers-in-law pay a heavy price. Without exception, the mother-in-law jokes are woven around a core of hostility. An analysis of marriage wit (Duvall, 1954) revealed that, in nearly all husband–wife jokes, women are the butt of the hostile humor. "This kind of wit tends to support primarily traditional views that the man should be the head of the house, should be in charge of the money and parcel it out to his wife, should not do household chores, and should accept marriage as a necessary evil, while the wife should be submissive, a good cook, and should consider marriage her only means of financial security" (p. 36). Just as marriages have changed over time (and it is rare to find traditional values of this sort), mother-in-law jokes, like marriage wit, quite possible support some older value systems that may or may not have meaning for modern families, says Duvall. To the extent that mother-in-law humor creates tensions around outworn values, it does more harm than good.

Duvall (1954) conducted a large study on behalf of a then-popular television show, "December Bride." People were asked to send in letters on the theme: "Why I think mothers in law are wonderful people." Large numbers of people responded by asking to be counted among those who believe the mother-in-law stereotype is unsound. They said that, in their own experience, the mother-in-law does not follow the negative patterns of recurring jokes, and that the stereotyped hostility is not only untrue but unfair. The stereotyping prejudices the young person against his or her mother-in-law, putting her in an unfortunate light before she ever gets a chance to prove herself a loving ally, and it produces unfortunate stresses and strains on the new marriage that are outgrown only through a long process of pleasant experience. "Therefore, say these challengers of the mother-in-law mythology, there should be an active campaign to reject hostility-humor as a powerful prejudice that civilized man can ill afford" (p. 37).

Many couples in therapy have reported ongoing tensions in early marriage that arose directly out of their preconceived ideas that their mother-in-law would be a meddlesome troublemaker to be avoided at all costs. The kind of stories and jokes we use can promote or undermine individuals as well as family relationships. In-law jokes are not, however, without their benefits. Anthropologists studying kinship relationships (Radcliffe-Brown, 1952) have found that joking and avoidance reduce potential conflict. Because points of conflict arise in relationships that pose the greatest threat to loyalty, the continued existence of mother-in-law jokes confirms an underlying tension associated with this kinship role (Schlien, 1962).

REAUTHORING OUTMODED STORIES AND STEREOTYPES

White and Epston (1989) have found that helping families externalize the problem—by telling their stories and then recreating (reauthoring) the stories in a more positive way—can have healing effects. The same thing can be done with jokes. Clients can externalize them by telling in-law jokes, rewriting them with other family members or individuals in mind, and then analyzing how and why the revision impacts the joke. According to White and Epston, negative stories about individuals and events can trivialize and minimize—or promote and empower—individuals. Our stories (and how we tell them) give meaning to our experience.

Byng-Hall (1988) discusses family behavior in terms of scripts and legends. He feels that families can create replicative or corrective scripts. A father-in-law might suddenly realize that he is treating his son-in-law as rudely as he was treated by his father-in-law. Byng-Hall discusses *The Legends*—stories that are time-honored, are told again and again, and are passed down through the generations. The Legends have constantly been re-edited to tell each new in-law something about how the spouse's family operates and how it expects members to behave. One client's in-laws had strong stories of community service. The husband's grandfather was head of the fire department and the Red Cross, and owned a small store that only barely supported his growing family. In contrast, the grandfather's son and grandson are successful investment advisers and bankers. By negating the example of the grandfather, the storytellers sent the message that it was more important to make money first and put community service second.

Another client's legend is related to the death of her father-in-law's mother after the birth of her fifth child. The legend was that the doctor had told her not to have another child because she had a bad heart, but the grandfather-in-law went ahead and "got her pregnant anyway," and for this he never forgave himself. My client's in-laws never forgave him either, and hence were highly critical when my client had four children in very close order. Small families and wide spacing between children had become part of the family legend and the in-laws' expectations.

The history of a client's story can be significant; past behavior and practices are often outdated. There is an old story about the daughter-in-law who always cut the end off a ham before she put it in the pan. When the mother-in-law asked why she did it this way, the girl said, "Because my mother did."

Being curious, the girl asked her mother why, and was told, "I did it that way because my mother did." The girl then went to Grandma. Grandma was amused that cutting the ham had become a tradition: the only reason she had done it was that her pan was too small for the entire ham.

It is important to look at how family stories support and perpetuate the survival of a problem (White, 1989). There is good reason why most of us have stories related to in-laws: they reflect the fact that we have not dealt with the real issues. In-laws will often mention the larger problem only peripherally and, when asked for specifics, will come up with an example of a slight, fight, or rejection. Through in-depth therapy, one can often find the larger picture, as was the case with the following two in-law families.

Jim, a 50-year-old police officer, said during the therapy session, "My father-in-law does not like me and has not spoken to me for five years." When questioned further, Jim replied, "He doesn't think I'm good enough for his daughter." Jim's wife, June, then said, "Come on, Jim, tell the whole story." According to Jim, "Well, June got mad and left me and went to her folks'. I went to get her and my father-in-law wouldn't let me in the house. I went to move him out the way and pushed him a little harder than I meant to. He fell and broke his arm, and hasn't spoken to me since."

In another family, Sue, a 31-year-old homemaker, said that she was upset because her mother-in-law would not stay with her. Her mother-in-law apparently "didn't feel welcome at Sue's house." Sue said that she never meant to give that message. Her mother-in-law looked dubious. When questioned further, Sue described an incident that had happened a year before. "We were all playing a very competitive game and my mother-in-law supported her son (my husband) in not letting me have my turn. So I told her to get out of my house, and now she won't stay with us."

The *real endings* of these client stories remind me of radio commentator Paul Harvey, who always concludes his program by saying, "And that's the rest of the story."

Building a Unique Outcome

In order to reauthor, the therapist might try to be playful. (Remember—you can lead a horse to water . . . .) If clients have excessive difficulty in reauthoring their more complex stories, the therapist may want to help them identify and build what White (1989) terms a *unique outcome* (p. 7). In looking for this unique outcome, the therapist would question the clients regarding the problem they were experiencing and try to find out whether there was a time when the problem had not occurred or when the problem had not happened in the way they normally described it. The therapist might say, "So, you say that your mother-in-law always gets frustrated when the family members are visiting for holidays and don't help out in the kitchen." The client nods and says, "She always blows up when she has to work in the kitchen and we're all around." The therapist might then say, "Was there ever a time when she didn't blow up?" The client would probably hesitate, think about it for a few minutes, and then say, "I guess there are occasionally times when she doesn't." The therapist would then probe a bit further and ask, "Can you give me a specific time when she didn't blow up?" The client might then say something like, "Well, we were over there a couple of Sundays ago and she was actually very congenial and we had an extremely good day." That extremely good day would be a unique outcome that the therapist would want to build on with a client, thus dispelling some of the negativity around the in-law experience.

Using these techniques can help the client to look at the in-law experience with some moderation, rather than identifying the glass as half empty or half full. Carrying around negative destructive stories is a heavy load, and externalizing the problem by reauthoring and identifying unique outcomes can be a very freeing experience. If we have enough negative encounters, we tend to magnify them in order to protect ourselves. Indeed, Byng-Hall (1988) states that our beliefs and practices are self-confirming. Again, looking at unique outcomes, the therapist can encourage clients to identify outcomes that differ from the usual. For example, "You say your mother-in-law is always rude to you, and think this is always the case (although it probably isn't). Now, think about one instance when she was polite and charming to you. If you can't remember one, imagine one."

I had a wise tennis teacher, Ted Backe, who used to say, "If you can hit one good forehand you can hit a thousand." Ted seized that *one good forehand* as a unique outcome we could build on. He would always finish the lesson with what he termed a *proper shot.* We sometimes finished early and sometimes late, but those early acceptable forehands were examples of unique outcomes that aimed at playing what Ted termed a "decent level of club tennis." The point is that when clients are telling their in-law stories, the therapist can help them to identify times when there were not problems with a particular in-law and then use these instances as a basis to develop a more functional story.

Clients all have a grab bag full of stories and jokes about themselves and their in-laws that they can pull out at will. Of interest to therapists is why clients remember certain in-law stories and why they choose to repeat them over the years. Therapists can suggest that clients think of themselves as screenwriters or book authors. Here are the steps therapists can give to clients who wish to reauthor negative stories:

1. Pick a story from your bag that you would like to reauthor. Start out with one that is the least hurtful.

2. Externalize the story by discussing it in therapy or writing it out and making detailed notes.

3. Ask three friends who were not involved to listen to your story without comment.

4. Approach those who were involved (keeping in mind unique outcome) and discuss their perceptions in light of the fact that you are trying to reauthor the event. If you are an artist, draw your story.

5. Go back and rewrite your story or look at your art. You may find that your story has changed.

In much the same way that many jokes against members of minority groups have disappeared from socially sensitive circles, so too might the old mother-in-law jokes and stories disappear, especially as people's actual experiences with their own in-laws refute any bearing on reality represented by the joke. According to Duvall (1954), at best, the stereotype calls forth a prejudiced response, and at worst, it adversely affects the new in-law relationship with strains and stresses arising directly out of anticipation of trouble that may be totally unwarranted.

At this point, it might be helpful for therapists to examine their own in-law stories and jokes and to ask themselves how these stories began and why they are relevant today. What would be the purpose of continuing to tell them in the future? The process of examining the jokes and stories will give the therapist experience in externalizing in-law problems and may lead to reauthoring some more negative narratives.

LETTING GO OF EXPECTATIONS: THE IN-LAW DREAM LIST

What happens when in-laws just don't click? Sometimes the reason has nothing to do with the individuals; instead, expectations patterned into the relationship are at fault. A therapist often has experiences where he or she does not click or relate with certain individuals.

People's negative attitudes may be connected to past experiences with other people of the same sex, gender, or age. For example, a young lady with whom I associate on occasion has had a difficult time with her mother. I assume her coldness toward me is related to the fact that I bear some resemblance in age or physical characteristics to her mother, because my encounters with this young woman have been very intermittent and her attitude toward me is unduly cool. It would stand to reason that similar kinds of prejudices will be brought into new relationships where in-laws are trying to learn to relate with a newcomer and integrate that person into the family. Dr. Pawll Lewicki (1992) of the University of Tulsa has shown that viewers' unconscious mind can be biased against certain individuals merely by showing them computer-generated faces and stating that these faces are fair or unfair. After only one session, Dr. Lewicki found that 20% of students showed bias against certain individuals which they were unable to explain. Dr. Lewicki feels these biases were learned through association with computer-generated faces.

Some in-laws don't live up to clients' expectations and the result is a tremendous disappointment with the in-laws. This can cause a sense of loss that may be manifested with either apathy or anger toward the in-laws. Again, externalizing the problem (White & Epston, 1989) might help in-laws to discuss their hopes and dreams for the relationship with other family members. How did they hope that the person would fit into the family? What were their expectations? The therapist might encourage clients to be very specific. For example, "They would have come over every Sunday for dinner," "We would have played cards," or "They would have spent family vacations with us." The client (or therapist) can write these expectations down as the first step in creating what might be called *The In-Law Dream List.*

The second step is to list what the in-law contributes to the family, as well as what one likes about him or her. This step may be hard: when people are angry or hurt, they naturally want to defend these feelings by being critical. Remember, the purpose of this exercise is to deal with disappointment and the loss of a dream in-law and to move on to more realistic expectations.

The third step is to have family members list what they have lost because of both the emotional absence and the physical absence of the ideal in-law. Lastly, the in-laws can list how they would like the situation to change or how they might compensate for the loss. Encourage the changes to be small and realistic; Rome wasn't built in a day. The dream list technique is effective with both individuals and families. Figure 7.1 shows how such a list might look.

IN-LAW DREAM LIST	CONTRIBUTIONS MADE BY IN-LAW
1. Play Scrabble™ together every Sunday night 2. Take a cruise to Alaska together 3. Stay up all night and talk	1. Always helps with the cabin each spring 2. Sense of humor and easy laugh help ease tense situations
EMOTIONAL AND PHYSICAL LOSSES TO THE FAMILY OF THE IN-LAW	REALISTIC GOALS
1. Realize that my brother-in-law will not stay at our house during Christmas 2. Realize that my sister-in-law isn't going to be my best friend	1. I will make an effort to get together with my brother-in-law at least once during the holidays 2. I will work on giving my sister-in-law some space

Figure 7.1 Changing a Dream List into Realistic Goals

CHOOSING ASSERTIVE VS. AGGRESSIVE IN-LAW BEHAVIOR

With some in-laws, assertiveness training can be very useful in helping them to deal with in-law problems. Many clients are reluctant to use a simple *no* with their in-laws; when they do say no, they feel guilty about doing so. This pattern leads to passive-aggressive behaviors and generates a great deal of anger. It might be suggested that a client take an assertiveness training course or read some books on assertiveness (Adams & Lenz, 1989; Smith, 1975).

Considering the difference between assertive-aggressive and nonassertive behavior can also be helpful for in-laws. Again, it is important to give simple explanations. The goal of the therapist is not to provide a course in assertiveness training, but to give the client an extra tool for staying out of in-law conflicts. The therapist might explain that the difference between an assertive person and an aggressive person is that an assertive person considers the feelings of others and an aggressive person just considers himself or herself. It also might be pointed out that people who are nonassertive tend toward aggressive behaviors when they are finally pushed into action. Therefore, nonassertive behaviors can be quite risky because, when the nonassertive in-law blows up, he or she is bound to make comments that are not easily taken back.

In their study of African American, middle-income women, Jackson and Berg-Cross (1988) found four prevalent problem-solving strategies between daughters-in-law and mothers-in-law:

1. Avoidance.
2. Tactful assertiveness.
3. Compliance.
4. Defensiveness.

This list of strategies used by in-laws would indicate that some people do need assertiveness training, especially in-laws using the avoidance, compliance, and defensive tactics. Through looking at triangles and transactional analysis (discussed in the next chapter), in-laws can be helped to understand and modify their problem-solving strategies. Compliance and avoidance might be good strategies in the short run. In the long run, however, those types of nonassertive behaviors can result in a nonsolution of problems and, because the in-law relationship is a very long-term relationship, may lead to annoyance and distancing in the family. When in-laws enter therapy, rather than seeing clients who use tactful assertiveness, the therapist will generally see the avoidance, overcompliance, or defensive stances; thus, in-laws can be encouraged to practice the in-law techniques previously mentioned when dealing with these long-term in-law relationships.

THE HEALING BALM OF FORGIVENESS

Forgiveness is an important part of the therapeutic process. At some point in in-law therapy, it is hoped that there will be a mutual forgiveness among the in-laws. Someone once said that we only really become adults when we learn to forgive our parents. However, many in-laws and many individuals in general seem to want forgiveness prematurely. Forgiveness is a process, not an event. This needs to be reinforced with in-laws so that they don't feel disappointed about not receiving instant forgiveness.

The idea that we forgive and forget is heavily laden with denial. To forgive and remember is a more functional strategy: remembering will help in-laws to identify and avoid future situations that predict in-law conflicts and problems. It is important to work with in-law families in slowing down the process by not rushing through discussions of the problem, possible solutions, and ideas each in-law has for healing the rifts between family members. Healing is a process, and in-laws need to be encouraged to go slowly in order to integrate the changes into their lives. It takes time to deal with the loyalty issues, as well as with feelings of hurt, exclusion, and misunderstanding.

WORKSHEET

Mending Broken or Bruised In-Law Relationships

1. Have I looked at the role in-law personality traits or style play in my relationships?
    a. Control needs
    b. Inclusion needs
    c. Intimacy needs
    d. Differing problem-solving techniques; i.e., assertive, aggressive, withdrawn
    e. Expectations of appropriate helping
2. Are there in-law issues around family holidays?
    a. Christmas and New Year's celebrations
    b. Easter
    c. Thanksgiving
    d. Fourth of July
    e. Mother's Day
    f. Father's Day
    g. Chanukah or Passover

3. Do I use in-law jokes to create barriers?

4. How can I reauthor stories around in-law problem areas to heal the wounds and build on unique outcomes?

5. What would go on my In-law Dream List?

6. What is the common denominator in my behavior—do I tend to be more assertive or more aggressive? How does this affect the in-law relationship?

7. What are my in-law problem-solving strategies?

   a. Avoidance

   b. Tactful assertiveness

   c. Compliance

   d. Defensiveness

8. Are there unresolved issues that fester within the in-law relationship?

9. If forgiveness is not possible, have I examined my role in the interaction and determined how to avoid a similar situation in the future?

CHAPTER 8

Therapeutic Interventions: Triangles and Transactional Analysis with In-Laws

Clients often say, "Your ideas of empowering and reauthoring are useful with in-laws in the long run, but what about the here and now? What do we do when we go home and my mother-in-law comments that our son's punk haircut is an embarrassment to the family?" Using a combination of Kerr and Bowen's (1988) theories regarding triangles and Berne's (1961) transactional analysis techniques can be valuable in helping clients conceptualize the problems in relationships with in-laws, as well as in instituting damage control for ongoing conflict situations. Recognizing that each of these therapeutic techniques is extremely complex, I present here only a broad view of the aspects I use in my own practice. Therapists interested in more in-depth explanations of triangles are encouraged to look at some of the earlier works of Bowen (1966, 1976) and Minuchin (1974).

IN-LAW TRIANGLES

Kerr and Bowen (1988) discuss how individuals who are not differentiated from the family emotional system naturally tend to feel more stable in interactions where three people are involved. Thus, if two people (a dyad) are having difficulty, they naturally bring a third person into the discussion, which forms an interactional triangle. These triangles usually result in the diffusion or the cover-up of conflict (Simon, Stierlin, & Wynne, 1985). The person brought in to form the triangle need not be physically present but can be included via verbal comments. Thus, individuals can be metaphorically triangled into a two-person interaction (or conversation). A common example is when parents who are having marital problems pull in (triangle) their child, "Little Willie," by focusing on his problems rather than their own (Figure 8.1).

Unresolved Parental Triangle

Here is an example of how the Little Willie triangle works. The original fight between the mother and father starts when Dad accuses Mom of overdrawing

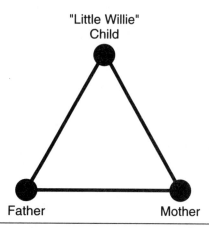

Figure 8.1   Parent–Child Triangle

the checking account. Her response is, "That's because we didn't have enough money to buy Willie the sneakers that the other kids are wearing. If you didn't stop at the bar every night on the way home from work, we would have more to spend. How am I supposed to take care of the children on the measly amount you give me?" Tension mounts. Dad says, "I don't know why a 13-year-old boy has to have such expensive sneakers anyway." Mom says, "I know it is a problem." The couple triangles in the problems of Little Willie, effectively covering up their marital conflict; both parents agree that Willie has a problem. The original problems—an overdrawn checking account, a possible alcohol problem, and allocation of money—are never resolved. The tension has now been diffused and is spread from the dyad to the triad. Mom and Dad may further diffuse tension by agreeing that Willie's sneakers cost too much money and giving him extra tasks to help pay for the sneakers. The parents will then leave the encounter feeling that something has been accomplished, Willie will be more responsible. The underlying problems of the husband's drinking and the family finances remain unaddressed.

For the therapist dealing with in-law relationships, the major purpose of teaching clients the triangle concept is to help in-laws understand the concept, recognize when it occurs, and try to stay *detriangled* (Bowen, 1966). Bowen also formulated the idea that the therapist should stay detriangled by having couples speak directly to each other in the therapy session, thus leaving the therapist to coach interactions rather than take part in them.

Siblings-in-Law Triangle

The same dynamics appear with the triangling of an in-law. Ronda and John had been married for a month when they came to see me in therapy. Ronda was feeling extremely angry because John was spending a great deal of time with his brother. Ronda conceded that John was needed by his brother, whose wife had recently left him for another man. However, it seemed to Ronda that John took every opportunity possible to spend time with her brother-in-law. John said he could see no problem with the relationship and didn't know why Ronda was so upset.

This couple's problem could be framed in many ways. We could look at the brother-in-law's problem, which was a need for comfort and support while dealing with the loss of his wife. We could look at the relationship between the brothers. But we could also look at it as an in-law problem. Looking at what was going on between the couple, John seemed to be spending as much time away from Ronda as possible and was enjoying the time with his brother. I discussed with the couple the options for framing the problem, and they chose to frame it as an in-law problem.

I then asked Ronda and John to position their chairs facing each other and to discuss their in-law issue directly, without covering up reactions or diffusing tension by triangling in me or the brother-in-law. Ronda then told John that she was uncomfortable because her new husband was spending so much time with a man who had recently been separated. She felt that John should adjust to life as a couple rather than resume his single-state activities. After a brief discussion of the issue, John said that he could see Ronda's point of view and that he would be upset if she were going out with a girlfriend who had recently been separated. The couple then agreed that an in-law problem encountered by many newly married couples is how to best consider the other's family while adjusting to their own marriage. John and Ronda decided that they would spend more time with the brother-in-law as a couple and that they would continue to try to solve their problems directly rather than triangling in a third person. Ronda and John have continued to be direct and honest in their disagreements. The interaction is not always easy because the couple sometimes lacks the desire or energy to deal directly with conflict.

In-Law Triangles and Their Meanings

Triangles are naturally occurring phenomena that help clients deal with stress. When emotional tension in the dyad is beyond what they can tolerate, they triangle in another person to relieve the tension.

To help clients understand the triangle concept, I have a large pad on an easel in my office. I draw a triangle using the sneakers situation mentioned earlier, and I demonstrate to in-laws how interactional triangles work. I draw the dyad, telling clients that dyads are naturally less stable than triangles. I ask the clients to describe some of the in-law triangles they have in their lives, and we jot them down on the pad. We then explore the complexity of in-law relationships using the concept of interlocking in-law triangles. The

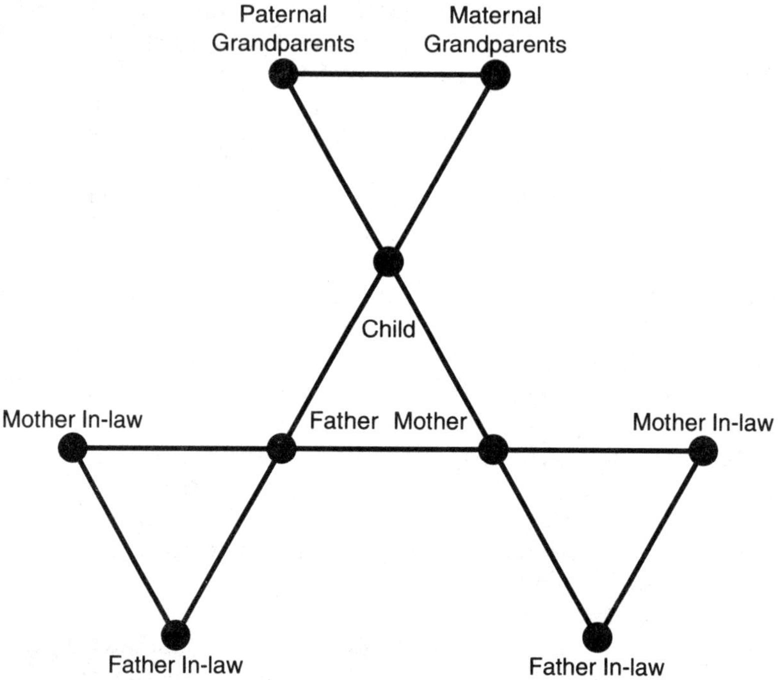

Figure 8.2 Interlocking Triangles

interlocking triangles show how one in-law interfaces with a number of in-laws. As I draw the interlocking triangles (Figure 8.2), the complexity of in-law relationships becomes clear to the clients.

I try to keep the diagrammed information fairly simple during the therapeutic process, because I want clients to be able to use this information in a practical way, to stay on task, and to not block a two-way discussion by bringing in a superfluous in-law issue. Knowing about triangles can help clients to avoid being the person triangled into an emotionally charged in-law situation.

Like reauthoring, learning about and identifying in-law triangles will help clients learn to externalize problems, which is the beginning of in-law damage control.

TRANSACTIONAL ANALYSIS IN IN-LAW RELATIONSHIPS

After teaching clients the tactics for avoiding being drawn into in-law triangles, I give them a brief and highly simplistic description of transactional analysis (TA). In the service of simplicity, I do not discuss complementary and uncomplementary transactions, cross-transactions, or nonverbal cues, because I am more interested in having clients think in terms of being drawn into

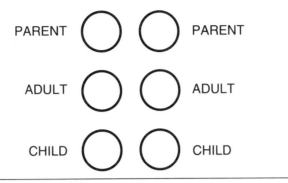

Figure 8.3   Three Ego States

old ways of reacting than I am in having them conversant with transactional analysis theory. To client in-laws who are interested in learning more about TA, I recommend *I'm ok, you're ok* (Harris, 1967).

As with the triangles, I get my easel out and draw three circles on the pad so that in-laws can visually conceptualize the ego states: Parent, Adult, and Child (Figure 8.3). I explain to the clients that each individual has a limited repertoire of ego states, which can be sorted into three categories: (1) Parent, (2) Adult (which is autonomously directed toward objective appraisal of reality), and (3) Child. Berne (1961) postulated that, in any given moment in a social situation, individuals would exhibit one of the three ego states and that individuals had the ability to shift with varying degrees from one ego state to another. Because it is not my purpose to go deeply into the analysis of the transactions, I do not attempt to look at the complexities of each interaction. I keep the descriptions very simple, to help clients identify and then avoid destructive in-law interchanges. My main interest is the ego interactions that are causing in-law conflict and discomfort, which, in my work, I find most often represented by the Parent–Child interaction. Such was the case with a young man named Albert and his mother-in-law; however, this case had an interesting twist. Albert (son-in-law) started in the Parent ego state, a reversal of the age hierarchy.

Son-in-Law/Mother-in-Law Interaction

Albert entered therapy because his mother-in-law was constantly asking to be taken care of and was demanding of her daughter Sheila's and son-in-law Albert's time.

MOTHER-IN-LAW: "Albert, I hope that you and Sheila will be able to drive me to my sister's on Saturday. It has been hard for me to drive since I sprained my wrist."

ALBERT: "I'll take you, but I'll only be able to go after four o'clock when the football game is over."

MOTHER-IN-LAW: "I so appreciate everything you do for me. I know you like to watch your sports. I guess I'm just a nuisance."

ALBERT (UNDER HIS BREATH): "Why the hell shouldn't I watch sports? I work hard."

MOTHER-IN-LAW: "Oh, I'm so sorry. I didn't mean anything by that."

In my conversation with Albert, he stated that an interaction with his mother-in-law always made him feel like a real heel, because he probably should be taking care of her. "God knows she is not taking care of herself." We analyzed the interaction and decided that Albert was in a Frustrated Parent role and his mother-in-law was in a Needy Child position (Figure 8.4). These positions reversed the age hierarchies, thus causing further imbalance.

We then talked about strategies that Albert might use to restore the age hierarchies, putting his mother-in-law in the Parent role and himself in the Adaptive Child role. Albert said that he wanted to encourage his mother-in-law to be more resourceful and competent, and to enjoy the respect he felt that an older person should receive. We discussed how using "I" statements and not needing to explain his day to her were important, as was speaking to her as a competent person. Albert felt that he would like to be more playful and less defensive with his mother-in-law. We then reworked how a similar interaction in the future might proceed (Figure 8.5).

MOTHER-IN-LAW: "Albert, I hope that you and Sheila will be able to drive me to my sister's on Saturday. It has been hard for me to drive since I sprained my wrist."

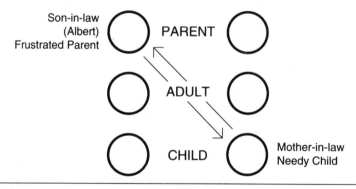

Figure 8.4   The Needy Child

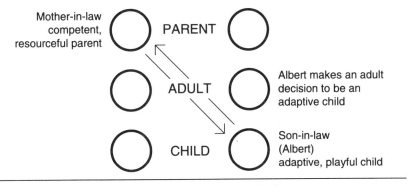

Figure 8.5   The Competent Patient

ALBERT: "If I were you, I'd want to see a doctor for that wrist. It is really slowing you down. One thing I have always admired about you is your independence."

MOTHER-IN-LAW: "I'd need to have you take me to the doctor."

ALBERT: "I would be glad to take you or pay for a taxi if I am tied up."

MOTHER-IN-LAW: "Tied up with what?"

ALBERT: "Just some stuff with the guys. You know some of us boys never grow up."

The important point in reworking the interaction with Albert and his mother-in-law is that he now views her in a new light as an adult. He is ready and willing to have her as the competent adult while he is the playful child. Albert continues to elevate his mother-in-law with affirming statements. He is also working hard at seeing her as a person able to take care of herself. Albert has asked his wife not to get involved; he feels that learning to deal with his mother-in-law in a firm but compassionate way will improve his relationship with his own mother.

According to Berne (1961), the first person's ego state will naturally elicit a complementary ego state in the second person. Thus, if one person hurts his knee and asks for sympathy, a second person will likely respond with a sympathetic parental response, like "Can I help you? Are you sure that you are okay?" Understanding possible ego responses and the direction of energy can help in-laws to alter and modify distressing interactions. There are positive and negative aspects to each ego state.

According to Berne's theory, individuals have ego state options and, at different times, may express themselves as, for example, Playful Child, Rebellious Child, Responsible Adult, or Punishing or Nurturing Parent. One stance that is helpful with in-law relationships is talking about the Adult-to-Adult role, which helps in-laws to avoid friction. Adult-to-Adult interaction is an information-giving stance. It is a direct answer to a request for information (Harris, 1973).

Sister-in-Law/Brother-in-Law Interaction

In the following sibling-in-law transaction, 35-year-old José started out feeling like an Incompetent Child in the first interaction and then role-played the Adult stance. José complained of always being treated like an Incompetent Child by his overbearing Parental sister-in-law (Lisa). José complained that when Lisa comes to town, she starts telling him what to do.

LISA: "We are coming to Las Vegas on business and we will plan on taking you and Virginia to dinner on Wednesday night."

JOSÉ: "I'll have to check with Virginia. I think we are going to my parents' house."

LISA: "I've already talked to Virginia. It will be fine. You can see your parents anytime."

This interaction left José feeling like an Incompetent Child. Figure 8.6 shows, in simple transactional terms, how the interaction would look.

In discussing the problem with José and drawing out the diagram, José stated that he was not in need of help or support from Lisa and really desired to be his own person; however, he did not want to upset her, because he seldom saw her and, after all, she was his sister-in-law. We then discussed how, by giving facts and being decisive, he might bring them both to the Adult ego state. José then role-played the following interaction.

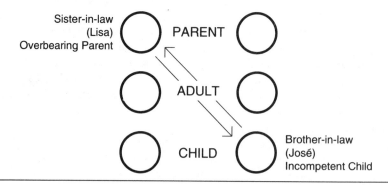

Figure 8.6   The Incompetent Child

LISA: "We are coming to Las Vegas and we will plan on taking you and Virginia to dinner on Wednesday night."

JOSÉ: "Gosh, I'm sorry, Lisa, but I am busy that night."

LISA: "What do you mean you're busy? I called Virginia and she said you could go."

JOSÉ: "Virginia doesn't know all my plans. Let's try to make it for another night. How about Tuesday or Thursday?"

LISA: "I guess that would be okay. What time and where should we meet?"

JOSÉ: "Give me the number of where you are staying and I'll get back to you."

By making "I" statements and assuming a friendly but firm stance, José stayed in control of his own life, which caused Lisa, his sister-in-law, to also take an Adult stance. (See Figure 8.7.)

Although this was only a role-play, José learned an important technique that he was able to use in his next interaction with Lisa. José continues to work on the tendency to get into a Compliant Child role with his sister-in-law, but he is taking responsibility for himself, even if his sister-in-law gets annoyed.

Typically, in an argument, one person starts in the Parent role, either as persecutor or rescuer, and another person is in the Child ego state as victim. As the argument progresses, the victim moves into the Parent ego state as persecutor, and the rescuer moves into a victim (Child) position (English, 1977). There is also a possibility that both parties in the interaction will move to the Adult or peer position. This is desirable especially to empower females in the family. One stays in the Adult position by being clear and by giving facts, thus avoiding the regressive pull that often accompanies interactions of children-in-law with parents-in-law.

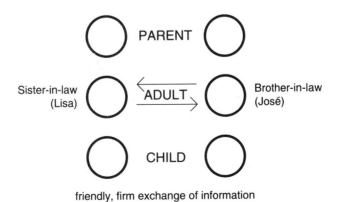

friendly, firm exchange of information

Figure 8.7   Moving to Adult Interaction

Mother-in-Law/Daughter-in-Law Interaction

The following case involved a young woman, Astrid, who complained of a highly critical mother-in-law, Dagmar. Astrid gave the following example of how her mother-in-law takes the role of the Critical Parent, making Astrid feel like a Naughty Child. The interaction had taken place the previous summer, when Astrid stayed with Dagmar for two weeks. Astrid said, "She was constantly after me for the way I treated her son and how I didn't take care of him." The interaction went like this:

DAGMAR: "Astrid, I can't believe you put Kent's shirts in the washer and then in the dryer."

ASTRID: "What else should I do? That's the way my mother did shirts."

DAGMAR: "I always hand-washed them and line-dried them so they wouldn't shrink. And, by the way, I also ironed his shorts and undershirts."

ASTRID (UNDER HER BREATH):   "What a witch."

Astrid and I diagrammed the interaction (Figure 8.8) and discussed the fact that she saw herself as a Naughty Child to her mother-in-law's Critical Parent.

We then discussed taking the Adult-to-Adult stance, making "I" statements, and respecting the feelings of her mother-in-law. Astrid then role-played the following interaction.

DAGMAR: "Astrid, I can't believe you put Kent's shirts in the washer and then in the dryer."

ASTRID: "I noticed that on the manufacturer's recommendations are that they be machine washed and dried."

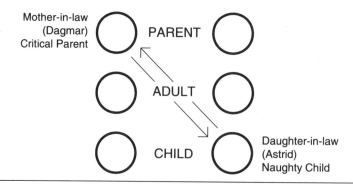

Figure 8.8   Adult–Child Interaction

DAGMAR: "I always hand-washed them and line-dried them so they wouldn't shrink. And, by the way, I also ironed his shorts and undershirts."

ASTRID: "Kent was lucky to have such a supportive mother, but Kent and I have decided to put his shirts in the wash. In fact, at home he does his own shirts. You raised him well."

DAGMAR: "I guess it is a new era."

During this interaction, Astrid stayed fact-oriented, gave information, and yet was highly supportive of her mother-in-law. The interaction then became an Adult-to-Adult interaction; the women basically agreed to disagree (Figure 8.9). Astrid is still struggling with her mother-in-law but says that Dagmar has become far less critical.

Problems arise when individuals have ulterior reasons (usually outside their immediate awareness) for assuming a given stance. Problematic ego states in in-law relationships are often seen when the son- or daughter-in-law is cast or operates in the Rebellious Child ego state with parents-in-law who accept or take the role of the Punishing parent. These negative positions often start quite innocently when the new bride or groom looks to the in-laws for advice, comfort, and a sense of togetherness. As the newness wears off, the Parent–Child ego transaction grows increasingly less desirable to the young couple, who have begun to assert their independence. Parents who stay in Critical Parent roles may find children-in-law spending increasingly less time with the family, avoiding family events, and becoming resentful of unsolicited advice. Such was the case with Catlin and her father-in-law. In their first transaction, the father-in-law was in the Critical Parent role and Catlin was in the Incompetent Child role.

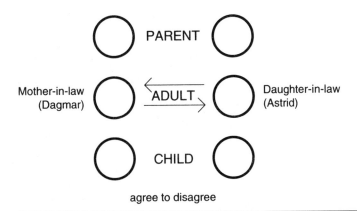

Figure 8.9   Adult–Adult Interaction

Catlin's father-in-law seemed to go out of his way to be rude to her. Her husband had asked Catlin to play it cool because the old man couldn't live forever. I asked Catlin to describe a typical interaction with her father-in-law. She said that they had had a problem several days earlier, when her father-in-law took her and her two-year-old son, Josh, to lunch. Toward the end of the meal, Josh started playing with his food and dropping it on the floor.

FATHER-IN-LAW: "Have you ever thought about not letting Josh feed himself? I think he is a little young to eat on his own."

CATLIN, BENDING DOWN, TRYING TO CLEAN UP THE SCRAPS: "Well, he does like to feed himself. If I try to take the spoon, he says, 'Me do it.' "

FATHER-IN-LAW: "If you don't get in some discipline right now, you will have no control when he is a teenager. Just give him a slap on the hand."

CATLIN: "OK. I won't slap him, but I'll try to feed him."

Catlin and Josh get in a struggle for the spoon. Josh then starts crying and Catlin picks him up.

FATHER-IN-LAW: "That's what I mean by giving in to him."

Catlin and I diagrammed the interaction (Figure 8.10). Catlin was put into the Incompetent Child role by her father-in-law's Critical Parent role.

Catlin did not want to confront her father-in-law head-to-head. She decided that she would make an Adult decision to be an Adaptive Child and not try to defend her parental role, in an effort to neutralize her father-in-law's criticism. Catlin then played the scene in the role of the Adaptive Child. To keep her father-in-law elevated by valuing his opinions, she kept in mind his age and the fact that he was her husband's father and her son's grandfather. At

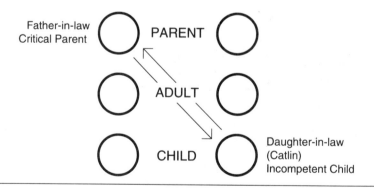

Figure 8.10   The Critical Parent

that point in the session, Catlin let some of the Playful Child come out, commenting with a laugh how much her family was going to enjoy Grandpa's money.

FATHER-IN-LAW: "Have you ever thought about not letting Josh feed himself? I think he is a little young to be eating on his own."

CATLIN: "You may be right, but your family has good coordination."

FATHER-IN-LAW: "It is important to discipline kids."

CATLIN: "That's a true statement. You know, I think this kid is probably not old enough to go to lunch with Grandpa. This was a good experiment, but I guess he isn't ready for the big leagues."

Play-acting the Adaptive Child brought Catlin into the Adult role (Figure 8.11). Another choice could have been to be Rebellious Child, but that role might have cut Catlin and her husband out of the father-in-law's will.

Externalizing the Problem

The therapist might suggest that the client begin to externalize the problem by writing down several uncomfortable transactions with the in-law. Then the client draws circles to identify the applicable ego states. Once the client has identified several interactions, he or she can begin to externalize the problem and choose strategies that can help movement toward a more satisfying ego state.

Caution is in order here. The therapist might wish to consider the fact that change can seem difficult but is not impossible. Human beings are comfortable with the familiar; they face change with reluctance and are somewhat fearful of change. To help move along the change process, the therapist might

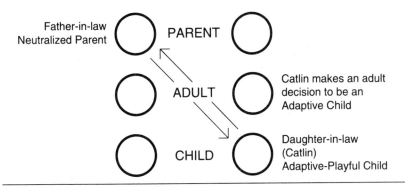

Figure 8.11   Neutralizing the Critical Parent

suggest that clients let their in-laws know that they have decided to make some changes in their own behavior. This should alert in-laws to the fact that they may not receive the predictable responses to in-law interactions.

Therapists can help in-laws by encouraging them to give themselves permission to grow and to make the same mistakes several times over before expecting to see change. It is helpful for the therapist to remind clients that all people have a right to change. Changes may include past attitudes and opinions as well as unwritten agreements made at the time of marriage, for example, "We will spend every Christmas with the in-laws." As one in-law so aptly put it, "If you're green, you're growing, and if you're not, you rot." Although in-laws tell me that they try to stay in the Adult position, the Child inclination is very active because that is where all the fun is.

Giving too much *free information* may cause conflict between a parent-in-law acting as a Punishing Parent and a child-in-law acting as a Child.

PARENT-IN-LAW: "Will you join us for dinner on Sunday?"

CHILD-IN-LAW: "Sorry, can't make it. We are going to get together with some friends from work and then I have to wash my car and network on the computer."

In this case, I would suggest that the child-in-law respond in an Adult role, "Sorry we can't make it, but we have previous commitments." If the parent-in-law demands more information (as a Punitive Parent), trying to force the child-in-law back into the Child role, the response should remain consistent: "Sorry, but we have prior plans."

When people are given too much information, it is natural to make a judgment on the behavior (a highly judging Parental activity). The problem with change, as with behavior modification, is that intermittent reinforcement has powerful consequences. Thus, if one says *no* most of the time, and then says *yes* only on occasion, people will push twice as hard as they would if one did the activity on a regular basis. Consistency is key.

Introduction of clients to the three ego states can make it possible for them not to be compromised by habit or as a reaction to an in-law's position (ego state). In-laws may sometimes have to adapt. Adult children may put up with an obnoxious father-in-law in order to inherit his money, or grandparents may make the best of a bad situation with a son-in-law in order to spend time with the grandchildren.

Imbalance in Sibling Interactions

In-laws can view themselves as actors on stage and decide in advance on all their options. One can keep going into the Parent role if one wants to be angry and to have an emotional cutoff with siblings-in-law, or one can take a Playful Child position and use humor or a conciliatory position if one wants to avoid friction. It is hoped that knowledge of transactional analysis can give options to in-laws; we all have selective, limited, and fairly predictable ways of re-acting to situations, and we often mistakenly think that our own point of view on issues is shared by those closest to us, including our in-laws. Change is by nature a slow process, and clients should be encouraged that if they don't at first succeed to try, try again. Clients might also be reminded that if the goal is to have more meaningful and healthy interactions, personal growth will be its own reward, even if they do not get the desired in-law changes.

ACKNOWLEDGING AND DEALING WITH EMOTIONAL AND PHYSICAL CUTOFFS

Therapy with in-laws requires working not only within the arena of a two- or three-generational family system, but also with individuals who have no bio-logical or formal legal ties. Because in-laws are not connected through biol-ogy, the therapist may need to appeal to their higher universal values, such as altruism, love, and humanity. These may be the only hooks available to pull distressed in-laws out of unsatisfying and destructive relationships.

When all else fails, the therapist may have to point out that if in-law issues are not dealt with, the family risks the emotional or physical cutoff of the bi-ological family member, or risks having the child-in-law choose his or her bi-ological family over the spouse or vice versa. When children enter the picture, children-in-law may retaliate for past problems by bad-mouthing parents-in-law or denying access to grandchildren (see Chapter 5), thus causing emo-tional cutoffs.

The problems created by not working out in-law emotional and physical cutoffs were evident in the Larson family, which included 7 children ranging in age from 8 to 18 years. The husband, Jeremy, and wife, Shawna, who had been married for 20 years and divorced for 7 years, had recently remarried each other. After having been remarried for a year, Shawna was ready to leave Jeremy again. He continually refused to let her see her parents. His rationale for this cutoff was that her family would not allow him in their house because 10 years earlier he had had a physical fight with his father-in-law. The father-in-law therefore wanted nothing to do with the son-in-law. Because Jeremy was not allowed in Shawna's parents' home, he refused to allow the children to visit. This cutoff from the grandchildren was upsetting for the father-in-law, mother-in-law, and Shawna, who was so angry with Jeremy about this separation from her family that she was considering divorcing him again, for the final time.

I encouraged the couple to invite the in-laws into therapy, but the father-in-law refused. Shawna was forced to make a choice between her biological family and her marriage. Several months later, she again filed for divorce. Now that they are living separately, Shawna sees her biological family on a regular basis and, interestingly enough, she also sees her ex-husband frequently. Thus, it seems that Jeremy and his in-laws needed more space than a marriage could offer. Shawna says that the arrangement is working out well and that she loves being reconnected with her family.

Avoiding In-Law Splitting and Projection

It is not unusual for children-in-law or parents-in-law to be involved in what therapists term *splitting* or *projection:* the person designates one member of the in-law couple to be the "good guy" and one to be the "bad guy." This cloning of the familiar good cop/bad cop framework produces good parent-in-law/bad parent-in-law, or good child-in-law/bad child-in-law roles. As has been noted in previous chapters, mothers-in-law are especially vulnerable to splitting. When splitting occurs, it is helpful for the therapist to bring the client to a problem-oriented framework that allows disentangling the personalities involved.

Again, the mothers-in-law seem most vulnerable with the children-in-law, and are seen as negative individuals. Paradoxically, the fathers-in-law are often viewed as the positive individuals. This identification may be somewhat linked to economic issues. In much of the current older generation, the father has had control of the financial resources and therefore any anger or discontent with the in-law relationship may be projected onto the mother-in-law, who has fewer financial resources to give (or deny). It is hoped that this is changing within the younger generations, where more women have equal control over financial resources. Projection of anger or frustration onto the in-laws may also be a reflection of the relationship that the child-in-law had with his or her own parents.

One way to deal with splitting or projection is to have the father-in-law or the other male in-laws take a more active role in relationships. Often, both the mother-in-law and the daughter-in-law are seen as being bitchy or hostile. The fact that the female counterparts in the family are historically more active in the social roles may allow the males to lie low and not take an active hand in dealing with in-law relationships. Women often pay too high a price as the keepers of the kin; they end up vocalizing discontent and problems for both themselves and their husbands. In-laws, both male and female, need to speak for themselves and become involved in problem situations. Some male in-laws stay out of the emotional relationships that need changes, withholding their opinion until the problem has escalated. When holdout males do state their case, rather than coming in with a reasonable discussion, they may take a dictatorial stance and recite a litany of *shoulds* and *oughts.* (It is interesting to note that, on psychiatric units in hospitals, vastly fewer violent incidents occur with female staff than occur with male staff, because males are not called in until the situation has escalated. This is reflected in domestic life: males are often put in the role of settling arguments rather than participating in the day-to-day workings of the household.)

Settling In-Law Arguments: The Geographic Solution

One way people avoid dealing with aggravating in-law issues on a daily basis is through a geographic move. However, this is often not the best solution. The therapist needs to counsel clients that if they do not work out these issues in the present, they may crop up in the next generation. Many families feel pleased that they moved away from their parents, but, paradoxically, feel that their own children will and should make the choice to live close to them. When children move away from their parents, they are frequently unable to work through issues from childhood. As humans, we need all of our support systems. One of my clients wisely put it, "If you don't encourage your spouse's relationship with your in-laws, you will end up having to fulfill the parenting relationship with your spouse."

It can be very stressful on the in-law relationship if one of the results of a new marriage is a geographic move away from the family. One mother stated her resentment clearly when she said that her son-in-law had betrayed her by looking for a job in another state. As my father-in-law always said, "Stay and work out your problems. Where the crow flies, the tale (tail) follows."

WORKSHEET

Therapeutic Interventions with In-Laws

1. When I have problems with my spouse or other family members, do I triangle in an in-law in order to avoid dealing with the original problem?

2. Do I allow myself to be triangled into difficult in-law situations?

3. Do I get co-opted into unproductive Parent or Child ego states in these interactions?

   a. With mother-in-law

   b. With siblings-in-law

   c. With father-in-law

4. Am I willing to identify and work on changing unproductive communication patterns with in-laws?

5. Do I tend to split my in-laws by looking at one in-law as being good and another as being bad?

6. Do I project often unfounded negative characteristics onto in-laws?

7. Am I especially critical or negative about my in-laws?

8. Have I emotionally or physically cut myself off from my in-laws?

9. Have I made a geographical move in order to avoid settling in-law disputes or working through problems with in-laws?

10. Am I missing out on the fun of having a positive relationship with my in-laws?

CHAPTER 9

The Broken Bond: Separation, Divorce, and Stepfamilies

When the family has finally adjusted to the expectations of being in-laws, new challenges may be brought by divorce. Bohannan (1973), an anthropologist, writes of six *stations* in the divorcing process: (a) the emotional divorce, (b) the legal divorce, (c) the economic divorce, (d) the co-parental divorce, (e) the community divorce, and (f) the psychic divorce.

Bohannan feels that each stage must be experienced and the tasks for that stage must be mastered if the family is to reach equilibrium. The roles of in-laws would be dealt with in what Bohannan terms the community divorce—which, paradoxically, is the divorce that is seldom addressed. The term refers to the changes that the divorced person (and community) must cope with. Because denial is such a strong factor in the process of dealing with the loss of a relationship, it is important that the client be aware of the possibilities and the pitfalls of in-law relationships affected by the divorce. These in-law relationships are often dear to the divorcing person as well as to other family members. It is hoped that those couples who are divorced and the in-laws of the divorcing couple will consider new options, ideas, and possibilities for in-law relationships. Some of these are presented in this chapter.

Prior to and after the divorce, families must address the changing status of the in-laws: they become ex-in-laws. This new status is seldom spoken of in our society, and the deterioration of the relationship is just allowed to happen. Often, this change in relationship is tumultuous and is done without flexibility or grace. Several authors have discussed some of the variables that will determine in-law relationships after divorce. After examining in-depth interviews with former spouses and their former in-laws, Duran-Aydintug (1993) found that the quality and quantity of relationships with the in-laws *before* separation and divorce determine the quality and the quantity of relationships with former in-laws *after* divorce. The majority of couples from the 60 couples interviewed for this study stated that society expected them to sever relationships with the in-laws after divorce and that choosing to stay connected with the in-laws was a conscious choice. In his study of remarriage and intergenerational relations, Furstenberg (1981) found that, for some in-laws, relationships after divorce continued as though the divorce had not occurred; for others, the home of the parents-in-law was a neutral zone where previously married couples could carry on the business of parenting.

STAYING IN THE FAMILY AFTER DIVORCE: RETENTION

Clarification of the role changes brought about by divorce involves important issues, and discussion of them in therapy can be helpful for both the child- and the parent-in-law. Johnson (1989) found the American kinship network to be mutable and flexible as people accommodate to the realities of marital change. She sees few normative mandates regulating the process of marital change, therefore she states, there are few guidelines on how to conduct these relationships. In-laws can be an important factor in the expanding of the kinship relationships by retention of former in-laws and introduction of new in-laws by divorce and remarriage.

When there are no children or grandchildren to consider, chances are high that the in-law relationship will end with the marriage. However, there are notable exceptions. In her autobiography, *Me: Stories of My Life* (1991), Katharine Hepburn writes of her family's relationship with her ex-husband, Luddy Ogden Smith. Ms. Hepburn visited her family's summer home in Fenwick, Connecticut, during the time she was living with Howard Hughes. In attendance for the weekend were not only Hughes but also her parents and her ex-husband. Luddy was taking pictures of the family on the golf course, and Hughes expressed his annoyance. Ms. Hepburn's father made what Katharine called his famous remark: "Howard, Luddy has been taking pictures of all of us for many years before you joined us and he will be taking them long after you've left. He is a part of this family. . . ."

This story says something about the importance of clarification of the ex-in-laws' role in the family. Ms. Hepburn's father was an unusual man, because we know from the small amount of research that has been done on in-laws that the mother-in-law usually plays the role of *keeper of the kin* (Johnson & Barer, 1987) and nurturer of relationships. Duvall (1954) found that many daughters-in-law divorced the sons, yet continued to enjoy the support and friendship of their mothers-in-law.

Indeed, some people become more deeply entrenched in their in-law families for a longer period than they lived in their family of origin. A question arises: Why should one have to be ejected from and rejected by the in-law families after a divorce? We need to take a hard look at how we deal with the in-law families. Rather than just ejecting the divorced spouses out of hand, we might think about what kind of relationships we would like to have with our families and give more consideration to the structure that the family will have after a divorce. In some cases, the in-law families have become the adopting families, where the spouse may have lost parents or may have somehow lost contact with the birth family. It is unfortunate that our society assumes that the relationship with the in-laws will end with the end of the marriage. When couples divorce, all of the unspoken contracts that have been made during the marital relationship need to be terminated or reexamined. Couples and in-laws and the entire family network need to grieve the loss of the relationship as it has been known and formulate a new ex-in-law connection (Kaslow & Schwartz, 1987).

CONTRACTION—FOCUS ON THE CHILDREN

A divorced son-in-law might want to try to connect with the ex-mother-in-law if he understands that she might be a key to the family and to access to his children. Hetherington, Cox, and Cox (1977) found that unless the divorced father has easy access to his children, maternal custody leaves the father feeling lonely and depressed. The father's involvement, according to Ahrons (1994), depends on what happens during the first two years after the divorce. Ahrons talks about the relationship between the spouses as being a key factor in the father's involvement, but the Duran-Aydintug (1993) study would lead us to believe that the relationships with both the former wife and the former in-laws are important.

I recently saw Dick, a 32-year-old doctor, the father of two children. Dick reported calling his ex-mother-in-law to tell her how depressed he was about the divorce. She said to him, "Dick, it is all over between you and Mary and you might as well face it." Dick said that he was very fond of his mother-in-law and that not seeing her in the future was an additional loss. I pointed out that the marriage may well be over, but not the roles of parenting and grand-parenting. The in-law role as related to the children had the potential, with nurturing, to be an important resource for Dick and his ex-in-laws. Even though Dick would like a retention relationship with his in-laws, the fact that the divorce was not amicable may cause the in-laws to side with his ex-wife (their daughter), thus contracting the kinship network. Dick and I then discussed how his relationship with the in-laws could continue outside the marital bond. Dick felt he might begin forming a new relationship by sending them cards on birthdays and holidays, not only to wish them a happy event, but to comment on something special about their grandchildren. Dick felt that, because the children represented a common bond of love, they would make an excellent bridge of friendship between himself and his in-laws.

Dick recently remarried and although he still has contact and news of the in-laws through his children, he is now highly involved with his second wife's family.

In looking at the transactional analysis paradigm, Dick said that he would be most successful at taking an Adult role with his mother-in-law by keeping her informed about the children and about how he related to the children. He saw himself in the Parent–Adult relationship when he asked her for information on parenting the grandchildren. He felt that asking her advice would be helpful. Because Dick's father-in-law was not involved in the actual day-to-day care of the children, Dick assumed that he would probably stay in the Adult role with his father-in-law. He would discuss the grandchildren with him and might at times even be able to talk about sports or some of the issues related to being a father or to the workplace.

Dick is well aware that he needs to work at not triangling in his ex-wife with her parents. Such a negative triangle might well eject him from his in-laws' family. Dick also realizes that his ex-in-laws need to remain elevated as *trusted advisers* and that his problems with his ex-wife need to be contained within that dyad. This will be a challenge for Dick. It is very tempting to stabilize a dyad with an ex-wife by bringing in either the children or the ex-in-laws and creating a triangle.

Maintaining the relationship will be especially challenging for Dick, not only as a divorced person, but also as a male. Johnson and Barer's (1987) interviews with 50 White, middle-class, paternal and maternal grandmothers point out some of the challenges for the divorced in-law. The study showed that 36% of the women in the study maintained at least weekly contact with a former daughter-in-law, but only 9% maintained contact with a former son-in-law.

The cutoff some people exercise toward their in-laws is interesting. When I told my lawyer that I was writing a book on in-laws, he said, "Well, I wouldn't be interested in it because I don't have any in-laws. I'm divorced." I replied, "Well, you have your in-laws of divorce." He said, "Well, yes, I guess I do have something to do with my in-laws because my wife has taken the kids off to the in-laws for Thanksgiving and I am, therefore, going skiing by myself. I guess I could use a book on in-laws. Send me a copy and I'll cut my fee."

However the in-law cut off after a divorce is not always the case, as seen in the following narrative:

My former husband was a middle-class Jewish prince. I was a brat. His parents owned a beach club. I was a poor girl. The first time I met my mother-in-law, I had fainted from heat and had gone into the shower at the club in my lovely flowered gown and hat. While I was sitting on the shower floor, my mother-in-law came in. She said, "Are you ready for lunch?" At that moment, I fell in love with her and even after our divorce I would visit her often. I didn't divorce her. I divorced her son.—Corky, 45, businesswoman

KINSHIP REORGANIZATION

Johnson and Barer (1987) grouped in-law kinship reorganization after divorce into the following three categories:

1. **Contraction of the kinship network:** 38% of the families become formal and distant toward in-laws, with each side trying to avoid conflict. The relationships become child-focused rather than based on being friends or relatives.

2. **Replacement of in-laws through remarriage:** 14% of parents-in-law felt pressure to exclude former children-in-law (their own children's ex-spouses) and to transfer loyalty to the new child-in-law in order to maintain a conflict-free relationship with their own child. This is an important area to consider in therapy with divorcing families, because 75% of divorced women and 83% of divorced men remarry (Kaslow & Schwartz, 1987).

3. **Retention of in-laws through in-law coalitions:** the most common expansion of the family was through mothers-in-law forming coalitions with former daughters-in-law. This was especially true if the son was unable to provide a link with the grandchildren. The expansion can go on to include multiple grandchildren and remarriage chains, making for very complex systems. Mothers-in-law in the study who were divorced or widowed were more likely to report expanding the system.

It may be useful to add one more area of kinship reorganization to the Johnson and Barer (1987) model: expulsion from the kinship network. There are cases where the in-law was so firmly expelled from the family that there is no longer any physical or emotional contact. Indeed, the person may even become a family secret. In these cases, the marriages were often of short duration or an in-law, usually the husband or partner, gave up any claim to family connection, including paternity rights. These expulsions are at times even formalized through the legal system with financial settlements and contracts of agreement not to be in contact with families. Other expulsions may happen, as in the following case, where the family did not give permission to marry and where no children are involved. As this story illustrates, some in-laws are directly involved in promoting divorce.

A young couple was referred to therapy by their ecclesiastical leader. They had many issues but one of the primary issues was that the 25-year-old woman was not yet ready to have children and, indeed, felt that she may never want to have children. The young man stated that his parents, particularly his mother, were very upset, because "they were ready to be grandparents." I suggested that we have a family therapy session with the in-laws. The couple was in agreement, but the young man was very frustrated because he could never find a date that was agreeable to the parents. With his permission, I called the parents and spoke to them about coming in for a session. His father was amenable but his mother said she had never wanted her son to marry the woman in the first place and that she was not happy that they were not having children. I tried to arrange an appointment with them, we arranged a date, and the parents canceled out. Eventually, the young couple separated. The young man called his parents and told them he was leaving his wife. With only one hour's notice, both parents were able to go to the couple's apartment and help the young man move out. They could easily find time to assist in the dissolution of the marriage, but could not contribute anything to saving it.

Opposition after divorce may not lie between generations, as Lévi-Strauss (1963) suggests, but along lines of tensions between relatives of blood and those of marriage. Bonds of affection and friendliness can be formed among ex-in-laws. "In-laws can be defined as one chooses, by norms of kinship, friendship, amity or enmity" (p. 97).

Sterling, a 40-year-old man with three children, had been divorced for several years. His ex-wife, Audrey, had remarried and they had, according to the ex-husband, a very cool relationship. There had been a great deal of anger in the divorce and, since the remarriage, Audrey had asked Sterling not to come to her home but to exchange the children (for visits) in a location such as a supermarket parking lot. Audrey was very angry at Sterling for fraudulent business dealings and had heavily relied on her parents for financial support during the divorce. Sterling had recently met Audrey in a supermarket parking lot to exchange their three children. During the course of the exchange, he saw his ex-mother-in-law, who, according to his account, turned her head and pretended he didn't exist. Sterling said this hurt him very much; he felt he had had a good relationship with his ex-mother-in-law, and it was difficult for him to think of himself as no longer being a *member of the family*. The stress of the divorce and the remarriage of her daughter no doubt left his ex-mother-in-law feeling burned, and she had no inclination toward a continued relationship with him.

As with any loss, family members may hold secret beliefs or theories regarding the in-law and the cause of a divorce or breakup. The healing process can be helped by expressing these theories and beliefs. Family members may feel guilt or shame and some sense of responsibility. This may be particularly true for siblings. "If I had been nicer to my brother-in-law, maybe he wouldn't have left."

There are cases where a total emotional and physical cutoff occurs for ex-in-laws. In a longitudinal study by Johnson (1992), the divorced father's link to his children progressively weakens over the years; thus, he may no longer be able to provide his parents access to their grandchildren. Because 74% of all divorces occur before age 40, the consequences are staggering for paternal grandparents who might get cut off from their grandchildren. Some in-laws are caught in a quandary: "If I do too much, I might have to keep doing it; and if I do too little, I may lose my grandchildren."

Johnson (1989) found that when the parent-in-law (most often, the mother-in-law) approved of the divorce or cohabitation, the person who was going through the divorce received more support. According to Johnson, the divorce situation resulted in overburdened parents-in-law and increased needs of grandchildren. Grandparents responded with money, baby-sitting, and other forms of assistance.

When I heard that my son and daughter-in-law were separating I feared that I'd never see my grandchildren again. Much to my relief, I now see them more than ever, because they often need backup baby-sitting now that they're not together and they have a rather rigid schedule of custody sharing.—Myrna, 62, real estate agent

Ahrons and Rogers (1987) interviewed 78 grandmothers and found that mothers provided support for divorced children, and few felt the divorce impacted them. However, Bohannan (1971) sees the U.S. divorce rate as being a greater problem than in other cultures, because of a lack of defined rights and obligations, as well as the relative isolation of the marital relationship from kin. Those in the study felt that individuals had a right to choose the relationships that added to their happiness, self-fulfillment, and personal growth. Interactions among kin were based on friendships rather than on recognized norms of obligation and mutual responsibility. The good news here is that individuals in the study were as permissive with themselves as they were with others, and thus were less likely to assign blame in divorce situations.

In-Laws Giving Assistance

The biological family can be expected to be more supportive after separation or divorce. According to Spanier and Hanson (1982), in a study of 205 individuals who had been separated from their spouses for 26 months or less, over three times more moral, financial, and services support was given by the extended birth family, as compared to the in-laws. Those who were separated received far more support from related kin than from in-laws. Friends and mothers offered the most moral support, and friends gave the most services support. Spanier and Hanson postulated that the reason friends showed more services support during separation was that the decision to separate was often made before the family was told; families only learned of the separation when it occurred. Divorced women have infrequent contact with their ex-husband's kin. The research of Rosenberg and Anspach (1973) and Spicer and Hampe (1975) confirms that divorced women's contacts with their ex-in-laws are less frequent than their contacts with their own families. Anspach (1976) postulates that this may be because the kin of the ex-spouse are perceived to be unreliable for aid or help. When a child grows up in a one-sided network, socioemotional support and resources are lost. In Anspach's study, 90% of the children who had no contact with their father had more contact with maternal than paternal grandparents. Regardless of marital status, consanguineous kin are more significant sources of socioemotional support than others.

The reality of divorce is that individuals tend to gravitate toward their family of origin rather than toward the in-laws. However, as Anspach points out, individuals are *the pivotal connecting links.* Pivotal denotes the idea of movement and the ability of human beings to make choices to connect with in-laws as well as with biological families.

Perhaps this book will broaden the horizons of those who divorce, in terms of the possibilities of in-law relationships. Divorce causes an imbalance in in-law networks; however, we know that crisis and imbalance can be reasons to rebalance in a new direction.

The Second Time Around: Reentering the In-Law System

It is not unusual to hear that a couple has gotten back together because of the difficulty, both financially and emotionally, of raising children alone. In-law support is not specifically mentioned but, as we have seen, it is a valuable support that is lost during separation and divorce, and its loss can create problems of ambiguity for the family. It may be helpful for in-laws to avoid getting locked into set attitudes toward ex-in-laws; they may think these exes have left the family and then find that their family member has brought the ex-in-law back into the family system. Such was the case with my client, Harris.

> *After a year of separation, my daughter Gail went back to her husband Rudy because she said she still loved him and that it was too hard to raise the kids on her own. Now she expects us to understand and welcome him back into the family with open arms. I just don't know whether I'm coming or going.*—Harris, 58, investment banker

The Role of Grandparents when Parents Divorce

At the unfortunate point when parents decide to divorce, the role of grandparents changes, sometimes not so subtly. According to Wilson and DeShane (1982), grandparents may be sued by the state or by individuals to support their grandchildren. Historically, if parents or stepparents are present, grandparents are not found liable. However, the legal rights of grandparents in most states are ambiguous. For example, the in-laws and grandparents in some states have no say if their daughter-in-law decides to put their future grandchild up for adoption. Courts do not want another additional party to interfere in the parent–child relationship. Further, in many states, grandparents do not have visitation rights in custody agreements, and end up paying a heavy price for the parents' inability to get along with each other. Because the courts are bound to look after the best interests of the child involved, the best interests of the grandparents are viewed as no more significant than those of unrelated individuals. (More on the legal ramifications of divorce and on custody of grandchildren in Chapter 11.)

TOOLS FOR HEALING THE EMOTIONAL AND PHYSICAL LOSSES BROUGHT BY DIVORCE

In-laws who feel ambiguity about whether a member is *in* or *out* of the family may make this their primary focus, rather than dealing with feelings of loss and considering how the absence of the in-law will affect the family. Boss and Thorne (1989) calls this uncertainty about the status of a family member *boundary ambiguity*. According to Boss, getting stuck or focusing on this boundary ambiguity can put the family in limbo and stop everybody from dealing with the loss.

One father-in-law put it this way: "Our son-in-law, John, was abusive to our daughter, so it was a happy day for the family when Carolyn left him. We felt that it was a chance for her to begin a new life, and for us a chance to get the bum out of the family. But then lo, and behold, only two months later, he's back in our life again. It's a matter of energy for me. It'll take a lot of energy to mend this relationship and then how do I know John won't be out of the family again."

Where there have been bad feelings or an even more difficult relationship, the therapist might want to encourage the couple or in-laws to plan a structured ritual such as the *bury the hatchet* ritual. During couples therapy, John said that he thought he would like to bury the hatchet in his father-in-law's neck, but for the sake of the kids, he would try for reconciliation. I suggested that the idea of burying the grievances was not a bad one—although the placement of the hatchet could have the potential to land him in more trouble than his father-in-law was causing. Then, during family therapy, which included the in-laws, Carolyn suggested that her father and John "literally bury the hatchet."

Carolyn, her mother, and her mother-in-law were given the assignment of going to the hardware store and buying what they considered to be an appropriate hatchet to bury. John, his father, and his father-in-law were then given the assignment to select a site for the hatchet-burying ritual. At the next session, Carolyn, John, and the in-laws came together to plan the hatchet-burying activity. They decided they would have the ritual on a Sunday afternoon and that they would invite other close family members. Afterward, they decided they would get together and have a party. Carolyn's father (John's father-in-law) was chosen to be the emcee for the hatchet burying. As a therapist, I was invited to the ritual. Lest someone consider digging up the hatchet, I brought along a small rosebush to plant on top of the site as a symbol of forgiveness, beauty, and the growth of this in-law family during the therapeutic period.

The preceding ritual was fairly complicated. Less complicated activities may accomplish the same purpose of integrating in-laws back into the family or healing old wounds. Such activities as simply inviting an ex-in-law to dinner, a movie, or a family outing may be all that is needed for the family to give permission to the ex-in-law to be a part of the family system.

Permanent loss of a key in-law, whether through death or divorce, may be looked at in terms of replacement and coping. Some losses can be coped with by replacement—another family member closes up the summer cabin or mows the lawn. Finances may be dealt with by getting a second job or moving into an apartment. But other losses, such as the loss of trust, are more difficult to deal with. All relationships are unique, and the client may miss a good sense of humor or the opportunity to see the son- or daughter-in-law, father- or mother-in-law. Loss of in-laws is difficult, but only through clarifying and defining the loss can clients move on and develop new relationships. The *In-law Dream List,* discussed in Chapter 7, is very helpful for families dealing with the loss of an in-law through divorce. Sometimes, a client will feel loss even before he or she becomes an in-law.

> As a young woman, I was engaged to Ruben and was very attached to his family. I well remember after we broke off the engagement, sitting in the living room with Ruben's parents and having his mother tell me that they were very sad about the broken engagement as they felt I would have been a wonderful daughter in-law. I never saw my potential in-laws again, but will always have fond memories of them based on my being a short-term member of their family.— Valentine, 27, graphic designer

It may be difficult for family members to understand that the ending of a relationship is a loss. The parties may be physically but not emotionally present during occasions of contact. As is often the case where children are involved, ex-spouses may be attending school activities together with in-laws, or they may be involved in exchanges of the children for visitation.

> I had one brother-in-law who was very nice. He coached me in football, and he gave me his football jerseys—he was like a brother I never had. Then my sister divorced him, so I was very sad because he was very popular within the family. He was well-liked by all the grandmothers and aunts and cousins and my mother, and so my sister faced a lot of pressure to try to make the marriage work. But he was a very violent person and so it was probably best that they were separated and divorced. I think they made multiple attempts at counseling but decided it was just not reconcilable. He still goes to all of his children's athletic events. So

my family inevitably sees him and it's very cordial. In fact, my wife and I saw him at a basketball game a year ago and he was very nice. When you lose an in-law through divorce or something like that and you liked that person or you enjoyed just spending time with them, it's kind of like losing a family member, because you can't really control it and it's quite frustrating and it's quite sad.—Rory, 28, athletic trainer

COMBINING TWO FAMILIES—STEP-IN-LAWS

The situation between families can get downright dicey when two families decide to become one. Rather than having only two sets of in-laws to deal with, the number increases almost exponentially, especially when close ties remain with ex-in-laws.

I have only one natural grandchild, but due to divorces and remarriages of my two children, I now find myself with seven new "grandchildren," none of whom I feel close to. During the holidays, it's very hard to give gifts without feeling that I'm showing favoritism (which I truthfully feel) when I give my own granddaugher a truly thoughtful gift. In fact, I've had to become kind of sneaky, but I think it's important for her to know that she's special to me.— Grace, 68, librarian

There is very little in the stepfamily literature about dealing with ex-in-laws. However, it is alluded to in the discussions of the grandparent roles because the grandparents are also ex-in-laws. Visher and Visher (1982) state that even if an adult child's parents have accepted the divorce, there is another psychological blow when the child tells them that he or she is planning to remarry. The remarriage will further change the relationship with the grandchildren. Visher and Visher state that parents are not only asked to adjust to the status of a new son- or daughter-in-law, but may also face diminished contact with grandchildren, and the new in-laws will likely have the same problem. The problem will be even greater, with less contact with the grandchildren, for the parents of the adult child who does not have physical custody of their grandchildren.

When working with stepfamily-in-law issues, it is helpful to use Tuckman's (1965) small-group process paradigm: forming, storming, norming, and conforming. (See also Tuckman & Jensen, 1977; this paradigm is discussed at length in Chapter 2.) The forming process will be very important for integration of the ex-in-laws and the new in-laws into the stepfamily. Just letting people know something about each other will be a large and long-term task. Who is who, where each person fits into the family, and what opportunities will allow introduction of in-laws and ex-in-laws to one another will be an important part of successfully moving into the next stage. The therapist might suggest that clients try to go very slowly through every stage—particularly the forming stage, where people need a long, easy time to get to know one another. At this point, the idea of shared family history may come in. Stories and jokes will have to be explained, along with the different nuances that are particular to the family history.

In the storming stage, breaking into the subsystems may be difficult for new in-laws. There may be cultural differences between families that will be recognized and will cause a certain amount of friction during the storming stage. In the early stages of forming, the stepfamily-in-laws will probably do no better than the couple. If the couple are experiencing storming regarding their in-laws, then the in-laws will probably not be able to get involved in creating a relationship. The newly formed couple may have to back off from in-laws until they are able to stabilize their own immediate family, particularly if they have children, who must be integrated into their new stepfamily system.

During the next stage, norming, relationships begin to settle in; all parties begin to figure out how they fit together and to learn what the new couple and stepfamily will require of them. Extended families can become very confused about their roles, but if their roles are explained, they can often run with them. It is important for couples to instruct in-laws on their expectations that in-laws can be integrated into the family.

In the last stage, conforming, there will be acceptance and peaceful coexistence for those in-laws who have been integrated into the step-in-law system. Support for the new family emerges as the in-laws help the two family cultures to blend. Some of the special issues that might come up in the in-law relationship with blended families are those that we've already explored: holidays, compromises, give-and-take, support for noncustodial in-laws, stepparenting, and parenting roles.

With a large stepfamily network, it is virtually impossible for the therapist to see the whole system in single settings. The therapist may want to break families that have in-law stepfamily problems into subsystems and subcompartments. Even though the therapist will not see all of the family all of the time, which is some therapists' preference, seeing subsystems of stepfamilies and their in-laws and ex-in-laws can be very powerful. These subsystems can find it supportive if they are able to see the stepfamily as a new family and to work in that family to develop healthy relationships.

SUPPORT FOR DIVORCING IN-LAWS

It is important for in-laws to support the divorcing couple, especially if there are children involved. Despite the divorce, ex-in-laws will often be involved in coparenting as long as there are underage children in the family (Ahrons,

1994). Peaceful coexistence, or at least a moratorium on conflicts in in-law relationships, is recommended for the good of the children and of the divorced couple who must go through the grieving process for their failed marriage. As well as having their own feelings regarding the break-up of the marriage acknowledged, in-laws can be a caring, supportive resource to an entire family shaken by divorce.

WORKSHEET

Sorting Out Trouble Areas for In-Laws and Families

The therapist may want to discuss the following questions with clients, or to use these as a starting point for a more in-depth look at problem areas.

1. What does your kinship reorganization look like after divorce?
    a. Contraction of the kinship network—formal and distant relationships toward in-laws
    b. Replacement of the in-law through remarriage
    c. Retention of the in-law through in-law coalitions
    d. Expulsion of in-laws
2. How would you like your in-law kinship network to look?
3. How would including an ex-in-law as part of the extended family affect the in-laws' loyalty to their own child?
4. When grandchildren are involved, have visitation expectations been delineated?
5. If you have difficult in-laws, have you looked at how you fit into the equation?
6. Have you taken steps to help resolve in-law issues or to neutralize their negative effects?

CHAPTER 10

Cultural Diversity and the In-Law Relationship

WHEN CULTURAL OR ETHNIC BONDS STRAIN FAMILY LOYALTY

When treating clients or families who desire to explore in-law relationships or problems, the therapist needs to be sensitive to diversity in ethnic and cultural backgrounds. In their work on ethnicity and families, McGoldrick, Pearce, and Giordano (1982) have found that the greater the differences in culture, the more difficulty couples experience in their marriages. It is not uncommon for clinicians to find that tension in the relationship is embedded in the cultural differences of the in-law family. As mentioned in Chapters 2 and 4, cultural or ethnic difficulties can put an enormous strain on family loyalty. This is especially apparent when issues regarding child raising are not resolved before a child enters the family. When this happens, in-law problems are exacerbated.

Therapists might want to consider ethnic differences when working with or thinking in terms of multigenerational family in-law systems. When there is conflict around cultural issues, McGoldrick (1982) suggests that the therapist might be seen as a *culture broker,* helping families to recognize their own ethnic values. Working in this role, McGoldrick reports positive shifts in couples' responses when the problem is put into the ethnic context, rather than seen as a personal attack. In my experience, there is often a great deal of unspoken tension around cultural and ethnic in-law issues, especially in bi-racial or cross-cultural unions. Diversity may have a subtle or a striking impact on how the clients view this in-law relationship. An example of this is seen in the experiences of Tony, who is White and is married to Shu Yen, a Chinese American. They came to therapy to resolve some cross-cultural in-law difficulties that were threatening their marriage.

According to Tony, the problems with the in-laws, who speak very little English, began before the couple was even engaged. When Tony told them he wanted to marry their daughter, they said he couldn't, because her father was 51 years old, which apparently was a bad luck year. The father asked Tony and Shu Yen to wait until he was 52, to avoid any bad luck. The next year, at the father's birthday, he said, "Oh, I'm 50 years old, I'm going to be 51 this year." Tony told him that they would not wait another year. Shu Yen's parents said they would not go to the Presbyterian church wedding, so the couple decided to also have a Chinese wedding and had two ceremonies. About 200 people showed up for the Chinese celebration, and they all brought money gifts—all cash. According to Tony, there was a surplus of $4,000, above and beyond the wedding expenses, and as Tony understood it, Chinese tradition was that this money usually was given to the new couple; however, his father-in-law kept it. In a couples therapy session, Tony said, "For some reason, at the time it didn't bother me, but it's starting to bother me now that I know more about the culture."

Tony talked about how angry he was at his mother-in-law, because she didn't come when Shu Yen's baby was born, and yet she had taken care of her son's two children. I asked if I was correct in thinking that, in China, when a girl marries she goes with her husband's family. Shu Yen affirmed that this was the case. I then asked Tony what his mother was doing to help with the baby. He became very defensive and said she was helping out as much as she could. I asked Shu Yen if there might be a cultural issue in the blending of the American and Chinese cultures. Indeed, this was the case. Shu Yen said that she and her parents felt that Tony's parents would lose face if her family gave more help than his family.

At our next couples session, Tony said that Shu Yen's parents had presented them with a new problem. In Shu Yen's family, it was a tradition to put little bracelets with bells on the newborn baby's legs or arms to ward off the bad spirits. Tony said, "I don't want to alienate my wife from her family by getting them upset, but I don't want these bracelets on my child." Tony and Shu Yen were in a bind and felt that resolution was impossible. Tony felt that a choice between the Chinese and the American culture had to be made for his newborn daughter. I suggested that, rather than make a choice, the couple could take the best from the two cultures, and then celebrate both of their traditions. Their daughter could be the bridge connecting Tony and Shu Yen with their in-laws.

With regard to wearing the bracelets to ward off evil spirits, I suggested that Tony might want to accumulate *goodwill points* with his father-in-law. Rather than try to take stands on small issues and prove to his in-laws that he was in control of his new family, he might want to give in on the small points, such as having the child wear the bracelets, which would be symbolic of his willingness to be amiable toward his father-in-law.

To further gain goodwill points, Tony would state that although it is not his belief that bracelets ward off evil spirits, he would allow the child to wear the bracelets, with his best wishes, because it was important to his father-in-law, his wife, and the goodwill of the family. I suggested that Tony might establish a pattern of announcing to his in-laws these goodwill points on the little issues, which would illustrate to them his ability to compromise and thereby allow him to take a stand on the larger issues.

It has been two years since I last saw the couple. However, I recently spoke to Tony and he said things are going well with his in-laws and he has collected many goodwill points.

As with Tony and Shu Yen, it is important for parents-in-law and children-in-law to consciously choose the issues they will take a stand on. Taking a firm stand on every issue labels a person as hard-headed, stubborn, and inflexible. It might satisfy one's ego to never budge, but, in the long run, the in-law who has the need to make a show of power only hurts those he or she most loves.

The Therapist's Cultural Bias

Regardless of their philosophy of therapy, therapists treating the individual or the family will bring their own cultural and ethnic biases to the therapy, and must recognize these biases in order to respect the cultures of the people with whom they work. We often hear clients and therapists state that, although they grew up in a culture or religion, they abandoned it when they became adults. It is still worth the effort to explore these backgrounds, because cultural issues run deep. As therapists, we cannot possibly have a total understanding of each culture's attitudes toward in-laws or in-law therapy; however, we can be curious and discover more about our clients' personal in-law histories.

Although an in-depth exploration of ethnicity and cultural diversity is obviously not within the scope of this book, I believe it is important for therapists to be aware of how different cultures may relate in the in-law system. To get some ideas about the differences brought by cultural diversity, attitudes of a few individuals were sought regarding their culture's views of in-law issues. The individuals interviewed are married to (or are) Hispanics, African Americans, and people from the Pacific Rim. Each was asked about permission to marry, in-law relationships, cultural views of in-laws, financial and emotional support, divorce, and grandchildren. The specific question–answer units appear later in this chapter. They represent just a sampling of the many questions possible, and I have not attempted to address the numerous in-law issues or the vast ethnic diversity present in the United States. Additionally, variables such as religion, social class, birthplace, and generation in the United States are not considered. As Martinez (1988) points out, there is a range between traditional and nontraditional cultural practices, and we should thus be careful not to stereotype. It is my hope that these brief interviews will be of interest and will make the point that although the United States is a melting pot, traditions change slowly and are deeply held.

AN OVERVIEW OF MULTICULTURAL ASPECTS OF THE IN-LAW RELATIONSHIP

To appreciate an individual's concerns, it is helpful for the therapist to understand the social and environmental milieu from which the client comes. This section gives a brief overview of each of the cultures covered in this chapter, with special focus on the peculiarities, within each culture, of the roles of in-laws in the extended family relationship. Following these general overviews are the responses from those interviewed.

Hispanics

With close to 6.5 million Hispanics in the United States, this group represents the second largest minority group, after African Americans. Hispanics have a higher birth rate than Anglo-American families (Falicov & Karrer, 1980), and the Roman Catholic church exerts an important influence. Martinez (1988) finds it likely that, among those of Mexican descent, many people will continue to maintain their own language and culture because of the close proximity of Mexico and the United States. However, he points out that the therapist should be aware that the Mexican people vary greatly in their degree of acculturation.

In traditional Hispanic families, the husband is the sole provider and the wife generally takes on the expressive role as homemaker and caretaker. There is a defined age hierarchy in the family, even among siblings, with the older siblings bearing more responsibilities. Godparents are an important part of the Hispanic family support system, and in-laws often fulfill this role. There has been a past history of residence in the patriarchal home, with the daughter-in-law moving in with the husband's family after marriage. The daughter-in-law takes on the same obligations as the birth daughter—she does domestic chores under the supervision of her mother-in-law. Falicov and Karrer (1980) state that this custom is the cause of marital conflict in current Hispanic families because many young women will not tolerate the role.

There is a good deal of in-law interaction in traditional Hispanic families because the extended family is very important. There is a prolonged parenthood cycle, with families living with or in the vicinity of one another. Quarrels and resentments are common among in-laws as well as siblings; however, Falicov and Karrer (1980) say these conflicts are seldom permanent, because life-cycle issues such as birth and death bring the siblings back together. It has been my experience that in-laws as well as biological kin are often brought into these resentments and quarrels.

Asian Americans

The Asian American family, impacted by Buddhism and Confucianism, stresses the good of the group (family) over that of the individual. As with Catholicism, there are age-specific hierarchical roles. The rules of behavior are formalized and the breaking of those rules reflects not only on the individuals but on the kinship they represent. In the traditional family, male offspring are more valued, and the roles of males and females are quite different. Family history is important, and many Asian Americans practice ancestor worship and keep family records that go back for generations. In traditional families, the choice of mate is heavily influenced by the family. Even in the United States, many Asian American children continue to desire the blessing of their parents, because marriage impacts not only the individual but the man's family line (Shon & Ja, 1982).

African Americans

African Americans currently represent 12.4% of the population of the United States. Because many African American males are absent from the family, African American families have become primarily matriarchal units, with mothers and grandmothers taking care of the children. African American women have historically worked and are comfortable with the role. Religion has played a strong role among African Americans and continues to be a force in many families. Where an African American father resides in the home, he is seen as the head of the household. Lack of skills and education has caused many African American males difficulty in making a living (Baker, 1988). Because of the drastically lower life expectancy of African American males, females outnumber the men; according to Hines and Boyd-Franklin (1982), the ratio is an astounding 44 to 1 in some geographical areas. The African American family tree can be extremely complicated because family boundaries are highly blurred. Children are often sent to live with extended family members or friends. Paternal and sometimes maternal identity is not always clear. Because of poverty and crime in African American communities, the welfare and legal systems often impinge on the African American families. A lack of role models to encourage youth to set academic or employment goals can result in escape into alcoholism and drug addiction. These outlets represent a large factor in the breakdown of African American families and contribute to the high percentage of African American males who are incarcerated. At the present time, 57% of African American children are born to young, poor, unwed mothers.

Southeast Asians

Many Southeast Asians have moved to the United States in the past 20 years in order to better their lives (Mollica & Lavelle, 1988). They live in densely populated "pockets" that are identified with their country people throughout the United States. Factions of families move to the United States, combine finances, and start small businesses. They then sponsor other friends, relatives, and in-laws to come to the United States (Besher, 1991). These cross-generational families living under the same roof present many in-law conflicts. If relatives remain in their home countries, they often expect to receive money from the United States on a regular basis. In the Thai culture (as well as many other Southeast Asian countries), women are given a lower status than men. Men are the heads of household, and women do the majority of the work. Once these families make a transition to the American lifestyle, many intergenerational in-law issues come forward. Children are greatly valued; however, in Southeast Asia there is a high infant mortality rate. In the Asian countryside, farming and agriculture are the primary industries, and the people are accustomed to a very simple life. Thais value control over emotions, and they stress politeness and deference to individuals considered senior to oneself (Piprell, 1991). Anger is not a welcome emotion, and people value a smile. Thais are very sensitive to criticism and do not appreciate those who find fault with their family or their country.

Tongans

There are approximately 10,500 Tongans in the United States and almost one million Pacific Islanders, who come from Samoa, Fiji, Tahiti, and other Polynesian countries. The Pacific Islander culture is represented in pockets throughout the country, but appears primarily in the Western states. Although each country has its own unique personality, the Tongans' experience in the United States is illustrative of Pacific Islander in-law relationships. The Tongan American people (Tongans) maintain their warm, relaxed lifestyle, and Tongan women have always had a more comfortable existence than anywhere else in Polynesia. Tongan Americans are devoutly religious and put a lot of focus on their children and the extended family. Age hierarchies play an important role, with the older members commanding more respect. Once in America, families tend to stay in close proximity, as they do in Tonga. Tongans have a long traditional history, according to Stanley (1993), and many can name up to 39 generations by heart. To a Tongan, great physical size is a measure of beauty, and Tongans are known throughout the world for their heft. To capitalize on this endowment, many Tongans work in jobs where physical strength and endurance are assets—construction, warehousing, and care giving. Unfortunately, these jobs tend to be at the low end of the income scale; hence, the Tongan experience in America frequently involves a lower-middle-class lifestyle. Because they tend to focus on relationships and family rather than material goods, the Tongan Americans I have met seem satisfied with their lifestyles.

A FOCUS ON IN-LAW ISSUES

To focus on the in-law issues that are affected by cultural diversity, members of the ethnic groups mentioned above were interviewed. A variety of topics related to the in-law relationship were covered, and excerpts from the responses are organized topically. The relevant questions appear in the text prior to the answers. As mentioned earlier, these viewpoints represent only those of the individuals interviewed and are not meant to characterize an entire ethnic group. The insights are valuable, however, in giving an inside look at how individual members of these groups view their extended family relationships. Before we move ahead with the questions, here are brief profiles of the ethnic or cultural representatives who agreed to share their in-law experiences.

Hispanic Profile

Rosa, a 35-year-old Hispanic accountant, is married to Max, a 39-year-old White engineer. Both are college graduates and they have no children. Both Max and Rosa were born in the United States. Rosa's parents immigrated to the United States in the 1940s.

Asian American Profiles

Sue is a 33-year-old first-generation Chinese American. Her parents came from Hong Kong in the mid-1960s. Sue, her parents, her husband Steve, and his parents are all of Chinese descent. Sue's parents are divorced. She is a computer programmer, and Steve manages business properties. They have been married for one year and have no children.

Gregory is a 25-year-old Chinese American born in Hong Kong. He has two children, a son and a daughter, and works in an auto body repair shop. His wife is also Chinese American and was born in the United States.

African American Profiles

Roger is a 32-year-old African American college graduate who works for the police department. He has twins, a boy and a girl, age 12. Roger was in a relationship with the twins' mother, Dena, for 10 years, but he left the relationship several years ago.

Lucy is a 60-year-old African American housekeeper. She is a divorced mother of one and has one grandchild.

Pacific Islander Profile

Tupou is a 60-year-old Tongan man, the father of four children by his first Tongan wife. He is currently married to Rita, who is White and American-born. They have been married for 18 years and have no children. They have a home in Tonga but claim California as their primary residence.

Profile of In-Law Relationship with Japanese National

Nelda is a 65-year-old White woman whose daughter recently married a Japanese national in Japan. Nelda's first husband is deceased and she is married to Leo, a White stockbroker.

Profile of In-Law Relationship with Southeast Asian

Dave, a 28-year-old White ski instructor, is married to Kim, a 26-year-old Thai woman. They have one child and live in the Midwest.

PERMISSION TO MARRY

Whether clients needed or received formal or informal permission to marry from their parents can tell the therapist a good deal about the family (see Chapter 3). This information can also reflect how much cultural power still exists in cultures that have a past history of arranged marriage, such as the Chinese and Tongan. Permission to marry can also be a powerful issue in cross-cultural marriages.

Question: In your culture, do you need permission from your parents to get married?

Rosa (Hispanic): *My father started talking to us about marriage when we were very young. He used to say when we were dating that we should look closely at the family because we weren't just marrying the man, we were marrying the family. When we were teenagers, he wasn't terribly thrilled about the prospect of us dating Anglos. I'll put it bluntly. He was afraid that we wouldn't be* *accepted by the Anglo family. So he thought it would save a lot of heartache if we just avoided a union with cultural differences. I appreciate what he said now, because my sister also married an Anglo and she does not get along with her father-in-law. He likes to tell others about her "humble beginnings," because he thinks all Hispanics are poor people living in some barrio.*

I left home at 17 for college and never really went back. I think my brothers-in-law asked permission of my father to marry my sisters, but I had been living with Max for several years, which made it even worse. We just announced that we were going to get married. Actually, Max asked if we should ask my father's permission, but at that point, it seemed a bit silly. I think my folks were glad we were getting married, as my mother is very Catholic and I think it was just in her faith that she thought I was going to go to hell, plain and simple.

Sue (Chinese American):   *In my family, I didn't need to have my parents' permission to get married. My parents are divorced and as the oldest child at home, I was the head of the house. But I know most of my friends had a pretty tough time in getting approval from both sides of the family. Their parents make a big deal about how many banquet tables the bride's side is going to get and how many tables the groom's side is going to get. Typically, the groom asks for permission to marry from the bride's parents, and in doing so he has to bring gifts. In essence, he is buying his bride by bringing pieces of jewelry or something that belongs to his side of the family. Nowadays, it's whatever the family can afford. I know for the engagement, they typically want at least a full-sized roasted pig, and wedding cookies to pass out, and you have a little buffet dinner for the bride's side of the family. My mom was really thrilled that after her two sons married Caucasians, I actually ended up with an Asian, and a Chinese to boot. She does, however, wish that her son-in-law could speak Chinese, as she speaks little English.*

Gregory (Chinese American):   *My wife was pregnant when we got married and when I asked my mother-in-law if it was OK to get married she said yes, but then she made me do all the work, like I was obligated to her because my father is dead and my mother couldn't afford to pay for the wedding. I had to remodel the whole house and do all the wedding plans. Everything had to be my mother-in-law's way.*

Roger (African American):   *We were never married so, of course, we didn't ask for permission. We met in college and just started living together. We lived together for 10 years and then separated. The kids and Dena are now back living at her mother's.*

Lucy (African American):   *I was raised in South Carolina and as far back as I can remember in my family, you always had to get permission to marry. The families had to know. They would investigate one another to see about their health problems and about their religious beliefs. The person you were going to marry had to be a member of a church. Usually the Baptists wanted their children to marry Baptists, or Methodists other Methodists. But mainly they insisted that you marry someone who belonged to a church.*

Tupou (Tongan):   *In the olden times in Tonga, all marriages were arranged. It is the current custom for the couple to go to their parents and their future in-laws and ask them for permission to get married. If the family says no, the couple will usually run off and get married anyway, and then they will apologize to their in-laws by giving a big feast for their families. At that point, the in-laws almost always agree to accept the marriage. My first wife was Tongan and we ran away and married, as many Tongan couples did. We didn't tell her parents. After we got married, I took my wife back to her parents, and they cried and cried and everything became good with the family. After the marriage, we made a big feast with a baked pig and took it back to our in-laws. We also took gifts to the in-laws, to show them that we still cared about them.*

Nelda (White, with a daughter married to a Japanese national):   *My daughter and son-in-law didn't need permission, but they asked for it. When they came back to the United States, Hiro stayed up all night and prepared the remarks he was going to give to me. He made a point of being with me because I'm Elsa's mother and her father isn't living, and he asked me if I would agree to the marriage. I kind of knew that's what was up but it was very formal. He said he thought I would be worried about her living in a foreign country and he wanted to assure me that his family would be good to her and that they wanted to have babies. It was a very sweet conversation.*

Dave (White, married to a Thai national):   *We were living in Thailand at the time, and I had to ask Kim's parents for permission, and I also had to give them sort of a dowry. I had to buy a water buffalo for the family and some chickens. That's generally the practice in their culture, the new son-in-law would give them some new things, like horses and things for the family. The water buffalo cost me about 1500 baht, about US $100, not even that. It wasn't a whole lot. My uncle-in-law helped me pick it out and helped me bargain for the price. At that time I spoke very little Lao or Thai, so that made it kind of strange. We had to drive way out near the mountains where people were selling their buffalo. When I told my parents about the coming wedding, it was pretty wild. They were in shock at first. They said, "Are you sure this is the right woman?" But they were very accepting and they went over to Thailand to meet her and they just fell in love with her. My whole family visited, and they were pretty hesitant at first. I could see that they were at first standoffish, but they've really taken to her and I can tell that they love her and they get along very well.*

IN-LAW RELATIONSHIPS AND CULTURAL DIFFERENCES

It is of interest to discuss with clients the relationships with in-laws within the family, as well as how they perceive their culture as opposed to the predominant culture. Determining whether the culture has a special name for their in-laws can shed light on the importance of the in-law relationships.

Question: How do you relate with your in-laws? Do you have a special name for in-laws? How do you think your culture differs from other cultures in relationship to in-laws?

Rosa (Hispanic):   *In my culture, in-laws are very close in terms of the circle, and relationships through marriage and through blood are very tight. You do things for those people. We were around our cousins but we never had friends over to the house.*

When I talk about my in-laws to other people, I refer to them by their first names. When I'm with them, I'm not consistent. I call them mom and pop sometimes, and sometimes I don't call them anything because they never came out and said, "Well, you just call me this." Mexicans call their in-laws comadre and compadre. It's a sign of respect.

My mother does not get along well with my father's family. Even though they're both culturally Mexican, my mother's family comes from Central Mexico, which has a colonial history. Her family is very light-skinned, so you have that whole light-skin, dark-skin thing operating. My father's family is very dark and is Yucca Indian. They were vacarros, cowboys, and very Wild West. My mother's family, on the other hand, is very cultured. And so you get this clash of class and education. My mother is very proper society and my father's family is anything but. So my mother always looked down on her in-laws.

Sue (Chinese American):   *In the old culture, the husband's siblings could boss the new wife around, but Steve's family has been here for three generations and they are totally Americanized. Steve has five brothers and sisters. They have been really good to me and we play with their kids all the time and see them a couple of times a month.*

My mother doesn't really speak English well and is one of those old-fashioned types. My oldest brother was supposed to take on responsibility for her but he has moved to Florida so, as the second-oldest child, I feel responsible. I have told Steve that if anything happens to my mother, she will have to move in with us. I know that it won't be great for him to have his mother-in-law live with us, but he realizes the Chinese sense of duty. I spend most of my time with my in-laws. They are a pretty close-knit family. I think my mother understands, as she is old-world and it is traditional for the wife to go with the husband's family.

Gregory (Chinese American):   *In the beginning, I got along well with my in-laws, but now because I live with them I'm kind of sick of them, especially my mother-in-law. In China, the wife typically goes to the husband's family after marriage, but my in-laws have a bigger house and we need to save up money to buy our own place.*

I think that my in-laws may be disappointed that their son-in-law, and not their own son, is living with them. One cultural difference from the Caucasian culture is that we all speak Chinese at home. My wife and I feel it important for our children to retain their cultural heritage. My mother speaks almost no English so I have always had to speak Chinese. We will try to encourage our children to go to both Chinese and American schools.

Roger (African American): *I have always looked upon Dena's mother as my mother-in-law. Dena's parents were separated when she was young. My parents are dead. I think it is a must for the kids to connect with Dena's family. Dena and I did create two beautiful kids and I am proud of them, as well as of her. She has a large family that is very close-knit, and basically, I consider them my in-laws because they're part of the tree, they're part of the kids. I address all of my in-laws by their personal names. I try to have good relationships with my in-laws because their daughter and I don't always agree on dealing with the kids and we have to meet someplace midway. Dena's and my way of looking at things are a bit different, and her mother and father often have input.*

Dena's mother appreciates that I am involved, especially because in many Black families the father is not around, unfortunately, to give his kids the support and strength they need.

Lucy (African American): *From the time I was 10 years old, I lived in a Jewish household where my mother was a housekeeper. I remember Jewish people wanting their sons and daughters to marry other Jewish people. If you married a non-Jew, you were really given a hard time, and basically this is the same type of thing that I saw with African Americans. In my family, if you marry out of your religion, it's just like marrying out of your race. And sometimes it would be really horrible the way you were treated by the in-laws.*

My father-in-law accepted me as a daughter and I was spoiled. My mother-in-law and my father-in-law gave me a lot of support because they knew their son was an alcoholic and it was a hard life for me. My father-in-law built a home for me, and he wanted to make everything convenient for me. He was from Virginia and they washed clothes on the washboard and carried water. When I got married, he made sure I had a washing machine. He wanted to make sure that I had all of the conveniences to make things easier for me. I felt very honored and I missed him when he died.

Tupou (Tongan): *In Tonga, the father-in-law is head of the family. The best food in the home is for the father and he sits at the head of the table. The main difference between the Tongan culture and the Caucasian culture is that we have great honor and respect not only for our in-laws but also for any older people. We look after our own. In Tonga, there are no nursing homes—people are taken care of in our homes. My island is so small that we all knew each other. I knew my in-laws before I got married. The people in Tonga are very loving. Just to give you an example of how they treat in-laws, my current wife's mother died when we were in Tonga and the community had a fi bong bong for her. That is a big memorial service. They didn't even know my mother-in-law, who was Caucasian and lived in California. The family prepared a big feast, and everyone brought cakes, sugar cane, and special dishes such as lamb curry. The in-laws came early to our house, cleaned the property, put up an awning and then all of the in-laws came to help her grieve. The women in the family sat in a circle with her and drank Kava, our national drink, and mourned the death of my wife's mother.*

In Tonga we call our mothers-in-law Fae'ahoku mali, *or mother of my wife. It is communal living, and often the in-law women will get together and do community projects such as weave the mats. Women are highly respected and are turned to for advice in times of trouble.*

Nelda (White, a daughter married to a Japanese national):   *Hiro's family is very traditional. We understood that they liked Elsa but they didn't like Americans. They thought it was high time for him to get married to her, but we were full of trepidation about going to Japan and being a guest in their home. We weren't sure whether they had some knowledge of English, but it turns out they're very traditional, very nice. Hiro calls me by my first name, Nelda. His father at one point suggested that Elsa call him Hiro-san, which is deferential to him, and she wouldn't do that and it was fine with him. The tradition in Japan is for the bride to move in with the husband's family. But, because her in-laws are in their 80s now, they would prefer to go to a home, and the translation is the friendship home. The Japanese do expect the first son to take care of them. I think it's quite a formal code that they have. And here, who knows what goes these days?*

Dave (White, married to a Thai national):   *I get along best with my uncle-in-law. My mother-in-law is very Asian, very old-time Asian. Rarely smiles and is very serious, very hard working. To start off with, we had a language barrier that meant we could never carry on a conversation. When my wife translated, I didn't know if she was always telling her exactly what I was saying. But, with my uncle, there's a lot more friendship, and they want to do things with you, whereas women are still very subservient. Even my mother-in-law kind of bows to me and brings me food and drinks. And I just felt more comfortable with the males where I could be more myself and enjoy their company and they would enjoy my company more as well.*

In Thailand, I have five sisters-in-law and four younger brothers-in-law. I didn't have a really close relationship with them at all. They're mostly younger and very shy, very threatened by an American or Caucasian, so I never got really close to them, but I was able to hang out with the older male in-laws. I do have a sister-in-law in California. She speaks very little English and she's very straight-faced, very serious, hard working. But we have a fairly good relationship. It's not exciting and lively by any means. We don't have the extended conversations, but I can sense that she accepts me and I accept them, because I understand their culture. Now my sister-in-law and her husband are going to Thailand for a year and they want us to take care of their 14-year-old daughter. They thought we were just obliged to, because we're a family. I'm still kind of in shock and wondering if I can actually do this. They never really asked. They just said, "We're going and Joy is going to live with you; we need you to come to California and work out all the details." In Asia, a lot of times the in-laws will actually live together at a certain point. But family is a really strong tie in Asia. I still see a lot more respect for in-laws in Asia than I do here. A lot of times here, I hear people talking bad about their in-laws, and that just wouldn't go over well in Asia at all. A lot of times they live in the same house together. So it's a big difference.

IN-LAW FINANCIAL AND EMOTIONAL SUPPORT

On the surface, ethnic or cultural differences may seem to be the salient points, but when one probes deeper with members of minority groups, finances may often override cultural considerations or the ability to be connected to in-laws or their children. It becomes clear, when interviewing individuals regarding their culture, that economics have a strong influence in determining with whom people live, as well as whether they have contact with their in-laws or parents. An understanding of Maslow's hierarchy of needs (1954) is useful in the context of in-law relationships, because survival issues may override cultural issues. Maslow saw human needs in terms of a pyramid-shaped hierarchy, with the needs moving in an upward direction.

Maslow felt that the individual must first meet physiological needs for food and water, and only after meeting these rudimentary survival requirements could safety needs, social needs, esteem needs, and, lastly, self-actualization needs be considered, in that order. Maslow saw human life as being organized to satisfy all of the needs save one, self-actualization, which allows the individual to grow to unlimited potential.

Meeting the needs as identified by Maslow, as well as maintaining the ethnic identity of the group, are key issues for groups such as the Pacific Islanders, Hispanics, Asian Americans, and African Americans. How in-laws impact the couple, family, or individual may be directly related to the strength of the relevant need. Physiological and safety needs impact strongly on the in-law relationship. These needs translate directly into financial issues.

This point is seen in the interview with Gregory, an Asian American male who is living with his wife's family. Conflict is created between the mother-in-law and the son-in-law over the treatment of the son-in-law's male child. His nephew is treated better by his mother-in-law because he is *her blood*. In the African American interview, Roger states that African American males and paternal mothers-in-law do not maintain contact with their children, grandchildren, and quasi-daughters-in-law because they can't afford to or don't want to have to pay child support, and that grandmothers don't want to cut into their social security payments.

Williamson (1994) suggests that therapists need to work with clients in terms of a core political issue—the equalization of power between generations (p. 16). There is some question in my mind as to whether ethnic groups and families-in-law are at a point in their developmental cycles where therapists could impact them with a political agenda. To equalize power within ethnic groups whose members are often struggling just to make ends meet, one must do more than change the emotional system: one must also change the economic system. As my grandfather often said, "Money is power," which takes us to the next question.

Question: How does your culture stand on giving financial and emotional support to in-laws?

Rosa (Hispanic):   *Mexican families are often open to having in-laws live with them if they need help; however, regarding finances in my family, they don't have much to give and I would never ask.*

Sue (Chinese American):   *Actually, my in-laws are always supportive in whatever we want to do. They wanted to pay for our wedding, but I said no. They want to help us buy a home, and I also said no. In my family, I have always had to earn things. So I guess for me, since I have always had to earn everything, why should I be given things now, at this stage?*

Gregory (Chinese American):   *Financially, whatever I need I can get, and if my brother-in-law would ask me for money, it would be no problem. The in-laws are very helpful in wanting to see us get ahead. Emotionally, it is hard to live with my in-laws, and to be expected to call them Mom and Dad when they don't act very nice.*

Roger (African American):   *I think that finances are key. Unfortunately, everybody doesn't have the financial resources they need, and I think that is part of the problem. Lack of money can cause a lot of stress and depression in the Black community. I know personally as a father I feel a certain pride. My pride gets to me sometimes because I want to do more for the kids than I can afford. My ex-mother-in-law has been a great financial and emotional support, as she is a critical care nurse and she lets Dena and the twins live with her.*

Tupou (Tongan):   *In Tonga there is not a lot of money; we grow our own food and people usually build their own houses. There is always someone in the family who will give you a helping hand with your house or your planting, and the in-laws would welcome you to stay at their house. In the United States, we continue to help one another. For instance, if one of the family is working, another person, such as an aunt, grandmother, or sister-in-law, might take over the care of the children. In Tonga, every Sunday the in-laws and others will bring food to share; it is thought to be a great shame not to share and to eat by oneself. The problem is that there are not a lot of jobs in Tonga and that is why families get separated by coming to the United States to seek employment. Tongans try to pool their money and resources for big feasts and funerals.*

Nelda (White, a daughter married to a Japanese national):   *The only financial experience we've had with the in-laws was the wedding, and the groom's parents were extremely generous, for what I would call a modest household. His father was a railroad worker, I presume with a regular income. He's retired, but they gave the couple a $5,000 piece of furniture, which I think is quite extravagant. It was a dining room table, a Western one with chairs—it was kind of a gift to her culture. And then her father-in-law's mother gave them matching sideboards, cabinets, china cabinets, and they were also expensive.*

Dave (White, married to a Thai national): *My mother-in-law was very excited about our marriage because she basically expects us to support her family in some way. She expects a check from us—she told me she wants $1,000 every three months, which is a huge amount of money there. It's a really big amount of money. She does have a large family to support. My father-in-law is a* samur *(taxi) driver and some days he doesn't work at all. It's just a matter of if he feels up to it. She really expects a lot of financial support from us which, at this present moment, we can't do. But I have every intention of giving her some financial support in the future.*

SINGLE AND DIVORCED IN-LAWS

Divorce can bring out many questions and problems that families have never considered. Questions of where the ex-in-law will fit in after divorce may cause a knee-jerk response. Families will often divide along biological lines; thus, if there are children, they will be a bridge between the two families. If there are no children, the in-law will often be lost to the family. With the high number of divorces annually in the United States (16.7 million), most families can expect to deal with a divorce. We take for granted that divorce and divorced in-laws are treated in a uniform manner without cultural bias. The following question explored the interviewees' cultural attitudes toward never married and divorced in-laws.

Question: In your culture, if you are divorced or never married, how does this impact your relationship with your in-laws?

Rosa (Hispanic): *As far as divorce, things have changed. Years ago, divorce would not have been possible due to the Catholic church. Now the family would tolerate a divorced in-law. I got married at 28 and at that point I was considered an old maid by Mexican standards because most of my cousins had been married by the age of 20. If I had never married, there would have always been a place for me in the family circle.*

Gregory (Chinese American): *My brother has been divorced and he has a child. His wife still brings the child to my mother's house for baby-sitting and he is still part of the family. We don't dislike our ex-in-laws just because they got divorced and in fact, I may like my sister-in-law better than my own brother. My mother invites her for family events, but it is really more for the benefit of the child and the fact that he is blood.*

Tupou (Tongan): *One of the things I have noticed in the United States is that White people's way of divorce is to become friends with their ex-spouse. In our culture, when you divorce, there is a cut in the relationship with your spouse. You don't have anything to do with them. The mother- and father-in-law might stay involved with the grandchildren, but they would be embarrassed to stay at* *the ex-daughter-in-law's house. In Tonga, they are slow to give a divorce. If you ask for a divorce, they say to come back in three years. If there is a divorce, it would depend on why. If there was drinking or abuse of the spouse or children, we might not want that person around, because Tongans don't like bad words or fighting.*

Nelda (White, a daughter married to a Japanese national):   *I've thought about divorce, in terms of Elsa, because I worry about what would happen if they have a couple of children and then she just can't take the culture or doesn't feel part of it. If the marriage doesn't work out, for whatever reason my understanding is that men don't tend to divorce in Japan, and that a lot of women who are not Japanese have a hard time adjusting. I guess if they should divorce, Elsa would come back home.*

Dave (White, married to a Thai national):   *With divorce over there, it's very one-sided. It's over. There's no support. There's no alimony. Child support is nonexistent. The extended relationship doesn't continue.*

GRANDCHILDREN AS A CULTURAL IN-LAW FACTOR

Grandchildren are an important cultural factor in in-law relationships because they are the biological bond between the parents and their in-laws. They may also be a bridge between the new and the old culture. How they are raised and who raises them can be a source of joy as well as of anger and disagreement. There are often differences between the in-laws regarding timing or, indeed, whether to even have children. Parents-in-law may feel strongly about these issues; however, in most cases, they have no choice but to take a wait-and-see attitude. In cross-cultural marriages, the entrance of children into the family can cause prospective parents to consider their ethnic origins.

Question: In your culture, how do grandchildren impact the in-law relationship?

Rosa (Hispanic):   *I know that my mother-in-law would very much like to have a grandchild, while my own mother has many grandchildren and really doesn't care. Max has been ambivalent about it and I don't think we'll have children. I notice that as I get older, I become more Mexican; I didn't notice it before, but my father says that it comes with age. When I think about children, there's a part of me that flinches at the thought of having mixed children, and it's irrational.*

Gregory (Chinese American):   *Living with my mother-in-law has created some problems for my three-year-old son, as my mother-in-law treats her biological son's boy better than my son. It is the old Chinese thing of the first-born male being very important. Whenever my brother-in-law's son comes over, my mother-in-law shelters him and doesn't let anyone get near him. As* *a grandmother, she neglects her son's daughter as well as my son. This fa-voritism creates a lot of tension in the family.*

Lucy (African American):   *Due to drugs and teen pregnancy, maternal grandmothers in the African American community have had to take the bull by the horns and take over, and not only raise the grandchildren, but re-raise their own adult children. Children, like my daughter in her mid-30s, have moved back home and we are left to take care of everyone. My ex-son-in-law is a drug ad-dict and the child has little contact with either the father or the paternal grand-parents. When the parents are not married, it is even worse. The paternal grandmother will usually not want any involvement with her grandchildren or their mother. Some don't want anything to do with illegitimate children, as they have deeply rooted beliefs that you should be married before you have children, and others are concerned about having dependents cut into their Social Secu-rity—they don't want the responsibility. I was talking to my friend this morn-ing and she said that not only did she have responsibility for her grandchildren, now she has her great-grandchildren, and it is really sad.*

Nelda (White, a daughter married to a Japanese national):   *My daughter is expecting, and I think the addition of grandchildren will enhance my rela-tionship with my son-in-law immensely. He's very excited. He's so thrilled. They're positive they're having a boy.*

Dave (White, married to a Thai national):   *The second time we visited Thailand, there was a totally different feeling because we brought the grand-child. I felt more like part of the family. I think that having my son was a big part of that. My mother-in-law and the whole family really took to Kelsey, and had so much fun with him. Whenever she writes, the first thing she asks about is how Kelsey is doing. And so, I really think it brought us a little closer together and it was a totally different feeling the first time. In Thailand, they love chil-dren. They're a lot more physical with kids there, and they really love their children.*

MAXIMIZING OUR UNDERSTANDING OF IN-LAW CULTURAL DIVERSITY

Understanding the cultural background of in-laws is important in order to un-derstand their thinking on issues and to determine their expectations of how to be a good parent and in-law. The therapist might suggest that the children-in-law ask the parents-in-law about *their* in-laws. The stories they tell about their in-laws will give the children a very good idea of how the parents see in-law relationships.

Cultural issues have an important impact on in-law relationships, as demonstrated by the Asian American culture's concept of the group being more important than the individual. Although ethnic minorities may buy into the American dream, it is very clear from the interviews that the Asian Americans, Hispanics, and Pacific Islanders are proud and sensitive regarding their cultures and fear the loss of their heritage. As Rosa puts it, "We Mexicans are proud of our culture. It was so insulting to me as a Hispanic when President Bush referred to his 'little brown grandchild.'" Cultural differences must be considered when working with or thinking in terms of family in-law systems.

CHECKLIST

Multicultural Variables

Following are some of the questions that might be asked of clients when looking at in-law culture:

1. In your culture, do you need parental permission to get married?

2. How do you relate with your in-laws? Do you have a special name for in-laws?

3. How does your culture relate to sibling in-laws?

4. How do you think your culture differs from other cultures in relationship to in-laws?

5. How much contact do you have with your in-laws?

6. How does your culture stand on giving financial or emotional support?

7. In your culture, if you are divorced or never married, how does this impact your relationship with your former and your current in-laws?

8. How do grandchildren impact in-law relationships?

9. Would you consider your family traditional or nontraditional regarding cultural heritage?

CHAPTER 11

Financial and Legal Considerations
of the In-Law Relationship

Despite the impact that a marriage has on the husband and wife, as well as on those who make up the extended family of in-laws, attempts are seldom made to examine the critical financial and legal considerations on which the marriage relationship is based. Because clients often look to their therapists for general advice about living, in addition to counseling on therapeutic issues, these legal and financial issues often surface. Although not regarded as traditional *family therapy territory,* this chapter provides an overview of some of the financial and legal factors that therapists are often called on to address with clients. The goal of this chapter is to provide therapists with an understanding of the potential impact of financial and legal matters on the husband and wife and the extended family of in-laws. Many suggestions are offered, but the therapist is advised to refer clients to the appropriate professionals for answers to specific legal or financial questions.

FINANCIAL CONSIDERATIONS FOR NEWLYWEDS

When does one become (or cease being) an in-law? Given the many different types of living arrangements, it is not unusual to hear a recently divorced or separated person state that he or she really misses the in-laws. Conversely, given the changing societal mores, it is not uncommon for couples who cohabit to have an in-law-like relationship with their partner's family prior to any legal in-law relationship.

Of all the contracts one enters into during a lifetime, the most significant is the marriage contract. Marriage has been defined as the joining together of two people in a legally binding and recognized contractual relationship. The partnership that is created by the marriage is far more complex and impacts more on the parties involved than any contractual relationship created in the business world. Nevertheless, most people consent to this legally binding contract with their eyes closed, oblivious to the host of potential problems that might have been avoided had they been addressed prior to saying "I do."

Sophisticated investors and businesspeople do not hesitate to ask for and to obtain complete information about all assets and liabilities of those with whom they consider becoming associated in business. It is difficult (if not impossible) for future in-laws to give similar caution to family members involved in romantic relationships. It is difficult to do something that may cool the growing ardor of the love affair. When a couple becomes romantically involved, they share a wish to be as desirable and pleasing to the other as possible, presenting to each other what Satir (1964) termed the *pseudo-self.* When it appears that a romance may lead to a marriage, it is very chilling to ask for an exchange of financial statements. Problems often develop following the marriage because false assumptions have been made by one or the other of the marriage partners. For example, if the bride-to-be has the impression that the groom-to-be is a wealthy financier, when in fact he is an impoverished sales clerk, problems are guaranteed to ensue when the truth is discovered. If the groom-to-be believes his future in-laws will welcome him into their company despite his prison record, he may be surprised.

If the couple can exchange financial information and the romance can withstand such truthful disclosure of financial standing, the marriage will have a far greater likelihood of success. This also applies, to a lesser degree, to the financial standing of the couple's parents, the future in-laws.

Prenuptial Agreements

One way of addressing (and often circumventing) many legal and financial problems is with a prenuptial agreement. Most people who have been married more than once or who have accumulated considerable assets insist on the execution of written prenuptial agreements (Kaslow, 1991). These agreements clearly document the understandings of the parties prior to the marriage and usually establish a positive agreement as to the division of assets in the event of the dissolution of the marriage. Normally, the parties to the agreement execute it after being advised by their respective legal counsel. Although these contracts clarify the positions and understandings of the husband and wife, they are not entirely foolproof.

Therapists encounter many brides- and grooms-to-be, especially those marrying for the first time, who feel that even the consideration of such an agreement indicates a lack of sincere love and trust, or that it would introduce the specter of divorce long before the marriage vows are taken. Nevertheless, many of the factors and considerations that are discussed in this chapter will normally be included in a well-drafted prenuptial agreement, and therapists who specialize in mediation may be a good referral source for working on prenuptial agreements. It is also wise to have a lawyer look over the documents before signing.

Meredith and Andrew came to couples therapy because, although they were in love and wanted to marry, Meredith's parents had advised her not to even consider a prenuptial agreement, despite the fact that Andrew had amassed considerable wealth and had had three prior wives. Meredith's father said she would be dooming the marriage to failure before it even had a chance, if they created such an agreement. Andrew was adamant in refusing to marry without one, primarily because he sought to protect his estate for his children from his earlier marriages. More immediately, he wanted to ensure that Meredith would understand not only the assets, but also the tremendous financial liabilities he had incurred in his many business dealings. Meredith felt that she was in a bind between taking her parents' advice or her future husband's. Andrew agreed to have his in-laws attend a session to explain his position. During the in-law session I worked with the family to help them separate the issues of romance and love (and the goal of creating a marriage that meant *until death do us part*) from the financial and legal entanglements that the prenuptial agreement would clarify. After much consideration, Meredith's parents assented to the agreement and the marriage took place. When I last inquired, the marriage was still going strong eight years later.

According to Kaslow (1991), legal prenuptial agreements are highly personal documents. These charts of the couple's future together can be creative and can build the marriage on a foundation of trust and honesty. However, if the parents-in-law are the instigators of the agreement, its terms can be divisive and can give a message that the marriage may not last. For example, Mr. and Mrs. Olsen spoke to their daughter's minister regarding their daughter's impending marriage. Because their daughter, Martha, was to receive a large inheritance from her parents, they felt that she should have a prenuptial agreement. Martha was against the idea; she felt that it was starting the marriage off on the wrong foot. The minister sided with Martha and said that if the Olsens were concerned that their son-in-law would inherit their money, they should consider putting the money in a living trust, with the income going to Martha and the principal being left to their future grandchildren upon Martha's death. He also advised them to stay out of their daughter's and new son-in-law's pocketbook.

Is a Premarital Background Investigation Warranted?

When a person applies for a position of responsibility or trust in governmental organizations, the candidate is required to successfully undergo a *security background investigation*. Such a requirement is designed to ensure that the candidate can be trusted with sensitive or important duties. The investigation discloses information about whether the person has a criminal record or has something in his or her past (or in that of a close relative) which would re-move him or her from consideration as a candidate. Few persons considering marriage (or their corresponding future in-laws) are likely to entertain the thought of such an investigation of a prospective marriage partner. However, many of the same types of questions should be asked—and answered—prior to the marriage. These might include the following: Have you ever been ar-rested? Have you been in the military? Were you honorably discharged? What was your service record? Have you been married before? Do you have any children? Have you ever been outside of the country? What were you doing? Have you ever been fired from a job? Why? Can I speak with a long-time contact who has known you all your life? What kind (and amount) of debts and/or assets have you accrued? Of course these questions have to be asked over time, and with great tact, especially if they are being asked by future parents-in-law.

It might seem overly suspicious or even ludicrous to ask some of the above questions, and clients might be warned that some people on the receiving end of the questions might feel they are being cross-examined. However, those who have nothing to hide will understand the need for disclosure of such in-formation and will usually answer with forthrightness and candor. Such dis-cussions should be reciprocal.

One of my clients, Alyssa, wishes she or her parents had asked such ques-tions prior to marrying Stuart. Swept away in the romance of marrying her longtime pen pal, Alyssa fell into an abusive relationship with Stuart, who, unbeknownst to her, had served two jail sentences and had left a string of wives across the country, some of whom he hadn't bothered to divorce. After two years and two children, Alyssa tried to find out why Stuart was away so much, because his job as a car mechanic clearly didn't warrant the frequent "business" trips. Her brother-in-law, who worked for the police, discovered that Stuart had resumed his husbandly duties 90 miles away, with a previous wife to whom he had not mentioned his present relationship. Alyssa was shat-tered, and realized that she had been duped. Stuart abruptly disappeared, but because of the community property laws, Alyssa found she was responsible for the substantial debts Stuart had brought to the marriage, and she was thus forced to declare bankruptcy. In therapy, we discussed the blind love that many people feel, and how it might explain their lack of inquisitiveness into the past of their spouses-to-be. Alyssa determined that any subsequent mar-riage partner she might later consider would be subject to a thorough investi-gation into his background by her entire family, including talking with her future in-laws.

Depending on the circumstances, the therapist may recommend a thorough professional background check by a private investigator. Such a check might probe not only the background of the intended spouse, but also that of the fu-ture in-law family.

Indebtedness and Money Management

Indebtedness and problems relating to money continue to form probably the single biggest cause of marital stress. Problems in this area can doom even the most promising relationships. Prior to entering into a marriage, the couple should be encouraged to frankly and truthfully discuss the indebtedness and assets of each party. Ideally, each party could prepare a complete and accurate listing of all indebtedness and a schedule of payments. The parties might wish to exchange signed copies of their listing and schedule, to eliminate unpleasant surprises as the two enter into their married life. Newlyweds who unexpectedly find themselves saddled with a heavy debt load may justifiably feel betrayed and may compound problems by being forced to turn to in-laws for a bail out. Neither spouse should assume that prior personal debts will be satisfied with the use of their common resources after marriage. Such assumptions often lead to misunderstandings and problems. It is far better for the couple to carefully examine the debts and to jointly develop a program for their payment, rather than let the debts become a cause of contention. Prior indebtedness can also impact the in-law relationship, especially if the parents-in-law are requested to help the newlyweds financially. Are the new parents-in-law expected to pick up the tab for their new son-in-law's student loans?

In today's mobile society, in-laws should mention the wisdom that both the husband and the wife establish their own lines of credit, so that in the event of the death of a spouse or the dissolution of the marriage, both parties will have established and preserved their own credit history. The husband and wife might be encouraged to reach an agreement or establish a cap for incurring new debts or new lines of credit during the marriage. Legally, both of the partners in a marriage are bound to pay the debts incurred during the marriage, so neither spouse should arbitrarily and unilaterally obligate the payment of debts without the prior concurrence of the other spouse.

After a couple has had an opportunity to examine and discuss their individual financial statements using responsible family members or professionals as sounding boards, they should reach an agreement, preferably in writing, regarding the sale or transfer of ownership of autos, homes, business interests, stocks, bonds, and other assets. Misunderstandings can arise regarding property owned by one or the other party prior to a marriage. If it is the intention of the owner to maintain sole and exclusive ownership of an asset, that fact needs to be clearly understood and agreed to prior to the marriage. This is particularly true when significant resources of the owner are to be devoted to preserving or securing an asset, such as the husband's cherished custom '67 Mustang that requires $700 a month in repairs and maintenance. Agreement in advance regarding all assets will decrease subsequent misunderstandings and strain.

A married couple may accumulate various amounts of joint property as the product of their individual employment rewards. In the absence of specific agreements regarding the management of these assets, erroneous assumptions may be made by either spouse. Parents and in-laws should encourage the couple to carefully discuss the management of jointly owned properties and reach an agreement regarding their disposition.

Therapists often see clients whose problem is that one or the other marriage partner has taken exclusive control of marital assets without consideration of the wishes of the other. This style is often a role model of in-laws' or parents' handling of money. Neither partner can, in wisdom, arbitrarily assume the prerogative of exclusive management and control of the other partner's solely owned property. The process of exchanging financial statements prior to marriage can open the door to discussions and agreements regarding the management of solely owned assets and of those generated during the marriage as a result of the joint work effort.

The couple might consider breaking the tradition of how the parents-in-law handled their resources, and setting their own norms, clearly stated (again, in writing), for who will manage the family cash flow, bill payments, savings, tax reporting, and similar matters. If clients have not had in-laws who shared financial responsibility, therapists can help clients understand that neither partner has exclusive right to control and allocate family resources.

Many marriages involve financial responsibility for the existing children of one or both of the parties. The couple might be encouraged to clearly reveal their existing obligations and to reach an agreement as to how those obligations will be met. Care must be exercised to ensure that obligations are not incurred that will bind the individual partners in the event of a dissolution of the marriage. Without such an agreement, a nonparent may be obligated to rear and support someone else's offspring.

Other questions arise: Who pays for my child's tuition? What about tax liens from a bankrupt company I previously owned? How do we handle support of my mother-in-law in the nursing home? Early discussion can prevent many problems.

INSURANCE ISSUES

The financial statements suggested above should indicate the existence (or absence) of insurance policies and the coverage they provide. Therapists and in-laws should encourage couples to discuss this matter with frankness and in detail, because the in-laws may be required to give support in the event of a death. If beneficiaries named before the marriage are to remain covered by insurance policies for which both parties are paying the premiums, the arrangement should have the agreement of both parties. If existing beneficiaries of insurance policies are to be changed in order to provide for the bride-to-be or husband-to-be, the couple should also reach a clear agreement on the timing of the change, the amount of the death benefit, and the schedule for payment of premiums. The extent of coverage and the deductible involved in insurance claims should also be clearly understood and agreed to. Instances where a husband or wife discovers that community income has been diverted to pay for insurance for the benefit of someone other than themselves cause severe strain on marital relationships. For example, Kent was extremely devoted to his widowed mother and had designated her as the sole beneficiary of his substantial insurance policy. After 22 years of marriage, when his mother died in a car accident, Kent realized that he needed to change his beneficiary designation. His wife Julianne was shocked and enraged to find that she had contributed for so many years to the potential financial comfort of her mother-in-law, while Julianne and her daughter had had no insurance protection. She justifiably felt betrayed.

Many couples starting out their married life foresee the need for insurance that will provide for the future financial needs of surviving spouses and offspring. For many families, the best means of accomplishing this security is to purchase the highest amount of *term* insurance coverage possible, at the lowest available rate, from a stable insuring company (Lynn, 1992). Without sounding like insurance salespersons, therapists and in-laws might encourage couples to plan to increase the amount until such time as they no longer need to provide for the financial security of survivors.

Lack of appropriate insurance coverage can put an enormous strain on the in-laws, who are often expected to assume the financial responsibility for the surviving family. This was the case with my clients, Melly and Ryan, who had planned to enjoy their retirement in Palm Springs on the golf course, until the unexpected death of their son-in-law, Paul. Apparently, the meager insurance policy Paul had obtained only barely covered the burial expenses and one month's rent. Rather than enjoying their well-deserved retirement years, Melly and Ryan opened their doors to their daughter Patrice and her three young children. Melly was stressed because she had already raised her own family and was now expected to baby-sit while Patrice worked. Although the couple was willing to help their own daughter, they continued to harbor resentment toward their deceased son-in-law for not adequately providing for his family, and this made for a very tense household. Therapy helped the two families reach agreement about realistic expectations and also brought to the open the guilt Patrice felt for being such a burden on her parents.

WILLS AND ESTATE PLANNING

One of the reasons for the growth and development of the laws relating to social relationships has been the need to resolve the rights of inheritance. Early courts of law looked with disfavor on those born outside the bounds of legally recognized wedlock. Such persons were generally not recognized as having the property rights or social privileges that a court was bound to honor and protect. It was generally felt that if a person was to have recognition "in the law," that person had to first have been given in-law status through the execution of a marital contract by his or her parents. Legislative bodies have codified and clarified many of the rulings of early courts. This combination of legislative action and court ruling has served as the basis for many of the legally recognized relationships we acknowledge today when we speak of *in-law relationships.*

Under early English law, in-law relationships had significant meaning. The father-in-law had jurisdiction regarding the welfare of his daughter-in-law, and, in some cases, also over his daughter's husband, the son-in-law. The oldest brother (who in most cases was the property holder) also had some clout as to the welfare of the brothers- and sisters-in-law. Today, the sense of being an in-law is not usually viewed as a formal legal connection, but as an informal affiliation. However, many financial and legal considerations must be addressed if one is to avoid the potential hazards that can occur as a result of assumptions and misunderstandings.

Without undue delay after a marriage, parents and in-laws might encourage the couple to make provision for the orderly transfer of their estates in the unhappy event of the demise of one or both of them (Lynn, 1992). The euphoria that exists following the marriage can lead the couple to overlook providing for the orderly settlement of their properties. It is generally advisable to seek legal counsel to assist in the making of wills. Family members have often been called on to settle the estates of a newlywed couple who died without making a will. A surviving spouse or family member should have the benefit of a clear expression of the wishes of the deceased persons.

Wills provide a means for the orderly transfer of assets upon the death of a person. The settlement of an estate by parents or in-laws can be time-consuming, costly, and frustrating. During the course of settlement, assets of the estate can be lost or dissipated. A means of avoiding this problem—and others related to the settlement—is for the individuals to execute and record *living trust agreements,* which permit them to transfer all or part of their holdings to a trust prior to their demise. This option permits them to supervise the settlement of their estates while they are still alive (Lynn, 1992). For many clients who are dealing with issues of grief and loss, the last thing they want to think about is the settlement of their loved one's estate. Living trusts enable people to, in essence, settle their own estates, thus making it easier for their surviving spouses, in-laws, children, and grandchildren.

WHEN AN IN-LAW BECOMES INCAPACITATED

The stresses of life are heavy for a husband, wife, or in-law who is confronted with handling the business affairs and providing for the care of a family member who is incapacitated by a physical or mental disability, or who has become incarcerated. The therapist might consider recommending that the couple discuss with an attorney the advisability of drafting legal documents that will empower each spouse (or other designated persons) to manage his or her affairs in the event of incapacitation. These documents can provide for the receipt and transfer of assets and can cover wishes regarding medical or other care, thus ensuring the orderly management of the invalid in-law's well-being. Some options an attorney might suggest include appointing a conservator or conservators in the event of incapacitation, drafting living wills, and creating agreements that designate durable power of attorney (Lynn, 1992). These documents can reflect the wishes of an incapacitated in-law regarding the receipt of prolonged medical treatment, efforts to sustain life beyond his or her wishes, and similar considerations.

One of my clients, Woody, was deliberating over putting together such agreements when he experienced a debilitating stroke that rendered him unable to perform his business or family responsibilities. Unfortunately, his produce business went down the drain because he had not appointed any line of succession or drawn up the necessary legal papers that would have allowed his wife or another designee to act on his behalf. Woody's son-in-law, who had worked his way up in the company, regrettably lost his stake when the business foundered. Had Woody made prior arrangements, the outcome would have been dramatically different.

In another situation, Holly and Anthony were unprepared when Anthony was convicted of tax evasion and sent to prison for three years. The in-laws were called upon to support the family while Holly tried to meet heavy legal expenses and to maintain their family business. Although people do not like to contemplate situations such as these, incarceration severely limits the power people have over their own affairs, and these issues should be addressed if the need arises.

GUARDIANSHIP OF CHILDREN

In-laws should strongly encourage married couples to make provisions for the guardianship of their children in the event of their deaths or incapacitation and to keep their desired guardians current. In the absence of such a provision, the decision regarding the guardianship of offspring is left to a court and often will not be in accord with the wishes of the incapacitated or deceased parents (Krause, 1986; Lynn, 1992). An attorney can assist a couple in drafting and executing appropriate documents. Care should be taken that the person(s) listed as guardian(s) is willing and able to accept and perform such a responsibility. This alone can save many in-law heartaches.

For example, when my client Peggy's daughter Lilly and son-in-law Pepper died in an airplane crash, leaving two young teenagers, Peggy assumed that, as the grandmother, she would raise the children. Unbeknownst to Peggy, at the beginning of their marriage, Lilly and Pepper had created a guardianship agreement that designated Pepper's brother and his wife as the children's guardians. In the meantime, however, Pepper's brother had added three children to his existing two, and he and his wife had divorced, leaving neither party ready or able to assume the care of Peggy's grandchildren. Peggy had to cross some very high legal hurdles in order to become designated the official guardian. When this subject arises in family therapy, therapists should encourage clients to review their existing documents to make sure they are still valid and reflect current circumstances.

One of the saddest situations therapists witness is when the parent of a child dies, or is separated following a divorce, and the loving grandparents of the child are suddenly deprived not only of their biological child but of the fulfillment and joy of sharing the life of the grandchild.

Another difficult situation occurs when a new marriage is entered into following the death of a parent or a divorce, and the new marriage partner has no interest in furthering the relationship with his or her spouse's former in-laws. The grandparents of the child or children are then denied a relationship with their loved ones. Because some grandparents feel a deeper love and affection for their grandchild than they did for their own child or children, the resulting loss of that love and the deprivation of that sharing constitute a bitter and damaging experience. The loss of the grandparent's love and affection is equally damaging to the children.

Grandparents' rights to visitation of a grandchild may be vigorously opposed by a bitter divorced partner. Nevertheless, the rights of grandparents have been recognized in the courts of many jurisdictions, and the courts have ensured those rights with legally enforceable court orders (Krause, 1986). Uncles and aunts of children whose parent or parents have become deceased or divorced are also often deprived of visitation rights to their nieces and nephews. The closeness of family relations is recognized as an important part of the mental and spiritual well-being of individuals, and when they are denied the bonding experience that can exist in a family, all of the parties sustain a loss. Regarding the in-laws, courts have not uniformly recognized the rights of uncles and aunts to visitation rights to their nieces and nephews. The loss to the children and to their uncles and aunts is inestimable. The therapist might suggest that opinion of legal counsel be sought to clarify rights and to enforce them, when necessary, to maintain bonds with relatives. Clergy may also help in establishing visitation rights from a reluctant parent and former in-law.

A very tender situation arises in the establishment of a new family unit where there are children from a prior marriage. The situation relates to the rights of survivorship between existing children and children born into a new family, as well as the rights and/or expectations of other dependents or relatives and in-laws of the spouses. This subject is so fraught with emotions and problems that it is often helpful for the family to seek professional counsel for resolution. The couple may wish to create an agreement, in writing, regarding this subject.

For example, Vince married Simone, and both have children from previous marriages. Both Vince and Simone brought solely owned assets into the marriage, and they anticipated creating additional ones. Vince had also been caring for and supporting a handicapped ex-sister-in-law who owns assets controlled by Vince. Simone had also been the sole provider of an elderly family friend. The older offspring of Vince were resentful of the prospect of possibly sharing Vince's estate with children born of the new union. Simone's offspring harbored the same misgivings. Both Vince and Simone wished to provide for their current offspring, as well as children born of their new union, and both desired to continue providing for their extended family members and to ensure that these provisions would continue after their demise.

I suggested that Vince and Simone work together to reach a clear understanding as to their wishes and intentions regarding providing for their various offspring and other responsibilities, and that those wishes and intentions should be made known to those who were impacted by them. In a large extended family session, we used a genogram to show the interrelated responsibilities and expectations, and this helped the existing offspring understand that they would not be left out when new children joined the family. The genogram also helped the extended family members see how they fit in, and, as it turns out, actually enabled the family friend, who had been dependent on Simone, to see the burden she represented. The friend realized that she should turn to her own family, rather than leaning on Simone. I encouraged Simone and Vince to seek legal counsel to develop a workable estate planning system that felt right to all involved. Solving these *rights of survivorship* issues helped smooth the road as Simone and Vince enlarged their family circle.

BORROWING MONEY, LENDING MONEY, AND BUSINESS DEALINGS WITH IN-LAWS

The day I got married, my father-in-law asked me to borrow a dollar from him. Although it seemed unusual, I agreed. He then said, "Now listen carefully. If anyone should ever ask you if they can borrow money from you, you can say, 'I'm sorry, but I owe my father-in-law money.'"—Chauncy, 40, diplomat

Experience has shown that one of the most common causes of problems in marriages relates to business dealings between the in-laws. Assumptions are made that are often not realized. As important as verbal agreements are in business dealings with strangers, they are even more important in dealings with in-laws. If loans to or from in-laws are contemplated, wisdom dictates that the agreement be in the form of a *written contract*. Some successful family transactions have resulted from not only reliance on a clearly drafted and executed contract, but also on the use of banks or trust officers who transfer and receive funds on behalf of the principals. The use of formal contracts may appear cold or be interpreted as a lack of trust, but, over the term of the transaction, the documentation and reliance on escrow or trust officers eliminate many problems before they arise.

Such problems occurred when Devon wanted to start a coffee house. She took out a second mortgage on her house and asked both her parents and her parents-in-law to invest in her business. After a somewhat successful first year, the business hit the skids and folded. Devon took a temporary job to forestall foreclosure on her house when she couldn't make the payments, and she was unable to make good on her other loan obligations. To lend her the money, her parents-in-law had taken out a home equity loan on their own house, and were now in a bind because Devon could not make the agreed-on repayments. They expected their son, Devon's husband, to make good on the loan, and when he was unable to do so, the parents-in-law were bitter.

This example illustrates that when in-laws contemplate either lending to or borrowing from other in-laws, or making investments in their in-laws' business ventures, it is of vital importance to everyone concerned that the transactions be in accordance with sound business principles. Every representation or agreement should be given a thorough *due diligence examination*—a complete investigation of all the business concerns—before the agreement is executed. Although it may seem harsh, the therapist may wish to encourage clients to consider employing the services of credit bureaus and business associations prior to any business transaction between in-laws.

When I mentioned to a colleague that I was including this topic in the book, she said, "A cardinal rule regarding business dealings between in-laws is that unless one is willing to reduce the transaction to a legally binding contract which can be enforced, then one should consider the investment or loan as a gift without expectation of repayment or the realization of a return on an investment." She said that simply gifting the money initially saves a lot of hard feelings later, and recounted Benjamin Franklin's adage, "It is better to give than to lend, and it usually costs about the same."

If the choice of simply giving the money is not feasible or desired, every transaction between in-laws should be set forth in a legally binding contract, which clearly states the remedies available to the parties in the event of default or other difficulty. As mentioned earlier, clients may wish to consider the use of trust officers to enforce contracts or to seek recovery of damages in the event of problems. Such services can be a valuable tool in keeping all parties at true arm's-length and can reduce friction within the extended family units.

When children-in-law have not completed their college degrees, parents-in-law are often expected or desire to provide financial assistance, either by giving the money, or via long- or short-term loans. As in all business dealings, and especially with regard to gifts, the tax consequences might be addressed with competent professionals.

In the study of blue-collar families mentioned in Chapter 2, Komarovsky (1962) found that most parents were not able to provide financial aid on an ongoing basis; however, financial aid was frequently provided in emergencies. Aid was also frequently given in terms of services, such as house painting, carpentry, repairs, and help in moving. Reciprocity of giving was an important principle with the extended family. Depending on the severity of need, aid could go in either direction. For instance, a grandmother in need of financial help could be paid for baby-sitting.

If in-laws agree to loan money or pay tuition for the in-laws' benefit, it is highly recommended that the terms of the agreement, as with any business agreement, be set in writing. Hard feelings can result when expectations are not met. An example of this outcome involved Jed and Nancy. Jed, who was a very successful dentist, loaned $40,000 to his son-in-law Harvey over the course of four years, to help pay for college tuition. Not only did Harvey disappoint Jed by not going into the career that he had suggested, but he also never graduated from college. Instead, Harvey changed from one major to another, and as Jed and Nancy viewed it, he "played at going to school at their financial expense and their daughter's emotional expense." Although Harvey had agreed that he would pay the money back, no date of payment or interest rate was agreed on. Five years after Harvey dropped out of school and took a job as an insurance agent, Jed had a massive heart attack and was required to go on disability. At that point, Jed and Nancy were extremely angry at Harvey because the money that had been loaned was now greatly needed. An ever-widening rift that had its roots in the good intentions of the father-in-law had expanded to the point where it could engulf the relationship. Harvey now avoids any encounters with his in-laws and discourages his wife from dealing with them as well.

GIFTS

If one agrees with Ben Franklin's maxim, and decides to give rather than lend, the road is still not clear for the in-law relationship. Gift giving is fraught with problems and can cause great discord within families. For example, during the holiday season a few years ago, a client was annoyed that she had to spend the same amount of money on her mother-in-law as she spent on her own mother. I asked her if this was a requirement of her husband and she said that it was not, but that she herself felt a moral obligation to spend equal amounts on both. She said that although she felt much closer to her mother and wanted to reflect this in her gift, she couldn't afford two equally expensive gifts. She felt a great deal of anger because she had to compromise on her own mother's gift, and resigned herself to giving a rayon scarf instead of the beautiful Hermés scarf that she knew her mother would love. She said she hated Christmas and birthdays, because she always had this dilemma over the gifts having to be equitable. I pointed out that this reflected loyalty issues, and suggested that perhaps she and her husband might agree to divide gift-giving responsibilities, with each handling his or her own family's gifts. She agreed that this might work and said they would give it a try.

Loyalty issues can often arise regarding gift giving. I recently overheard a young couple in a baby furniture store with the wife's parents, who had spent a good deal of money on a stroller. When a bill for $700 was presented, the son-in-law said, "My parents are going to give a car seat and probably something else, too." It was obvious the young man was somewhat overwhelmed by his in-laws' gift and that he wanted them to know his parents would reciprocate. The need to have one's parents do as much as the in-laws is a natural reaction.

I remember after the death of my mother-in-law, my father-in-law (who was a coin collector) gave his new wife of one year and his daughter, my husband's only sister, a gold coin on a gold chain for Christmas. He gave me a silver dollar on a silver chain. Although the gift was nice and I like to think that it's the thought that counts, I must say I was rather hurt and felt slighted not only that my sister-in-law would receive a gold coin, but that my father-in-law's new wife would receive the same gift, while I (who'd had a 25-plus year relationship with him) had received a less expensive gift. My husband and I never discussed it, but a few years later, after the death of my father-in-law, my husband gave me a gold coin with a gold chain for my birthday. I never wore the silver coin—in fact, in annoyance, I actually took it as a white elephant to a gift exchange party. The woman who received the silver dollar on the chain was delighted, as it did not carry the symbolism of inequity it carried for me.—Larisa, 43, therapist

One set of in-laws handled the gift-giving loyalty issues by giving each of their children and children-in-law a dollar for each year of life on birthdays, and Christmas gifts were calculated in the same way. Although this worked for this family, not every family likes to give money. There are some who consider it crass to give cash as gifts.

One needs to understand a family's traditions in order for the effort to result in an appreciated gift. Gift giving represents a very important ritual in today's society, and those who take it lightly often regret doing so. Just as the Japanese have a long-standing tradition that makes the gift wrapping every bit as important as the quality of the gift inside (Engholm, 1991), each family has rules regarding gifts that can make or break the in-law relationship. It behooves the family to discuss expectations, themes, and even requirements for thank-you notes, and in lieu of a discussion with the extended family, the spouse can often provide the cues needed to successfully navigate this area.

CHECKLIST

Some Legal and Financial Issues

It is acknowledged that few romances would survive the close scrutiny suggested in this chapter. Nevertheless, in the same way that sophisticated businesspeople would never consider embarking on a business relationship or making an investment without an intense review of the financial and legal factors and the personalities involved, clients might be encouraged to consider taking these same factors into consideration before beginning their marriage relationships.

1. Would I encourage family members or future in-laws to have a prenuptial agreement? What should be included in it?

2. Have in-depth questions been asked—and answered—regarding the background of the future in-laws?

3. Have expectations regarding finances and assets of future in-laws been discussed? Has the couple prepared a financial statement?

4. Has agreement been reached regarding pre-existing indebtedness of future in-laws?

5. Have insurance issues been addressed?

6. Do the in-laws have adequate estate planning, including wills, living trusts, or appointments of conservatorship?

7. Has guardianship of the children been resolved? Are in-laws aware of who has been designated and has approval been received?

8. If money has been borrowed or loaned to in-laws or other family members, is there a written agreement with a repayment schedule, and remedies if expectations are not met?

9. Have biological family and in-law gift-giving issues been discussed?

CHAPTER 12

Pulling It All Together

QUALITIES OF POSITIVE IN-LAW RELATIONSHIPS

In today's society, there seem to be more questions than answers regarding in-laws. In his *Life Cycles of Man*, Erickson (1950) saw the healthy adult as being an interdependent person. As with the healthy individual, I believe the healthy family is interdependent. But interdependence has gotten a bad name. We are all encouraged to be independent, self-sufficient, autonomous units—indeed, nuclear families in a nuclear age. Yet this autonomous unit does not reflect reality, especially the reality of cultures such as Hispanic, African American, Asian American, and Pacific Islanders, who are highly involved in the network of the family.

In-Laws—An Odd Space between Friends and Relatives

As Framo (personal communication, December 5, 1994) put it, parents (and therefore in-laws) are in the middle of the family. Like it or not, individuals thrive on and need community, and in-laws are an intricate and basic part of that community, although they in many ways represent an unacknowledged, undefined web of relationships. As a cab driver told me on the way to the airport, "I think that the reason people don't relate as much to in-law relationships is because biological relationships are more primal." He further stated: "In my family, I have seen my spouse automatically rally to her brother's defense if I attack him. In a way this gives me comfort, because I know she would do the same for me. I'm sure my father-in-law *likes* me more than my brother-in-law, but he *loves* his son. My father-in-law wouldn't take his arm off for me, but he would for his own son." As this cab driver saw it, "In-laws fall in this odd space between friends and relatives."

What is that odd and undefined space, and how do we by choice or default fill that space? Recently, I heard a young man say with pride in his voice, "I just read about my brother-in-law's company in the paper. It's neat to have a relative connected with a project that is written about in the *New York Times.*"

This young man was at that moment filling his brother-in-law space with pride in the accomplishment of another, which is some of the best we humans have to offer one another.

The point is that each therapist, client, and family needs to decide how it will fill that space between friends and relatives. Will the space be filled with friendly words, kind deeds, loving acts, caring behaviors? Will it be filled with pride for accomplishments, support for failure as well as success, understanding of faults and slights? Or will the space be filled with contention, animosity, disappointment, and jealousy? Will the space be all-inclusive and welcome new in-laws as well as existing in-law relationships? Will the space be flexible and able to tolerate fluidity in welcoming new members and retaining those in-laws who without an open system space might lose their connection through divorce or death of the biological family member? Can the family space allow for change of intensity in in-law relationships through time by keeping out the in-law welcome mat as life cycles, developmental family issues, and stressors cause individuals in the family to wax and wane regarding the intrusion or inclusion of extended family?

What of connections that have not been legally formalized through marriage, those people one might term quasi-in-laws, such as parents who have more than one child by a different spouse? What of those in-laws? Is it possible to have enough space to draw in those special in-laws who have no legal ties to the family system and make claim only to the biological ties of grandchildren? Is it possible to draw in their energy to support space between limping isolated family systems with few resources?

What maintains a space for in-laws as family and friends? The two major energies I see are love and hate. Hate is a strong energy that represents one of the strongest bonds in relationships. It is a powerful connection with few productive results. As one male client stated, "I hate my in-laws. Every time I think about them, it puts me in a bad mood for days." A female client stated, "If I want to get into a big fight with my husband, I bring up something my parents have said. There is always energy around my family and it is mainly negative." Another client was highly disappointed to find that his new sister-in-law was so flighty. "I thought because they were brought up in the same family, there would be some consistency."

These negative comments regarding in-laws indicate a negative energy in the family emotional system representing cognitive distance rather than interdependence and growth. Therapists may do well to think in terms of their own in-law relationships as well as their clients'. It is surprising how helpful it is to distance the problem from the biological family's energy and to look at that in-law space, which can also be looked at as neutral territory. Taking in-law energy away from being seen as an interpersonal issue and reviewing it in a more global, generic way as an in-law issue can be powerful and can help clients deal in a new way with tension between themselves and their ings-in-law, parents-in-law, and children-in-law. When we think of in-laws, we can view any conflicts in terms of: What is really going on in the in-law space? What kind of in-law energy do clients have? Is it positive, negative, or ambivalent energy? Can that energy be transformed by love into successful in-law relationships? Clients (as well as therapists) might be encouraged to explore the space, starting at the beginning of the relationship.

IN-LAW RELATIONSHIPS: WHERE ARE WE?

This book has called for a paradigm shift in dealing with in-laws and has pointed out the need to identify and work with the variables that are unique to in-law relationships. It is unfortunate that much of the literature (especially that in the public domain) is geared to viewing in-laws as a problem rather than a resource. A brief survey of recent magazine article titles says it all: *Family ties: How not to let in-laws (yours or his) come between you* (Pauker & Arond, 1995); *Understanding your marriage: Should you outlaw your in-laws?* (Hendrix, 1991); *Do your in-laws drive you crazy?* (Parvin, 1994).

Fortunately, in the body of these articles is some good advice, including:

- Try to overlook flaws in relatives and be sensitive to their feelings (Pauker & Arond, 1995).
- Recognize that it may be a couple's problem rather than an in-law problem (Hendrix, 1991).
- In-laws are often blamed for traits one doesn't like in a spouse (for example, a fear of intimacy, or a perverse satisfaction in having the in-laws pick on him or her) (Pauker & Arond, 1995).

There is also appropriate advice regarding letting grandparents know the boundaries and rules; however, when it comes to talking about how to deal with the intrusive in-law, the articles emphasized how much it is resented when the mother-in-law tells the parent or child what to do (Pauker & Arond, 1995). Here is one segment of some positive advice.

- Be clear with grandparents about the role you want them to play so that you as a couple present a united front and so that relatives don't intrude on your marriage (Pauker & Arond, 1995).

These articles also contain highly punitive remarks and reflect the old stereotype of the meddlesome, overbearing mother-in-law. One article (Parvin, 1994) even goes so far as to pick out what I call *trophy mothers-in-law,* those mothers-in-law who were infamous for being difficult, like Madge Gates Wallace, Harry Truman's difficult mother-in-law. The same article describes how the wife of Winston Churchill had to bear the brunt of her overbearing mother-in-law, who redecorated the couple's new home while they were on their honeymoon. There is also mentioned the mother-in-law who was baby-sitting and had the audacity to rearrange the living room furniture, which I understand is not uncommon (Hendrix, 1991).

When fathers-in-law enter the picture, they are given a totally different slant, as illustrated by a story of Ulysses S. Grant's extended family, where the two fathers-in-law didn't get along and, thus, had *manly fights* (Parvin, 1994).

In these articles, the moniker *in-laws* seem to denote only the couple, while the mothers-in-law are identified almost generically by the term *dysfunctional in-laws*.

What I find most disturbing about these articles, however, is that two were written by psychotherapists (Hendrix, 1991; Pauker & Arond, 1995) or consist mainly of quotes by psychotherapists. One of my favorites is that you should not rely on the in-laws for financial help or child care (Parvin, 1994), which I believe is unrealistic advice, since several studies show that the majority of parents-in-law have at one time or another given financial or other support to their children-in-law.

Rather than starting from a negative point of view and depending on old stereotypes, therapists and clients alike might come to terms with the fact that in-laws are here to stay and that one's in-laws just happen to be one's spouse's parents and blood relatives. When there are problems with an in-law, clients (as well as therapists) might be well advised to look at the issue in the singular: "There is a person in the family system with whom I am having problems. Is it my problem or is it their problem?" Recognizing that it may not be a global "in-law problem" and may instead reflect a problem with an individual in-law is helpful for many clients. Or, if clients are caught in an individual issue, the therapist may then move it to a more global perspective.

The lack of attention to the in-law relationship is not because there is not energy around the issues. There are few people who, when focused on the in-law relationship, don't have a comment, story, or joke about their in-laws. I believe this lack of attention by professional therapy circles to the extended family, especially the nonbiological family, has strong early biblical roots: "Cleave unto your spouse" (KJV Genesis, 2:24); in other words, ignore the in-laws. But the Bible also states: "Honor thy father and thy mother that thy days may be long upon the land" (KJV Exodus, 20:12). If you cleave to your spouse and honor your father and mother, then the logic would have it that having your partner honor your parents (your spouse's in-laws) promotes a positive energy for love and understanding in the family system.

WHERE DO WE NEED TO GO?

Rereading Duvall's 1954 study of 7,000 in-law relationships shows that, during the ensuing years, not much has changed. This is echoed in nearly all subsequent in-law studies. The relative lack of literature, studies, and even interest in the topic by the therapeutic community points to an enormous vacuum that beckons attention. A quick perusal of the meager amount of professional research available on the topic of in-laws indicates that most data are generated only peripherally, in studies on grandparents, divorce, and marital therapy. Additionally, the dearth of sibling-in-law studies invites the opportunity for future in-law research in this area.

As pointed out earlier in the book, therapists can go a long way in helping families to see—and use—in-laws as a valuable resource rather than an antagonistic force that must be endured. It's a tough world out there, and with increasing numbers of single-parent households as well as families where both parents work outside the home, in-laws can bring an added dimension of energy, joy, love, and fun.

In-law problems and relationships cannot all be painted with the same brush—they are unique and filled with as much variety as the people they represent. Solutions to these problems are also unique to each family system dealing with the problems. Setting down hard-and-fast rules does not work with a system as large and fluid as the extended family. However, in the following sections are some ideas—a synthesis of my observations of many hundreds of families—about how to develop in-law relationships that work.

Identifying In-Law Problems and
Staying In-Law-Problem Oriented

It is important, when working with a system as large and as varied as the in-law system, for the therapist to remain focused so as not to lose the forest for the trees. In other words, instead of looking for problems, the therapist may wish to let the clients define them. The therapist might encourage clients to try to keep situations simple and resist the therapeutic urge to want more for the in-laws than they want for themselves.

McGoldrick (1980), in her book on family life cycles, states that the majority of marital problems arise from unresolved extended family problems. She sees unresolved family issues as being significant factors in marital choice. With a divorce rate close to 50%, it would seem that the future in-law family should consider trying to work out issues with the potential daughter- or son-in-law as early as possible in the relationship. And a daughter- or son-in-law might be encouraged to recognize that working out a relationship would be to his or her benefit.

In looking at differing coping styles of an in-law, simple identification of the feeling structure held by each member of the in-law system can be useful in providing a groundwork for future communication and problem solving. According to Weeks and Treat (1992), when nuclear family members believe certain feelings should not be felt or expressed, questions about how feelings were handled in the family-of-origin can help the individuals understand the historical basis of the problem.

Some questions the therapist may ask in-laws include the following, based on those suggested by Weeks and Treat (1992):

1. Can you describe the dominant feelings for each member of your family?
2. Was there one predominant feeling in your family? Who set the mood?
3. In your family, which feelings were expressed most often, most intensely?
4. Were there feelings that you felt could not be expressed?
5. Were members ever punished when an unacceptable feeling was expressed? If so, how?
6. Did specific members of your family have the responsibility to know how others felt?

Recognizing and Respecting In-Law Differences

The initial stages of the in-law relationship are crucial. This is when many mistakes are made that only become amplified with the years. One way of ensuring harmony with one's in-laws is to marry someone whose family is congenial. Do good in-laws run in families? My father always likened families to horses, and would say, "Now, you wouldn't want to pair a sleek quarter horse with a big draft horse like a Clydesdale. The union wouldn't be productive and you'd have two very unhappy animals. If you're a thoroughbred who likes to run fast, find a partner like you. If you're a wild stallion, you'd better find a similar horse." According to Duvall (1954), when you share a similar way of life with your spouse and his or her family, you already have a great deal in common with them and they with you. Your ways of behaving are understandable to each other. Your roles with each other are in harmony because you have similar expectations as to what is appropriate (p. 315).

In-law systems are comprised of unique individuals with diverse backgrounds. These individuals marry for many reasons and bring with them their own family history, including likes and dislikes. Wherever possible, it is best not to personalize negative in-laws' responses; they may be holdovers from the past.

Henry Clay said, "I'd rather be right than president," and so it is with some in-laws who feel that being right is more important than being liked. Many parents-in-law end up with children-in-law who are their direct opposites. One of my clients who is conservative in his political leanings now has a son-in-law who is a dyed-in-wool liberal. The client's idea of fun was a ski trip to Idaho; his son-in-law's idea of heaven was working in a homeless shelter or getting involved in a demonstration against the establishment, carrying signs that proclaim, "Down with the Capitalist Pigs." Because my client could be considered to fall into the category of *capitalist pigs,* the air around this in-law relationship was often charged with emotional intensity. My client said that his father-in-law had always maintained that "Nothing good ever comes from discussing politics or religion," but after discussing it in therapy, my client decided that with his new son-in-law, he would make a brave effort to discuss those touchy areas. My client reports that the tension sometimes mounts, but that he is rather enjoying the lively discussions.

On the other hand, sometimes a client may enjoy hating his or her child-in-law's family, or may not want to put in the time or energy needed to develop a relationship. However, if one takes this negative approach, it will probably impact the relationship with the child's spouse in subtle ways. There will be questions regarding who comes first when babies are born and where the family will spend the holidays. Because this could put a good deal of stress on the child, one might want to consider putting some energy into developing these relationships.

You Can Talk Yourself Out of an In-Law

One father-in-law said, "I really can't stand my daughter-in-law; she is ruining our grandson and I wish they would get divorced." I asked him to take a look at what a divorce would mean. Number one, she would still be involved with his family through the son and grandson. Number two, he and his son would have to deal with all the problems of divorce, including visitation, missing holidays, and child support, along with the loss, depression, anger, and hurt that go along with divorce. He agreed that there was enough divorce in the world, and said if a couple no longer wants to live together, that is one issue, but for him to put energy into seeing the marriage fail would be misplaced judgment, unless there was physical or emotional abuse.

But, what if one really doesn't like one's daughter- or son-in-law? What if one hates the spouse's parents? If this is the case, the therapist may wish to suggest that the client investigate whether he or she is dealing with one or more of the following hidden in-law agendas:

- In-laws who have a need to be perfect.
- In-laws who need to be the center of attention.

- In-laws who have a need for special recognition of their achievements.
- In-laws who desire to be seen as special and unique.
- In-laws who are highly protective of their time, money, and energy.
- In-laws who scan for danger in order to avoid being slighted by others.
- In-laws whose agenda is to keep the maximum number of options open.
- In-laws who want to be in charge.
- In-laws who want to achieve balance and avoid conflict.

If clients feel that their in-laws do have hidden agendas, they might look at their own agendas to see whether they conflict. If the agendas conflict, a compromise might be in order. If they do not conflict, one might just identify, acknowledge, and even learn to appreciate in-law differences.

Going from In-Law Permission to Acceptance

For a person to be accepted by the in-laws, he or she must first receive implicit or explicit permission to be a member of the clan. If potential new in-laws feel that permission has not been given, they need to confront this directly either on their own or with professional help. Only with permission, blessings, and welcome can the in-law system really move toward acceptance. A shared commonality can bring family members closer.

> *I think that the reason my mother-in-law and I got along so well together was because we had three things in common—golf, a sense of humor, and her son.—* Maddie, 55, professional golfer

Families wishing to integrate new members may wish to explore the feelings, interests, and hopes they hold in common. The success of this in-law integration can be viewed in different stages. What would be felt as an extremely successful relationship in the forming stage would be deemed unsuccessful once the conforming stage has been reached. However, the chances for success seem to be greatly improved when the parents-in-law enthusiastically and warmly welcome their new child-in-law to the family.

Once a couple is married, many in-laws find that restraint and consideration are invaluable in avoiding stepped-on toes. It is often best to wait until asked before moving in with some kind of assistance or advice.

> *I'll never forget coming home one day after my sister-in-law had been at my home baby-sitting. She was so proud that she'd "helped" me clean out the kids' closet and had tossed out a lot of old toys she'd found. I viewed her assistance as a slap in the face regarding my housekeeping abilities and priorities. And I can guarantee that she'll never be asked to baby-sit again.—*Cecilia, 35, sales representative

Realizing that helping is a skill that must be learned is a good first step for any person who would become a better in-law. Here is some free advice: When you see in your in-law's family something different from yours, you are a good in-law if you respect the difference and refrain from immediately leaping in with "help."

Respecting and Honoring In-Law Connections

Achieving balance is a worthy goal in connection with the extended family. This balance can be precarious when a newcomer tries to make his or her way through the maze of biological connections. Making extended relationships work requires the love and goodwill of all concerned. Making decisions jointly with others in the family is an established method of getting along well in the family. As the relatives who are concerned are consulted, each feels in on the decision and shares responsibility for it. When the channels of communication among in-laws are kept open, real feelings can become expressed and hidden meanings are less common.

People who accept the fact that they do differ learn to resolve their conflicts in ways that protect—and respect—the values of each individual. Open discussion and mutual respect are recommended procedures. A sincere willingness to see all possibilities and to avoid thinking that there can be only one solution is important for success.

Family members may find it useful to identify whether they are experiencing loyalty "pulls." Boszormenyi-Nagy and Spark (1973) have identified a number of areas where there may be loyalty problems. Included in these are the following, which seem especially problematic for in-laws:

- Split loyalty.
- Intergenerational loyalty conflicts.
- Couple vs. in-law loyalty.
- Individual vs. multigenerational loyalty.
- Loyalty obligations of spouse.
- Filial loyalty.
- Disloyalty to self.
- Unresolved loyalty.

The Path Is Not Always Straight

Clients need to be aware that there will be disruptions in in-law relationships as family members transit the life cycle. Identifying predictable and unpredictable life-cycle issues can aid in-laws in adjusting to the ups and downs in the family system. Birth of children causes many role changes in the in-law system with parents-in-law becoming grandparents and siblings-in-law becoming aunts and uncles. There can be a number of issues around discipline and general matters of the best ways to care for children.

The death of a family member can create havoc in the family, especially if there is a family estate or family home to be disposed of. Untimely deaths, such as the death of a child, represent enormous trauma for families, and everyone wants to rush in and help. Tensions run high with funerals to be planned and people to be housed. Hurtful things said by in-laws and other family members during these times of stress and crisis are not soon forgotten.

Another life-cycle problem that can stress the family system is the illness of an in-law, and most often an aging parent-in-law. Many is the daughter-in-law who has taken care of a cantankerous mother- or father-in-law during the parent's later years. The son-in-law seldom performs this same valiant effort. With the advent of more available nursing home care, custody of the elderly is now often left to professionals.

At times, in-laws may be welcomed as helpers and supporters; at other times, family members may be immersed in their own individual needs and hence may see the presence of in-laws as an intrusion. There will be times when help is needed, but, because of lack of resources, or knowledge, or energy, in-laws do not respond. At other times, unwelcome in-laws will arrive to *rescue* a biological family member. This intrusion can be highly positive in cases of spousal abuse, alcoholism, or other types of neglect:

> *I was married for two years and had a one-year-old boy. My husband used to get drunk and push me around. He was a blackjack dealer in Vegas and my father never felt good about his son-in-law. One night, my husband came home drunk and sat my son on his knee and said he couldn't wait until he was old enough to get drunk and go out with the showgirls. I called my dad that night and told him what happened. He said, "You may let your own life be influenced by that man but don't let my grandson's life go down the drain." An hour later, my dad and brother came over with the truck and we were out of there. I have never regretted the decision.*—Rachel, 43, accountant

Heightening the Sibling-in-Law Profile

Siblings are an important factor in the in-law system. Family members will find that the relationship between siblings prior to marriage is echoed in the sibling-in-law structure. In-laws may be used by the spouse to pull the sibling out of the family soup, and if this is the case, there may be a physical or emotional cutoff that will not be welcomed by other family members. On the other hand, a sibling-in-law can be used as a scapegoat by the spouse in order to deal with the couple's unresolved problems. Siblings may blame the sibling-in-law when they have little or no contact with their beloved sibling (who, if the truth were known, is often happy not to have family contact). Even though they bring a potential for conflict to the family, siblings-in-law, with their close age proximity, can also be a source of fun and entertainment.

Duvall's (1954) study confirms that if one's attitudes are primarily those of acceptance and of mutual respect, one has little to dread in relationships with siblings-in-law.

Strategies for Mending In-Law Rifts

Taking responsibility for one's own part in the in-law problem is a good beginning for change. If one person in the family system makes a change, it creates a ripple effect of positive in-law energy and offers a role model for change. New in-laws often bring in the voice of change. As newcomers, they can often see where the in-laws are having problems, and thus, give in-laws who want change the opportunity to see the problem in a different light. Change happens slowly because it usually has taken years to build up problems, and it takes months to break down those in-law barriers and walls. The most important underlying component for change is the *desire* to be a helping, caring, and loving in-law. Coupled with this desire are the willingness and flexibility needed for change. Relationships are fluid, and understanding some simple techniques can free up energy and creativity for the entire family.

If clients are on a negative track, it is important for the therapist to emphasize that it is never too late to renegotiate in-law relationships. Basic nutrients for the growth toward positive in-law interactions are love and respect. Gottman and Silver (1994) identified four warning signs of potential marriage meltdown. My clinical experience leads me to believe that these could also hold true for in-law relationships:

1. Being unduly critical of in-laws.
2. Contempt (as shown by comments intended to insult the in-laws) or hostile humor.
3. Defensiveness or feeling victimized by in-laws; in response, in-laws may deny responsibility or make excuses.
4. Stonewalling, or the in-law's emotional or physical withdrawal.

Controlling advice and criticism is an important step in healing wounds. Here is an example:

Shortly after I married Blaine, I heard my aunt complaining about her mother-in-law. I told her that I had the best mother-in-law in the world, and she replied, "Then that means she never gives you any advice." After thinking about it, I realized how lucky I am that even now after 25 years of marriage, she has never interfered. And we continue to have an excellent relationship. Her example has really taught me how to be a good mother-in-law as my own children marry.— Sherise, 46, homemaker

Many of the old stereotypes about in-laws just aren't true. By renouncing the old jokes and reauthoring the stories, we can make positive changes in the relationships. Those who would become better in-laws must refrain from telling the old jokes and from encouraging those who do. The use of labels also erects barriers between in-laws. It is better to recognize that in-laws are individuals who have their own needs, interests, and habits. The better understood, the more understandable the in-law behavior will be. When we understand people, we can learn to love and respect them.

Clients can be encouraged to watch out for inner in-law scripts such as righteous indignation or feeling the victim. Here are some quickly accomplished strategies that can help diffuse these in-law situations:

- Calm down. Take time out. It takes time to rewrite your inner in-law script. Practice relaxation. Take a walk.
- Speak and listen nondefensively. Be the architect of your own thoughts. Try to be a good in-law listener. Remember the major differences between the ways males and females communicate (Gray, 1992).
- Validate your in-laws. Let them know that you appreciate them. Try to put yourself in their shoes.
- If you don't succeed, try, try, try again.

If people practice these skills, they will have gone a long way to improving a marriage relationship. If these are good for strengthening couples, they should be great for in-law systems (Gottman & Silver, 1994).

Balancing the In-Law System after Separation and Divorce

To balance the in-law system after separation and divorce, circumstances and events must be known by the family. Secrecy is not helpful if support and help are needed. Families are often very skilled at coping if they know what they are coping with. In-laws need to talk with each other and let it be known how they stand on having the divorced in-law included as a part of their life. Because children must bridge the in-law gap between their mother's and father's families, it is preferable for in-laws to treat the divorced in-law well, if only for the sake of the children. In remarried families, grandparents will have an especially difficult time. If the new spouse has children, they need to think about how these stepgrandchildren will be treated. Will the in-laws bring gifts at Christmas and birthdays, or will these stepgrandchildren be treated differently than the biological grandchildren? How will the ex-in-law be treated if he or she is the custodial parent of the grandchildren? These issues need to be discussed and brought out into the open where they can be dealt with on a consistent basis.

The high divorce rate in the United States makes it clear that the dyad of husband and wife or significant others must be strengthened and supported. The expectations of the in-law relationship are often not realistic. It makes sense to enlarge the resources available to meet the heavy demands of the nuclear family with a supportive extended family system. If there is divorce in the family, the options multiply and the need for in-laws to stay involved with empathy and understanding expands.

After we divorced, my ex-husband still wanted to come to my family's really fun gatherings, like Thanksgiving and the New Year's tamale feed. But he wasn't willing to make the effort to show up at the less fun events, like baby christenings, my niece's piano recitals, or other events where his presence was required to support our sons. I told him that if he wanted to be invited to the A-list celebrations, he had to put in time at the B-list events, to "earn" an invitation. This way, I didn't feel like he got to enjoy all the best my family has to offer without having to endure the downside of marriage and in-law responsibilities.—Gwendolyn, 36, pharmacist

Vive la Différence—Cultural Diversity and In-Laws

Not all in-laws dance to the same beat, especially those who have different cultural or ethnic backgrounds. As recently as 20 years ago, cross-cultural marriages were frowned on; today there is a great deal of intermarriage between ethnic groups. Even among in-laws, there are wide differences between the generations. Many in-laws cling to their old ways and languages after immigrating to the United States. Some choose not to assimilate, in the hope that their children and grandchildren will maintain some of the family's rich culture.

There are differing attitudes among ethnic groups regarding responsibilities and expectations of the in-laws. Rather than assume that because an in-law is of a certain ethnic background he or she will have certain traits and characteristics, it is best to check with in-laws and see what their attitudes are on such issues as permission to marry, living together, and expectations of the role of in-laws. Ethnicity may indicate a ballpark idea of what the in-laws may be like, but only by finding out their personal opinions can one have the full story. These ideas regarding in-laws should be brought out in the open and talked about freely because only by being honest can people avoid feeling shame at letting others down. Ethnicity and heritage can bring great diversity, interest, and richness to the in-law system, and, with agreement among all concerned, meaningful traditions can be passed down through the generations.

Further study and research on other cultures are much needed. Expanded knowledge of ethnically diverse families could be especially helpful when grandparents and other in-laws, along with parents, are raising the children. More thought could be given to how in-laws on both sides of the family can pool their financial and emotional resources to support the next generation. As therapists, we need to find support for these multicultural families wherever we can, and what better resource to tap than the extended families? I am also sure that there is much more to be learned from other cultures about in-law relationships and about how we can weave the best of these cultures into the fabric of American families in order to support the family system.

In addition to exploring the diverse cultural approaches to extended family relationships, special attention might be given to the young and the aged—two groups in need of functional and supportive family and extended family structure.

Money Talks, But Doesn't Talk Back

Contractual, legal, and financial matters are important underlying issues for families. In-laws can be unwittingly drawn into in-law control conflicts connected with financial resources, family businesses, and the time and resource demands that test the nerves of the most well-adjusted in-laws. Pride and loyalty issues, involving financial support or being helped out in ways that one's biological parents cannot afford, also put stress on the in-law structure. Financially well-off in-laws who are generous with their resources often receive more attention from their biological children and thus the in-laws are drawn in. It is difficult to turn down weekend trips or paid vacations.

There may be problems around family businesses or issues of in-laws being involved in wills and estates. Is there a will? Who is the executor? Who gets what, and when do they get it? Who gets mother's diamond ring and dad's watch? Who gets the family car and the antique rocker? It is important for therapists to help clients remember that these are only *things* and they are not worth bad family feelings. In-laws often get caught in the fray by simply trying to support their spouses.

BUILDING SUCCESSFUL IN-LAW RELATIONSHIPS

Becoming a good in-law is a lifelong task for all of us, says Duvall (1954). Most of us want to become more effective in our interpersonal and intrafamily relationships. If we are wise, we know that the best way of improving relationships with other people is to change our own ways of thinking, feeling, and behaving. We may run into a wall of resistance if we try to make others come over to our ways. But, as soon as we look for what we ourselves may do to adapt more skillfully to the realities of the situations and persons involved, we make progress. The inference here is: If you want to get along better with your in-laws, your best approach is to start with yourself. As you learn how to become a better in-law, you will have more success with your in-laws.

In-law relationships are unique; they are like no other relationships. They do not have the primality of the biological ties; however, as we have already observed, they are not just relationships of convenience. In-law relationships carry a great deal of power, and to offend one's in-laws is to touch the very heart of a significant other (to demonstrate this, all you have to do is offend one's partner's parents).

Ten Commandments for Building Positive In-Law Relationships

Gottman (1994), one of the foremost therapists in couples and family therapy, has studied over 2,000 married couples in two decades and has found the following strategies for how people can strengthen foundations of their fundamental relationships. These strategies have been modified from Gottman's focus on couples to a focus on in-laws.

1. Negotiate your in-law style.
2. Pick your in-law battles carefully.
3. Acknowledge your in-laws' viewpoints.
4. When dealing with in-laws, moderate your emotions.
5. Choose to be polite, regardless of in-law actions.
6. When possible, be direct and honest with in-laws.
7. Be careful about teasing in-laws—one person's humor is another's poke in the eye.
8. Learn to level with in-laws when necessary.
9. If in-laws get you down, turn to others for support.
10. Use friendly humor with in-laws in order to diffuse tension.

IN-LAW INVENTORY

The therapist may wish to help clients explore the space available for in-law relationships with the following inventory of issues covered throughout this book:

1. When I think of the word *in-law*, what comes to my mind?
2. Do I have negative in-law stereotypes represented by stories and jokes?

3. Can I identify the stages that my in-law relationships have transited?

    a. Forming: Being introduced into the family.

    b. Storming: Looking at and expressing differences.

    c. Norming: Accepting what can't be changed and changing what can.

    d. Conforming: Settling into a comfort zone with the in-laws.

4. Have my in-laws and I successfully negotiated the stages of the relationship?

5. How was I (and am I currently) received by the in-laws?

6. How do I receive other in-laws joining the family?

7. Did my significant other and I have permission from the in-laws to be together? Is approval of mate still an issue?

8. Have we dealt with family and in-law loyalty issues?

9. Are individuals in the in-law space empowered? Are the age hierarchies honored?

10. Have I considered that my personality may conflict with my in-laws' in terms of the following characteristics?

    a. Control needs.

    b. Inclusion needs.

    c. Intimacy needs.

    d. Differing problem-solving techniques; i.e., assertive, aggressive, withdrawn.

    e. Worldview.

11. Is the in-law space filled with cultural, ethnic, or religious bias issues?

12. Is there undue stress and tension around holidays or other special occasions or family events?

13. Are there unsettled accounts or hurt feelings?

14. Are there family secrets or myths that impact my in-law relationships?

15. Are grandchildren (and the way the in-laws interact with them) an issue?

16. Are in-laws aware of (and comfortable with) possible grandparenting styles?

    a. Detached grandparent.

    b. Passive grandparent.

    c. Influential grandparent.

    d. Selective investment grandparent.

17. Have I been able to recognize and let go of unrealistic in-law expectations?

18. Am I comfortable with the relationships between myself and divorced in-laws?

19. Have I learned how to accept what I cannot change with difficult in-laws?

20. Are my in-law relationships flexible enough to tolerate change in myself and others?

21. Have the in-laws established informal guidelines for dealing with divorced, separated, or step-in-laws?

22. Is the in-law space open to mending relationships with understanding, forgiveness, and acceptance of differences?

23. Do I experience stress with family secrets or myths that aren't dealt with?

24. Are there in-law inheritance or financial issues?

25. Have the in-laws been able to storm, norm, and conform around life-cycle changes, such as a death of a spouse, an empty nest, or a geographical move?

26. Do I or my in-laws have hidden agendas? Do they conflict?

ISSUES FOR THERAPISTS

Therapists might wish to look at their own issues, to avoid the risk of projecting their own unresolved in-law problems onto the clients. While supervising nursing students on a psychiatric unit at a major medical center, I often felt that psychiatric residents took their own family issues out on many of the patients' parents and in-laws.

Therapists who work with in-law issues may wish to:

1. Look at their own in-law rituals and customs in terms of ethnicity.

2. Describe their sibling-in-law and parent-in-law relationships.

3. Explore their own in-law bias, as expressed through stories, jokes, family secrets, and myths.

4. Discuss the pros and cons of in-law focused therapy for themselves and their in-laws, identify the areas that need to be addressed, and then describe the interventions they would use to address these areas.

A CALL TO ACTION

Not all clients or therapists can, or even wish to, improve their in-law relationships. However, by reading this book, you have already made a shift: you have identified the in-law relationship as a space to be considered. I have attempted to explore various aspects of in-law relationships familiar to me in my research, clinical practice, and personal experience. There are, no doubt, many areas left to explore on a macro level regarding in-law relationships. On a micro level, each family and individual could write his or her own story of in-law relationships. I hope that this book will inspire further research in the area and will encourage dialogue and discussion, on an individual as well as a clinical level, regarding the extended family. On an individual level, the book should enable in-laws to step back and to observe, with a bit more objectivity and compassion, the intricate web of these relationships.

This book is not the last word on in-laws. It is intended to be a catalyst for future dialogue and research on an important and neglected area of study.

References

Adams, L., & Lenz, E. (1989). *Be your best.* New York: Perigree.

Ahrons, C. R. (1994). *The good divorce. Keeping your family together when your marriage comes apart.* New York: HarperCollins.

Ahrons, C. R., & Rogers, R. H. (1987). *Divorced families: A multidisciplinary developmental view.* New York: Norton.

Anderson, T. B. (1984). Widowhood as a life transition: Its impact on kinship ties. *Journal of Marriage and the Family, 46*(1), 105–114.

Anspach, D. F. (1976). Kinship and divorce. *Journal of Marriage and the Family, 38,* 323–330.

Aponte, H. J., & VanDeusen, J. M. (1981). Structural family therapy. In A. S. Gurman & D. P. Kniskern (Eds.), *Handbook of family therapy.* New York: Brunner/Mazel.

Baker, F. M. (1988). Afro-Americans. In L. Comas-Diaz & E. E. H. Griffin (Eds.), *Clinical guidelines in cross-cultural mental health* (pp. 151–181). New York: Wiley.

Barnes, G. (Ed.). (1977). *Transactional analysis after Eric Berne. Teachings and practices of three TA schools.* New York: Harper's College Press.

Baron, R., & Wagele, E. (1994). *The enneagram made easy.* San Francisco: Harper San Francisco.

Bateson, G. (1980). *Mind and nature: A necessary unity* (p. 74). New York: Bantam.

Beck, A. T. (1976). *Cognitive therapy and the emotional disorders.* New York: International Universities Press.

Beck, A. T. (1988). *Love is never enough: How couples can overcome misunderstandings, resolve conflicts, and solve relationship problems through cognitive therapy.* New York: Harper & Row.

Berg-Cross, L., & Jackson, J. (1986). Helping the extended family: In-law growth and development training program. *Psychotherapy in Private Practice, 4*(1), 33–50.

Berle, M. (1989). *Milton Berle's private joke file.* New York: Crown.

Berne, E. (1961). *Transactional analysis in psychotherapy.* New York: Ballantine.

Besher, A. (1991). *The Pacific Rim almanac.* New York: HarperPerennial.

Bilofsky, P., & Sacharow, F. (1991). *In-laws/outlaws: How to make peace with his family and yours.* New York: Villard.

Black, H. C. (1990). *Black's Law Dictionary* (6th ed.). St. Paul, MN: West.

Bohannan, P. (1971). *Divorce and after.* New York: Anchor.

Bohannan, P. (1973). The six stations of divorce. In M. E. Lasswell & T. E. Lasswell (Eds.), *Love, marriage and family: A developmental approach* (pp. 375–388). Glenview, IL: Scott Foresman.

Boss, P., & Thorne, B. (1989). Family sociology and family therapy: A feminist linkage. In M. McGoldrick, C. M. Anderson, & F. Walsh (Eds.), *Women in families: A framework for family therapy* (pp. 78–96). New York: Norton.

Boszormenyi-Nagy, I., & Spark, G. M. (1973). *Invisible loyalties.* New York: Brunner/Mazel.

Bowen, M. (1966). The use of family therapy in clinical practice. *Comprehensive Psychiatry, 7,* 345–374.

Bowen, M. (1976). Theory in the practice of psychotherapy. In P. J. Guerin (Ed.), *Family therapy.* New York: Gardner.

Bowen, M. (1978). *Family therapy in clinical practice.* New York: Jason Aronson.

Boyd, L. M., (1995, February 23). For Your Information. *The Houston Post,* p. A16.

Bradt, J. O. (1980). The family with young children. In E. A. Carter & M. McGoldrick (Eds.), *The family life cycle: A framework for family therapy* (pp. 121–146). New York: Gardner.

Byng-Hall, J. (1988). Scripts and legends in families and family therapy. *Family Process, 27,* 167–179.

Byng-Hall, J. (1991). Family scripts and loss. In F. Walsh & M. McGoldrick (Eds.), *Living beyond loss. Death in the family* (pp. 130–143). New York: Norton.

Carter, E. A., & McGoldrick, M. (Eds.). (1980). *The family life cycle: A framework for family therapy.* New York: Gardner.

Cherlin, A., & Furstenberg, F. (1985). Styles and strategies of grandparenting. In V. L. Bengston & J. F. Robertson (Eds.), *Grandparenthood* (pp. 97–116). Beverly Hills, CA: Sage.

Cryster, A. (1990). *The wife-in-law trap.* New York: Pocket Books.

Duran-Aydintug, C. (1993). Relationships with former in-laws: Normative guidelines and actual behavior. *Journal of Divorce & Remarriage, 19*(3, 4), 69–81.

Duvall, E. R. (1954). *In-laws, pro and con: An original study of interpersonal relations.* New York: Association Press.

Engholm, C. (1991). *When business east meet business west: The guide to practice and protocol in the Pacific Rim.* New York: Wiley.

English, F. (1977). What shall I do tomorrow?: Reconceptualizing transactional analysis. In G. Barnes (Ed.), *Transactional analysis after Eric Berne. Teachings and practices of three TA schools* (pp. 287–347). New York: Harper's College Press.

Erickson, E. H. (1950). *Childhood and society.* New York: Norton.

Falcon, A., & Graham, G. H. (1993, August). *Presentation on in-law relationships.* 111th Annual Convention of the American Psychological Association, Toronto, Canada.

Falicov, C. J., & Karrer, B. M. (1980). Cultural variations in the family cycle: The Mexican-American family. In E. A. Carter & M. McGoldrick (Eds.), *The family life cycle: A framework for family therapy* (pp. 383–426). New York: Gardner.

Famighetti, R. (Ed.). (1994). *The World Almanac.* New York: World Almanac Books.

Fischer, L. R. (1983). Mothers and mothers-in-law. *Journal of Marriage and the Family, 45,* 187–192.

Framo, J. L. (1965). Rationale and techniques of intensive family therapy. In I. Boszormenyi-Nagy & J. L. Framo (Eds.), *Intensive family therapy: Theoretical and practical aspects* (pp. 143–212). New York: Harper & Row.

Framo, J. L. (1976). Family of origin as a therapeutic resource for adults in marital and family therapy: You can and should go home again. *Family Process, 15,* 193–210.

Framo, J. L. (1992). *Family of origin therapy: An intergenerational approach.* New York: Brunner/Mazel.

Friday, N. (1987). *My mother my self: The daughter's search for identity.* New York: Dell Brooks.

Furstenberg, F. F., Jr. (1981). Remarriage and intergenerational relations. In R. Fogel (Ed.), *Aging: Stability and change in the family* (pp. 115–140). New York: Gardner.

Gluck, N. R., Dannefer, E., & Milea, K. (1980). Women in families. In E. A. Carter & M. McGoldrick (Eds.), *The family life cycle: A framework for family therapy* (pp. 295–327). New York: Gardner.

Gottman, J., & Silver, N. (1994). *Why marriages succeed or fail.* New York: Simon & Schuster.

Goulter, B., & Minninger, J. (1993). *The father daughter dance. Insight, inspiration, and understanding for every woman and her father.* New York: G. P. Putnam's Sons.

Gray, J. (1992). *Men are from Mars: Women are from Venus.* New York: Harper-Collins.

Haley, J. (1976). *Problem solving therapy: New strategies for effective family therapy.* San Francisco: Jossey-Bass.

Harris, T. A. (1967). *I'm ok you're ok.* New York: Avon Books.

Hendrix, H. (1991, September 24). Understanding your marriage. Should you outlaw your in-laws? *Family Circle,* pp. 39–41.

Hepburn, K. (1991). *Me: Stories of my life.* New York: Knopf.

Hetherington, E. M., Cox, M., & Cox, R. (1977). Divorced fathers. *Psychology Today, 10*(11), 42–46.

Hines, P. M., & Boyd-Franklin, N. (1982). Black families. In M. McGoldrick, J. K. Pearce, & J. Giordano (Eds.), *Ethnicity and family therapy* (pp. 84–107). New York: Guilford.

Hirsh, S., & Kummerow, J. (1989). *Life types.* New York: Warner Books.

Holmes, S. A. (1994, July 20). Birthrate for unwed women up 70% since '83, study says. *New York Times,* p. A1.

Horsley, G. C. (1988, September). *Network therapy with Mormon families.* Paper presented at the meeting of the American Association of Mormon Counselors and Psychologists, Salt Lake City, UT.

Horsley, G. C. (1989, January). Baggage from the past. *American Journal of Nursing, 89*(1), 60–63.

Imber-Black, E. (1993). *Secrets in families and family therapy.* New York: Norton.

Jackson, J., & Berg-Cross, L. (1988). Extending the extended family: The mother-in-law and daughter-in-law relationship of Black women. *Family Relations, 37,* 293–297.

Johnson, C. L. (1989). In-law relationships in the American kinship system: The impact of divorce and remarriage. *American Ethnologist, 16*(1), 87–99.

Johnson, C. L. (1992). Divorced and reconstituted families: Effects on the older generation. *Generations, 16*(3), 17–20.

Johnson, C. L., & Barer, B. (1987). Marital instability and changing kinship networks of grandparents. *The Gerontologist, 27*(3), 330–335.

Kaslow, F. W. (1991). Enter the prenuptial: A prelude to marriage or remarriage. *Behavioral Sciences and the Law, 9,* 375–386.

Kaslow, F. W., & Schwartz, L. L. (1987). *The dynamics of divorce: A life cycle perspective.* New York: Brunner/Mazel.

Keirsey, D., & Bates, M. (1978). *Please understand me.* Del Mar, CA: Prometheus Nemesis Book.

Kerr, M. E., & Bowen, M. (1988). *Family evaluation.* New York: Norton.

Kivnick, H. Q. (1982). *The meaning of grandparenthood.* Ann Arbor, MI: UMI Research Press.

Komarovsky, M. (1962). *Blue collar marriage.* New York: Random House.

Krause, H. D. (1986). *Family law in a nutshell* (2nd ed.). St. Paul, MN: West.

Kubler-Ross, E. (1969). *On death and dying.* New York: Macmillan.

Kushner, H. S. (1981). *When bad things happen to good people.* New York: Avon.

Landau-Stanton, J., Clements, C. D., & Stanton, M. D. (1993). Psychotherapeutic intervention: From individual through group to extended network. In J. Landau-Stanton, C. D. Clements, R. E. Cole, A. Z. Griepp, & A. F. Tartaglia (Eds.) with J. Nudd, E. Espaillat-Piña, & M. D. Stanton, *Aids health and mental health: A primary sourcebook* (pp. 214–266). New York: Brunner/Mazel.

Landau-Stanton, J., Horsley, G. C., Stanton, M. D., & Watson, W. (1994). *Church and family: The religious community as a resource in therapy.* Manuscript submitted for publication.

Landis, J. T., & Landis, M. G. (1973). *Building a successful marriage* (6th ed.). Englewood, NJ: Prentice-Hall.

Lash, C. (1977). *Haven in a heartless world.* New York: Basic Books.

Leader, A. L. (1975). The place of in-laws in marital relationships. *Social Casework, 21,* 486–491.

Lear, P. (1992, July 12). A Tale of Two Swimmers. *New York Times Magazine,* section 6, pp. 30, 36, 42.

Leman, K. (1985). *The birth order books: Why you are the way you are.* New York: Dell.

Lévi-Strauss, C. (1963). *Structural analysis.* New York: Basic Books.

Lewicki, P. (1992, June 23). Your unconscious mind may be smarter than you. *New York Times,* p. B-5.

Lynn, R. J. (1992). *Introduction to estate planning in a nutshell* (4th ed.). St. Paul, MN: West.

Marotz-Baden, R., & Cowan, D. (1987). Mothers-in-law and daughters-in-law: The effects of proximity on conflict and stress. *Family Relations, 36,* 385–390.

Martinez, C. M., Jr. (1988). Mexican-Americans. In L. Comas-Diaz & E. E. H. Griffin (Eds.), *Clinical guidelines in cross-cultural mental health* (pp. 182–203). New York: Wiley.

Maslow, A. (1954). *Motivation and personality.* New York: Harper & Row.

McCullough, P. (1980). Launching children and moving on. In E. A. Carter & M. McGoldrick (Eds.), *The family life cycle: A framework for family therapy* (pp. 171–195). New York: Gardner.

McGoldrick, M. (1980). The joining of families through marriage: The new couple. In E. A. Carter & M. McGoldrick (Eds.), *The family life cycle: A framework for family therapy* (pp. 93–119). New York: Gardner.

McGoldrick, M. (1982). Ethnicity and family therapy: An overview. In M. McGoldrick, J. K. Pearce, & J. Giordano (Eds.), *Ethnicity and family therapy.* New York: Guilford.

McGoldrick, M., & Gerson, R. (1985). *Genograms in family assessment.* New York: Norton.

McGoldrick, M., Pearce, J. K., & Giordano, J. (Eds.). (1982). *Ethnicity and family therapy.* New York: Guilford.

Minuchin, S. (1974). *Families and family therapy.* Cambridge, MA: Harvard University Press.

Mollica, R. F., & Lavelle, J. P. (1988). Southeast Asian refugees. In L. Comas-Diaz & E. E. H. Griffin (Eds.), *Clinical guidelines in cross-cultural mental health* (pp. 262–302). New York: Wiley.

Myers, I. B., & Myers, P. B. (1980). *Gifts differing.* Palo Alto, CA: Consulting Psychologists Press.

Nerin, W. F. (1993). *You can't grow up till you go back home: A safe journey to see your parents as human.* New York: Crossroads Publishing.

O'Hanlon, B. (1994, November/December). The promise of narrative. The third wave. *The Family Therapy Networker,* pp. 18–26.

Palmer, H. (1995). *The enneagram in love and work: Understanding your intimate and business relationships.* San Francisco: Harper San Francisco.

Parkes, C. M., & Weiss, R. S. (1983). *Recovery from bereavement.* New York: Basic Books.

Parvin, J. (1994, June). Do your in-laws drive you crazy? *Reader's Digest,* pp. 165, 166, 168, 170.

Pauker, S. L., & Arond, M. (1995, December/January). Family ties. How *not* to let in-laws (yours or his) come between you. *Child,* pp. 67–68, 70–72.

Perls, F., Fefferline, R. F., & Goodman, P. (1972). *Gestalt therapy.* Great Britain: Souvenir Press.

Piprell, C. (1991). Bangkok. In Fodor's Travel Publications, Inc. *The Wall Street Journal Guides to Business Travel: Pacific Rim.* New York: Fodor's Travel Publications.

Popenoe, P. (Ed.). (1945, January). What do you call your mother-in-law? *Family Life Education.* Los Angeles: American Institute of Family Relations.

Radcliffe-Brown, A. (1952). *Structure and function in primitive society.* New York: Free Press.

Riso, D. T. (1990). *Understanding the enneagram: The practical guide to personality types.* Boston: Houghton-Mifflin.

Rohrbaugh, M., Tennen, H., Press, S., & White, L. (1981). Compliance, defiance, and therapeutic paradox: Guidelines for strategic use of paradoxical interventions. *American Journal of Orthopsychiatry, 51*(3), 454–467.

Rolland, J. S. (1991). Helping families with anticipatory loss. In F. Walsh & M. McGoldrick, *Living beyond loss. Death in the family* (pp. 144–163). New York: Norton.

Rosenberg, G. S., & Anspach, D. F. (1973). *Working class kinship.* Lexington, MA: Lexington Books.

Satir, V. (1964). *Conjoint family therapy: A guide to theory and technique.* Palo Alto, CA: Science and Behavior Books.

Satir, V. (1988). *The new peoplemaking.* Mountain View, CA: Science and Behavior Books.

Schlien, J. (1962). Mother-in-law—A problem in terminology. *Etc., 19,* 161–171.

Shanas, E., Townsend, P., Wedderburn, D., Friis, H., Milhhoj, P., & Stehouver, J. (1968). *Older people in three industrial societies.* New York: Atherton.

Shon, S. P., & Ja, D. Y. (1982). Asian families. In M. McGoldrick, J. K. Pearce, & J. Giordano (Eds.), *Ethnicity and family therapy* (pp. 208–228). New York: Guilford.

Simon, F. B., Stierlin, H., & Wynne, L. C. (1985). *The language of family therapy: A systemic vocabulary and sourcebook.* New York: Family Process Press.

Simon, R. M. (1972). Sculpting the family. *Family Process, 11,* 49–57.

Sluzki, C. E. (1978). Marital therapy from a systems theory perspective. In T. J. Paolino & B. S. MacCrady (Eds.), *Marriage and marital therapy.* New York: Brunner/Mazel.

Smith, M. J. (1975). *When I say no, I feel guilty.* New York: Bantam.

Spanier, G. B., & Hanson, S. (1982). The role of extended kin in the adjustment to marital separation. *Journal of Divorce, 5,* 33–48.

Speck, R. V., & Attneave, C. L. (1973). *Family networks.* New York: Brunner/Mazel.

Spicer, J. W., & Hampe, G. D. (1975). Kinship interaction after divorce. *Journal of Marriage and the Family, 37*(1), 370–379.

Stanley, D. (1993). *South Pacific Handbook* (5th ed.). Chico, CA: Moon.

Stanton, M. D. (1981a). An integrated structural/strategic approach to family therapy. *Journal of Marital and Family Therapy, 7*, 427–439.

Stanton, M. D. (1981b). Marital therapy from a structural/strategic viewpoint. In G. P. Sholevar (Ed.), *Marriage is a family affair: A textbook of marriage and marital therapy*. New York: SP Medical and Scientific Books.

Stanton, M. D., & Todd, C. (1982). *The family therapy of drug abuse and addiction*. New York: Guilford.

Stern, E., & Ross, M. (1952). *You and your aging parents*. New York: A. A. Wyn.

Toman, W. (1993). *Family constellation. Its effects on personality and social behavior* (4th ed.). New York: Springer.

Tomm, K. (1989). Foreword. In M. White & D. Epston (Eds.), *Literate means to therapeutic ends*. Adelaide, South Australia: Dulwich Centre Publications.

Troll, L. E. (1983). Grandparents: The family watchdogs. In T. Brubaker (Ed.), *Family relationships in later life* (pp. 63–74). Beverly Hills, CA: Sage.

Troll, L. E., Miller, S. J., & Atchley, R. C. (1979). *Being a grandparent or great-grandparent. Families in later life*. Belmont, CA: Wadsworth.

Tuckman, B. W. (1965). Developmental sequence in small groups. *Psychological Bulletin, 63*, 384–399.

Tuckman, B. W., & Jensen, M. A. C. (1977). Stages of small group development revisited, *Group & Organizational Studies, 2*, 419–427.

Uhlenberg, P., & Myers, M. A. P. (1981). Divorce and the elderly. *Gerontologist, 21*, 276–282.

Van Heusden, A., & Van Den Eerenbeetmt, E. (1986). *Balance in motion: Ivan Boszormenyi-Nagy and his vision of individual and family therapy*. New York: Brunner/Mazel.

Visher, E. B., & Visher, J. S. (1982). *How to win as a stepfamily* (2nd ed.). New York: Brunner/Mazel.

Wallerstein, J. S., & Blakeslee, S. (1995). *The good marriage: How and why love lasts*. New York: Houghton Mifflin.

Weeks, G. R., & Treat, S. (1992). *Couples in treatment. Techniques and approaches for effective practice*. New York: Brunner/Mazel.

Whitaker, C. A. (1976). A family is a four dimensional relationship. In P. J. Guerin (Ed.), *Family Therapy*. New York: Gardner.

Whitaker, C. A., & Keith, D. V. (1981). Symbolic-experiential family therapy. In A. S. Gurman & D. P. Kniskern (Eds.), *Handbook of family therapy* (pp. 187–225). New York: Brunner/Mazel.

White, M. (1989). *Selected papers*. Adelaide, South Australia: Dulwich Centre Publications.

White, M., & Epston, D. (1989). *Literate means to therapeutic ends*. Adelaide, South Australia: Dulwich Centre Publications.

Wilson, K. B., & DeShane, M. R. (1982). The legal rights of grandparents: A preliminary discussion. *The Gerontologist, 22*(1), 67–71.

Williamson, D. S. (1991). *The intimacy paradox: Personal authority in the family system.* New York: Guilford.

Worden, J. W. (1982). *Grief counseling and grief therapy. A handbook for the mental health practitioner.* New York: Springer.

Author Index

Subject Index